Wittgenstein on Universals

American University Studies

Series V
Philosophy

Vol. 56

PETER LANG
New York · Bern · Frankfurt am Main · Paris

Robert Fahrnkopf

Wittgenstein on Universals

PETER LANG
New York · Bern · Frankfurt am Main · Paris

Library of Congress Cataloging-in-Publication Data

Fahrnkopf, Robert
Wittgenstein on universals / Robert Fahrnkopf.

p.   cm. — (American university studies. Series V. Philosophy
; v. 56)
Bibliography: p.
1. Wittgenstein, Ludwig, 1889–1951—Contributions in theory of
universals. 2. Universals (Philosophy)—History—20th century.
I. Title. II. Series.
B3376.W564F27   1988
111'.2'0924—dc19   87-34193
ISBN 0-8204-0707-0   CIP
ISSN 0739-6392

CIP-Titelaufnahme der Deutschen Bibliothek

Fahrnkopf, Robert:
Wittgenstein on universals / Robert Fahrnkopf.
– New York; Bern; Frankfurt am Main; Paris:
Lang, 1988.
(American University Studies: Ser. 5,
Philosophy; Vol. 56)
ISBN 0-8204-0707-0

NE: American University Studies / 05

© Peter Lang Publishing, Inc., New York 1988

Printed by Weihert-Druck GmbH, Darmstadt, West Germany

CONTENTS

PREFACE

Wittgenstein has frequently been interpreted as being ill-disposed in principle as well as in practice to the realist solution to the problem of universals. The contention of my book is that this interpretation is unwarranted. In both his earlier and later periods, I shall argue, Wittgenstein includes non-particular items, i.e., universals, in his ontological inventory. In calling such a position 'realism', in distinguishing between what I call 'Platonic' and 'Aristotelian' versions of realism—this distinction bearing on whether or not universals are held to have an ontological status apart from being instantiated in particulars—and in calling the view which holds that the ontological inventory of the world includes only particulars 'nominalism', I am admittedly framing the issues concerning universals in an unexcitingly traditional way, and I concede that there might well be more sophisticated perspectives for a discussion of these issues from which my own characterizations would appear crude and superficial. This does not greatly concern me, however, since my purpose is not so much to use Wittgenstein as a springboard for an in-depth treatment of the problem of universals as it is to use the topic of universals as a springboard for a more general exploration of the philosophy of Wittgenstein, and for this latter purpose the distinctions as I have drawn them will suffice.

Except for Chapter Eight, where I critically examine Wittgenstein's attack on privacy, I am almost exclusively concerned to give an exposition of his views rather than a critical evaluation of them, and my book is therefore primarily a work of scholarship, rather than an example of creative philosophy in its own right. Nevertheless, Wittgenstein is so often these days appealed to in support of this or that philosophical position—his role as an authority-figure among contemporary Anglo-American philosophers approaching that of Aristotle during the medieval period—that a thorough and accurate exposition of his views can be a positive and worthwhile contribution to the philosophical enterprise it-

viii

self. As Wittgenstein scholarship has amply demonstrated, however, even this more modest goal can prove to be elusive; how well I have succeeded in the task must be left to the judgement of the reader.

It has been approximately fourteen years since the original version of the manuscript on which this book is based was completed. I thought at the time that it contained some important and original interpretive insights, but after trying unsuccessfully to find a suitable publisher, I put the manuscript aside and moved on to other areas of philosophy. In arranging for the publication of my research at this time, I have tried to go through the relevant secondary literature that has accumulated in the intervening years, and I have been gratified to find that the views I expressed in 1973 have on the whole not been duplicated or superseded by other scholars, and still seem to me to be worth saying. Although I have made some attempt to update my work by taking into account a number of primary and secondary sources available only after my initial research was completed, I have for the most part continued to rely on the older secondary literature to serve as a foil for my interpretation of Wittgenstein, since it continues to serve this purpose as well as it did before.

While generally relying on the standard translations of Wittgenstein's works for quotations cited in the text, I have continued to use my own translations of passages from Wittgenstein's *Philosophical Remarks* (listed in the bibliography under its German title, *Philosophische Bemerkungen*) and *Philosophical Grammar* (*Philosophische Grammatik*), as well as Waismann's *Ludwig Wittgenstein and the Vienna Circle* (*Ludwig Wittgenstein und der Wiener Kreis*); I have also felt free to make occasional, minor modifications of existing translations, especially as regards the Pears and McGuinness version of the *Tractatus*.

Finally, I wish to thank all those individuals who have read earlier versions of my manuscript, offered constructive suggestions for its improvement, and encouraged its publication.

INTRODUCTION

That Wittgenstein was a philosopher of great creativity and originality is beyond dispute; nevertheless, he was not an isolated genius, working in an intellectual vacuum, though the distinctiveness of the style of his prose and the frequent obscurity in the presentation of its content no doubt encourage this impression. My own view is that Wittgenstein's philosophy owes more to the works of others than is commonly supposed. I cannot in this book attempt a comprehensive defense of this claim, but shall instead concentrate on a particular topic where the tracing of historical antecedents is especially fruitful. In the first half of the book, which deals with the early Wittgenstein, I shall examine the ontology of the *Tractatus* with the purpose of showing that Wittgenstein, following the lead of Russell, embraced a version of realism, by which I mean that the 'objects' of the *Tractatus* comprise not only particulars but also properties and relations.

This is by no means a novel interpretation of Wittgenstein. Ramsey seems to have taken this line in his review of the *Tractatus* over a half-century ago, and the position has since been advocated by others, notably Stenius, Allaire, Hacker, and Canfield.[1] Furthermore, if we accept the accuracy of Desmond Lee's recently published reports of conversations he had with Wittgenstein during the academic year 1930-31, the issue is no longer seriously in doubt. One of these discussions concerned the first four propositions of the *Tractatus*. Concerning the third proposition, 2.01, which Lee translates as "An atomic fact is a combination of objects (entities, things)...," he has recorded as the gist of Wittgenstein's remarks the following:

> Objects etc. is here used for such things as a colour, a point in visual space etc..... "Objects" also include relations; a proposition is not two things connected by a relation. "Thing" and "relation" are on the same level. The objects hang as it were in a chain.[2]

Nevertheless, as this interpretation of Wittgenstein's ontology has generally found a less favorable reception than a competing interpretation—put forward by Anscombe, Copi, Pitcher, and Griffin, among others[3]—which holds that the *Tractatus* does not treat properties and relations as objects, there might be a reluctance in some quarters to take Lee's notes here at face-value. Such reluctance, if it exists, cannot be taken too seriously; while it is reasonable to wonder of any second-hand report of Wittgenstein's views whether it has accurately captured the subtle nuances of his position, it is unreasonable to suppose that Lee could have been so confused as to take Wittgenstein to be telling him that colors and relations were objects, in the sense intended by 2.01, when Wittgenstein really meant to deny this. However, even if Lee's notes should now be regarded as having settled the matter, it is in any case a useful undertaking to confirm Lee's account through an independent examination of the evidence, since much can be learned through such a process about the development of Wittgenstein's thought in general. Accordingly, I will proceed on the assumption—if only for its effectiveness as a heuristic device—that Lee's notes are not decisive, and attempt to meet the interpretation of Anscombe *et al.* head on, primarily through examining Wittgenstein's own writings, but also by taking note of other corroborative evidence as well.

The interpretation of the *Tractatus* which I am opposing rests largely on the conviction that Wittgenstein's distinction between what can be shown and what can be said implies that symbols for properties and relations are theoretically eliminable. According to this view, Wittgenstein is maintaining that a logically perspicuous symbolism requires only names of particular objects and certain conventions whereby the sorts of ways objects can be configured in possible states of affairs are directly displayed in the symbolism by a corresponding configuration of the names themselves. Following Allaire, I shall call this interpretation of the *Tractatus* 'nominalistic', but we cannot assume that proponents of this interpretation want altogether to deny ontological status to properties and relations, especially to the latter. To be sure, the sort of view I here call 'nominalistic' denies that relations exist as objects, but at the same time it might be thought to allow that relations somehow exist, either by having a kind of content different from that possessed by objects, or by way of contributing to the form (or structure), though not the content, of facts. Despite such qualifications, 'nominalism' seems a convenient label for this position, if only because the ontological implications of this position are sufficiently unclear that I do not know what else to call it. In any case, my contention is that this commonly received interpretation, however we label it, is mistaken. I intend to show this, not only by examining the textual evidence of the *Tractatus* itself, and other writings of Wittgenstein prior and subsequent to the *Tractatus*, but also by placing his views in their proper historical context, which will show that his ontological concerns and assumptions are, with a few qualifications, basically those of the early Russell.

It is the close connection in this matter between Russell—the realist *par excellence*—and Wittgenstein that has allowed me, with a clear conscience, to characterize Wittgenstein's view that properties and relations are objects as a version of ontological *realism*, i.e., as an endorsement of the existence of *universals*. While this way of putting the matter might seem innocent enough, there is at least one commentator, Erik Stenius, who would agree with me that the *Tractatus* includes predicative and relational entities among its objects, but who would deny that such entities ought to be characterized as universals. Stenius does not really argue for this position; he simply states that the grammatical distinction between subject and predicate is irrelevant to the traditional distinction between particular and universal, so that Wittgenstein could presumably have regarded properties and relations as objects without supposing that they were universals.[4] But even if Stenius were able to produce convincing arguments for his claim that the subject/predicate distinction has no bearing on the particular/universal distinction, this would not show that Wittgenstein himself entertains any such scruples. Certainly Russell, as we shall see, assumes—with certain qualifications—that the grammatical distinction between subject and predicate corresponds to, and is the best way to characterize, the ontological distinction between particular and universal. Lacking any evidence that the early Wittgenstein parts company with Russell on this point, I feel justified in characterizing the ontology of the *Tractatus* as realistic. Still, although I find these traditional distinctions useful, the following terminological substitutions can be made without substantially affecting my argument: for 'realism' read 'the view that includes properties and relations among objects'; for 'nominalism' read 'the view that denies that properties and relations are objects'; and for 'universals' read 'properties and relations'.

The appropriateness of using any of these expressions to characterize Wittgenstein's ontology could, however, be challenged on another ground. One could argue that we have no reason for supposing that the *Tractatus* acknowledges the existence of universals, not—as Stenius would claim—because entities which function grammatically as predicates should not on that account be called universals, but for the quite different reason that, on the basis of views expressed in the *Tractatus*, we cannot know that there are entities having any such grammatical function, and thus we cannot presume anything at all about the nature of objects on the basis of the grammatical functions of their names. Such a view is, I believe, at least implicit in Ramsey's paper "Universals."[5] If so, Ramsey does not, contrary to the impression given by his review of the *Tractatus*, give unqualified endorsement to a realistic interpretation of the *Tractatus*. In any case, as an account of what Wittgenstein's position ought in all consistency to be, such a view is undoubtedly correct. The *Tractatus* does maintain that the ultimate analysis of language into elementary propositions has not yet been achieved and therefore that we do not yet know the logical form of any particular elementary proposition. But, as I hope to show in the course of my argument, Wittgenstein does in practice assume that there are, e.g., propositions of the subject-predicate form, and that the grammatical difference between subject and predicate reflects an ontological distinction between particular and universal. If I am right, then Ramsey's view is untenable as an interpretation of the ontological position actually taken up by Wittgenstein in the *Tractatus*.

After setting out and defending my interpretation of the *Tractatus*, I will argue in the second half of the book that although the later Wittgenstein repudiates the Platonic realism of the *Tractatus*, in which properties and relations are held to have full ontological status apart from their instantiation in particulars, his later position provides some support for Aristotelian realism, i.e., the view that universals exist, but only as instantiated in particulars as their common qualities; in Wittgenstein's case this is a modest sort of Aristotelian realism limited to items such as specific sense-qualities.

This claim requires two qualifications. First, I am not maintaining that the later Wittgenstein thinks of himself as an advocate of a limited Aristotelian realism; indeed, it seems clear that he thinks he has originated a revolutionary method of philosophizing which obviates the need for taking sides in traditional disputes, including ontological disputes. My contention will be that, whatever he may think, his method of philosophizing is not ontologically neutral, and that his standpoint is one of a limited realism. Secondly, I will show that even though Wittgenstein is a realist, his ontological position differs radically from Aristotle's, or from other traditional positions, in being held to be determined by and dependent upon language, a position which is the reverse of the more orthodox view that language is a reflection of ontology. So, whatever ontological position Wittgenstein can be said to hold, in his view it is to language, rather than to an independent reality, that we must ultimately address ourselves.

CHAPTER ONE

UNIVERSALS AS INDIVIDUALS

Paragraph #46 of the *Philosophical Investigations* offers a comparison of Wittgenstein's own earlier position in the *Tractatus* to that of Russell:

> What lies behind the idea that names really signify simples? —Socrates says in the Theaetetus: "If I make no mistake, I have heard some people say this: there is no definition of the primary elements—so to speak—out of which we and everything else are composed; for everything that exists in its own right can only be *named....*"
>
> Both Russell's 'individuals' and my 'objects' (Tractatus) were such primary elements.

This passage has sometimes been cited in support of the view that the *Tractatus* does not include universals among its objects.[1] The argument is that since (1) Wittgenstein equates his objects with Russellian individuals, and (2) Wittgenstein must understand Russellian individuals to include only particulars, therefore (3) Wittgensteinian objects must all be particulars as well.

The obvious challenge to this argument would focus on premise (1). One could claim that #46 equates Russellian individuals and Wittgensteinian objects only with respect to their being primary elements, so that nothing in this passage bears on whether such elements are particulars or universals. Surprisingly, however, premise (2) is vulnerable as well. In Moore's notes on Wittgenstein's lectures of 1930-33 he tells us that Wittgenstein spoke of colors as well as atoms as if they were 'individuals' in Russell's sense.[2] Since a color, unlike an atom, is presumably a universal rather than a particular, premise (2) seems undermined. This interpretation of what Russell means by an individual is so unusual, however, that we might be tempted to suppose that Wittgenstein is here talking about an instance of color rather than the color itself, i.e., a particular red sense-datum rather than the universal redness. Such a strategy, though, can scarcely explain away Wittgenstein's remark in the *Blue Book* where, in the course of characterizing his earlier view of the *Tractatus* in which he had held that it was only the arrangement of elements, and not the elements themselves, which need not exist, he says: "...[T]he elements, the individuals must exist. If redness, roundness, and sweetness did not exist, we could not imagine them."[3] Here it is clearly the universal redness—not a particular instance of a red sense-datum—that is called an individual.

It is not my present purpose to contend that this passage in the *Blue Book* shows that objects in the *Tractatus* do include universals. Even though such a conclusion seems the most natural reading—and it will be the burden of the subsequent argument to show that the natural reading is indeed the correct reading—we must for the time being allow the possibility that Wittgenstein is not here precisely characterizing his own earlier view in the *Tractatus*. My present claim is only that #46 of the *Philosophical Investigations*, taken in conjunction with the above passages from Moore's notes and the *Blue Book*, is—to the extent that premise (1) is plausible at all—evidence in favor of the interpretation of Wittgensteinian objects as including universals, rather than evidence against this interpretation. But given the weakness of premise (1), the net result is that #46 provides no evidence one way or the other on this question.

How, though, shall we explain the surprising collapse of premise (2) of the above argument? If Wittgenstein does regard universals as individuals, what sense can we make of the puzzling situation in which a philosopher of his competence attributes such a view to Russell? After all, as Müller says, Russell's individuals "...are identified by their inventor with 'particulars' and circumspectly enough defended from every suspicion of universality...," whereupon he quotes Russell himself as saying: "We shall further define 'individuals' or 'particulars' as the objects that can be named by proper names."[4] One possible solution to the puzzle is that although Wittgenstein may himself use the Russellian expression 'individual' to refer to universals, he is for reasons of his own deliberately and radically departing from Russell's own use of this expression. It might seem that this would have to be the solution, in light of Russell's own unequivocal identification of individuals with particulars, in the passage cited by Müller. But perhaps we are being too hasty. *Introduction to Mathematical Philosophy*, from which this passage was taken, was not published until 1919, and the period of Wittgenstein's own intense involvement with Russell's philosophy was some years before that (the period of his close personal contact with Russell extending approximately from 1912 through 1914). Might it not be possible that Wittgenstein's characterization of universals as individuals is consistent with Russell's own position, at least as it stood at some earlier time, when Wittgenstein would have had occasion to be exposed to it either through the study of Russell's writings or through discussions with Russell himself?

To explore this possibility, let us begin by examining Russell's views as they would have been when Wittgenstein first encountered them. For a definitive account of what Russell understood by the notion of an individual at that time, one might reasonably turn first to Volume I of *Principia Mathematica*, which was published less than two years before Wittgenstein began his studies under Russell in October of 1911. What *Principia* says, first, is that individuals are those "...objects which are neither propositions nor functions...,"[5] and secondly, that an individual is "...something which exists on its own account."[6] Are either of these characterizations incompatible with the view that universals are individuals? As to the latter characterization, there is clearly no incompatibility, given the early Russell's Platonism, which allowed that universals exist quite independently from particulars. The first statement, however, which distinguishes between individuals and functions, would seem to present a problem for the view that universals can be individuals. If functions are not individuals—a position which *Principia* underscores by holding that functions and individuals are of different logical types—then it would seem that universals, which in the logical symbolism of *Principia* would correspond to the function-part of the proposition rather than to the argument-part, could not be individuals either.

There is a way of trying to get around this conclusion that involves some exegetical hair-splitting. The distinction drawn in *Principia* between functions and individuals does not, strictly speaking, show that universals are not individuals, because universals are not functions. That is, predicates and relations are constituents of elementary propositions, but functions are not. As *Principia* says,

> [i]t should be remembered that a function is not a constituent in one of its values: thus for example the function 'x is human' is not a constituent of the proposition 'Socrates is human'.[7]

Thus, if for the sake of illustration we take 'Socrates is human' as an elementary proposition of the subject-predicate form, we must distinguish the function 'x is human' from the predicative constituent expressed by the words 'is human'; therefore, from the fact that the individual Socrates differs in type from the function 'x is human' we cannot conclude that Socrates and the predicative constituent of this proposition differ in type as well. The possibility remains open that both sorts of constituents could be individuals.

This strategy, while resting on a distinction which is technically correct, is nevertheless implausible as an account of the authors' own intentions, because the distinction is one which Russell and Whitehead themselves more than once fail to observe. We have already considered their remark that individuals are those objects which are neither propositions nor functions, which suggests that functions are indeed a kind of propositional constituent. Again, they say that "...propositions which contain no apparent variables we call elementary propositions, and the terms of such propositions, other than functions, we call *individuals*."[8] This suggests that there can be two sorts of terms in elementary propositions, individuals and functions. Of course, 'term' can only be taken here in the broad sense of 'constituent'; even so, however, the statement cannot be correct, since we have already seen that a function cannot be any sort of constituent of an elementary proposition. Still, it is clear that what is intended by this statement is to single out only one sort of constituent in elementary propositions as individuals. That the contrast has been drawn incorrectly between individuals and functions rather than between individuals and universals is no consolation, since it is obviously the latter sort of contrast that is intended.

Given this conflation of functions with predicates and relations, we also have some reason to assume that the difference in logical type between individuals and functions is intended by the authors of *Principia* to reflect a difference in logical type between individuals and universals as well, which would again show that universals could not be individuals. And this is hardly a bold exegetical leap; to posit a type-difference between individuals, which serve as the subjects of predication and the terms of relations, and these predicates and relations themselves, would seem a simple matter of common sense. What could be more obvious than that these various sorts of propositional constituents have different logical jobs to do, a difference which is appropriately expressed by saying that these sorts of constituents are of different logical types?

The text of *Principia* thus seems to offer no support for the view that universals are individuals; rather, it seems to present powerful evidence against this view. How, given this sort of textual evidence to the contrary, could Wittgenstein have thought that Russellian individuals include universals? Perhaps the answer lies in the realization that, although the difference between individuals, on the one hand, and predicative and relational constituents, on the other, is indeed genuine, to focus exclusively on this difference is to tell only part of the story. To explore this line of inquiry, we need to examine still earlier writings of Russell. Let us turn first to Russell's 1908 paper "Mathematical Logic as based on the Theory of Types." Since this paper contains essentially the same account of the theory of types as presented in Volume I of *Principia*, we have *prima facie* grounds, in the absence of evidence to the contrary, for supposing that Russell's views about individuals expressed in the earlier paper would be those of *Principia* as well. What Russell actually says in this paper is as follows:

> In an elementary proposition we can distinguish one or more *terms* from one or more *concepts*; the *terms* are whatever can be regarded as the *subject* of the proposition, while the concepts are the predicates or relations asserted of these terms. The terms of elementary propositions we will call individuals.[9]

In Russell's text there is a footnote following the first sentence of the above quotation. This footnote, which is presumably intended to throw further light on the distinction between terms and concepts, refers us to #48 of *Principles of Mathematics*. In this still earlier work, written around the turn of the century, Russell informs us that concepts have a curious two-fold use which allows them to function not only in their predicative or relational capacity, but also as terms—though not, of course, in the same proposition. So, for example, the two propositions 'Socrates is human' and 'Humanity belongs to Socrates' are equivalent, but nevertheless distinct, since the first proposition makes an assertion about Socrates while the second makes an assertion about humanity, the difference between the two propositions being that the concept which functions in the first proposition as a concept functions in the second proposition as a term.[10] Things, i.e., particulars, are opposed to concepts, i.e., universals, in that the former can occur in propositions only as subjects, whereas the latter can occur predicatively or relationally in addition to being able to occur as subjects.

It would thus appear that by referring to #48 of *Principles of Mathematics* in the footnote of his 1908 paper, Russell is indirectly allowing that universals could be individuals; specifically, they are individuals in those contexts in which they function as terms in elementary propositions. The trouble with this conclusion is that, although Russell's footnote occurs in the context of a discussion of elementary propositions, so that it is natural to take him to be implying that it is elementary propositions which could have universals as logical subjects, such a conclusion seems to be inconsistent with his theory of types. If, despite my earlier argument that concepts are not to be identified with functions, we concede that in the system of *Principia* (as well as in the 1908 paper) concepts are symbolically represented as functions, then it is obvious that functions could not serve as logical subjects of elementary propositions; the symbolism of *Principia* rules this out straightaway, since individuals are there explicitly said to be denoted by "...such letters as a, b, c, x, y, z, w...,"[11] rather than by the small Greek letters used for function-signs. Furthermore, any proposition which had a concept serving as its logical subject would symbolically be represented as the function of a function.

And any such proposition containing a higher-order function, though perfectly permissible in the system of *Principia*, would by definition not be elementary, since an elementary proposition could contain only individuals and first-order functions. The only way around these difficulties would be to deny that concepts must always be symbolized as functions. We would have to contend that when a concept acts as the logical subject of an elementary proposition, it assumes a different logical type than it has when it functions predicatively or relationally, and that this change in logical type is accompanied by the appropriate change in symbolic representation.

Whether or not this is a plausible interpretation of Russell, it is at least aesthetically pleasing, since it would bring the solution of our original puzzle full-circle. Not only would Russell be the source for Wittgenstein's broad notion of an individual, but Wittgenstein, in turn, would be responsible for Russell's subsequent abandonment of that notion in favor of the view that individuals must be particulars—though a view which, as we shall later see, Wittgenstein had his own reasons for declining to adopt. That the responsibility for Russell's change of position would be Wittgenstein's stems from the fact that, whether or not during the time of their interaction Russell had allowed that universals could be logical subjects of elementary propositions, it is clear that during this same period he never questions that there are propositions of some level of complexity or other in which universals do serve as logical subjects.

Thus, for example, we have Russell's theory of judgement (and of propositional attitudes generally) in which one's judgement of the truth of a proposition is not a relation of two terms—one's mind and the proposition (the latter considered as a complex object)—but rather a multiple relation between the mind and the constituents of the proposition, where all the constituents are regarded as terms of the judgement-relation. As Russell explains his theory in *Problems of Philosophy* (1912), the proposition 'Othello believes that Desdemona loves Cassio' contains the relation 'loving', not as the relation which creates the unity of the complex whole, but as "...one of the objects—it is a brick in the structure, not the cement. The cement is the relation 'believing'."[12]

Again, in *Problems of Philosophy*, general propositions are given as further examples of propositions having universals as logical subjects, since general propositions are there thought by Russell to contain only universals as constituents.[13] Russell continues to hold the view that universals can function as logical subjects through the writing of the 1913 manuscript *Theory of Knowledge*.[14] Finally, however, Russell's ongoing discussion with Wittgenstein concerning this manuscript brings about a change of view. Here is how Russell himself later expresses that change in his 1918 lectures on "The Philosophy of Logical Atomism":

> I pass on from particulars to predicates and relations.... A very great deal of what I am saying in this course of lectures consists of ideas which I derived from my friend Wittgenstein. But I have had no opportunity of knowing how far his ideas have changed since August 1914.... Understanding a predicate is quite a different thing from understanding a name. ... To understand a name you must be acquainted with the particular of which it is a name, and you must know that it is the name of that particular. You do not, that is to say, have any suggestion of the form of a proposition, whereas in understanding a predicate you do.... The importance of that is in connection with the theory of types.... It is in the fact that a predicate can never occur except as a predicate. When it seems to occur as a subject, the phrase wants amplifying and explaining, unless, of course, you are talking about the word itself.... Exactly the same thing applies to relations.... A relation can never occur except as a relation, never as a subject.... The different sorts of words, in fact, have different sorts of uses and must be kept always to the right use and not to the wrong use, and it is fallacies arising from putting symbols to wrong uses that lead to the contradictions concerned with types.[15]

The change in Russell's position here openly proclaimed is already subtly manifest in the 1914 lectures on *Our Knowledge of the External World*. In these earlier lectures Russell does not explicitly say that relations cannot be logical subjects, but he does allow that "when we say there are relations of more than two things, we mean there are single facts consisting in a relation and more than two things...,"[16] and generally he is careful to speak of properties and relations only in connection with their occurrence in facts, i.e., where they are said to be predicated of, or to relate, things.[17] It is as though he feels that Wittgenstein must be right, but is sufficiently unsure about this new development—not yet being able fully to assess the consequences for his own philosophy—so as to prefer to underplay the whole matter until he can get his own position sorted out.[18]

Of course, once Russell has come to hold that universals cannot be logical subjects, then, according to his characterization of individuals as logical subjects, it follows that universals cannot be individuals. If the preceding interpretation of Russell is correct, then both views concerning universals would have changed at the same time, and it would therefore not be surprising that the first explicit identification of individuals with particulars does not come until *Introduction to Mathematical Philosophy*, a work roughly contemporaneous with the 1918 lectures in which Russell's view that universals cannot be logical subjects also receives its first explicit expression. However, even if we decide against this account of Russell's development, and we opt instead for the view that Russell's theory of types, as it appears in the 1908 paper and subsequently in *Principia*, rules out the possibililty that universals could be individuals, even while allowing that they could be logical subjects, the earlier paper nevertheless provides us with the necessary clue for solving our original puzzle about Wittgenstein. It does this by drawing our attention, by means of the previously discussed footnote, to *Principles of Mathematics*. The following passage from that work gives us our desired Russellian precedent for Wittgenstein's broad notion of an individual:

> Whatever may be an object of thought, or may occur in any true or false proposition, or can be counted as *one*, I call a *term*. This, then, is the widest word in the philosophical vocabulary. I shall use as synonymous with it the words unit, individual, and entity. The first two emphasize the fact that every term is *one*, while the third is derived from the fact that every term has being, *i.e. is* in some sense. A man, a moment, a number, a class, a relation, a chimaera, or anything else that can be mentioned, is sure to be a term; and to deny that such and such a thing is a term must always be false.... Every term...is a logical subject: it is, for example, the subject of the proposition that itself is one. Again every term is immutable and indestructible. What a term is, it is, and no change can be conceived in it which would not destroy its identity and make it another term.[19]

If we ignore the Meinongian extravagances expressed here, which Russell himself soon repudiated by using suitable methods of analysis to show that what seemed to be constituents of propositions were not always really so, the passage is important to our inquiry on two counts: first, there is the extraordinarily wide scope given to the notion of a term and, by implication, to the notion of an individual; secondly, we find terms characterized in a way which minimizes the difference between particulars and universals—not only can both sorts of entities be logical subjects, but they are both immutable and indestructible as well.

It is instructive to contrast this passage with Russell's view in the later *Theory of Knowledge*, where the total emphasis is on the difference between particulars and universals. While Russell there allows that both sorts of propositional constituents "...occur in the logical inventory of the world...,"[20] the two sorts of objects differ so significantly in their "logical character"[21] that Russell is unwilling to say that they both exist, in any univocal sense. Thus: "...when we say 'there are' predicates, it is rash to affirm that these words have precisely the same meaning as when we say 'there are' particulars."[22] It is this growing emphasis on the difference between particulars and universals— found to some extent in the *Problems of Philosophy*, where the contrast between the immutability of universals and the transitoriness of particulars is sharply drawn,[23] and found most pronounced in *Theory of Knowledge*—that provides the best, though not conclusive, evidence that Russell might have given up the view that universals could be individuals before he gave up the view that universals could be logical subjects. That is, if universals and particulars are as unlike as *Theory of Knowledge* portrays them to be, then what is the point of obscuring these differences by classifying both sorts of objects as individuals? And if to say that universals and particulars differ in logical character is to say that they differ in logical type, even in the context in which both are functioning as logical subjects, then, according to the account of *Principia*, in which individuals are all of one logical type, the case against universals being individuals would be complete. Since I am not altogether confident that 'logical character' and 'logical type' can be thus equated,[24] the issue as to exactly when Russell gave up the view that universals could be individuals must remain unresolved.

For our purposes, the important point is that we have shown that this view was definitely Russell's, at least at the time of the writing of *Principles of Mathematics*. Moreover, when we examine the development of Wittgenstein's own views, we will see that he ultimately finds Russell's earlier tendency to emphasize the similarities between universals and particulars much more congenial than Russell's later tendency to emphasize their differences. A more detailed examination of likely connections between *Principles of Mathematics* and the *Tractatus* will be found in Chapter Three. Our more immediate concern is to trace the course of Wittgenstein's philosophical development to see how his own assimilation of particulars with universals eventually comes about—or, more accurately, his re-assimilation of these two sorts of entities, since his development will be shown to exhibit a three-stage dialectical development of (1) assimilation, (2) emphasis of differences, and (3) re-assimilation.

CHAPTER TWO

THE THREE STAGES OF
WITTGENSTEIN'S DEVELOPMENT

Wittgenstein's three positions can be distinguished by their different attitudes towards the relation of particulars to universals with respect to a distinction which I shall call that between dependent and independent symbols. This distinction roughly corresponds to Russell's distinction between proper names, which have meaning in isolation, and incomplete symbols, which have meaning only in certain contexts. The difference between Russell's distinction and mine is that whereas incomplete symbols are mere technical devices which are supposed to disappear upon analysis and so do not really symbolize anything at all, I do not wish to deny that dependent symbols have a genuine, indispensable, symbolizing role. They differ from independent symbols in that their symbolizing role requires that they be in relation to other symbols, a relation which for our purposes in this discussion will always involve their occurrence within the context of a proposition (or at least within the schema of a proposition, where variables or blank argument-places take the place of one or more constants).

Given this distinction between dependent and independent symbols, which, it is hoped, will become clearer as we proceed, the development of Wittgenstein's thought can be characterized as follows: (1) views both particulars and universals as represented by independent symbols, all such symbols therefore being names of objects. (2) views only particulars as being represented by independent symbols and sees this as a reason for supposing that the symbols which ostensibly stand for universals, since they are dependent symbols, are not really names of objects, and that they instead contribute only to a symbolization of the form of the proposition in which they occur.[1] (3) recognizes that *every* symbol in a proposition has meaning only in the context of the proposition, so that both universals and particulars are represented by dependent symbols, a situation which removes any reason for supposing that only symbols for particulars are names of objects and therefore puts universals again on a par with particulars. I shall now support this interpretation with a detailed examination of the relevant texts.

Unlike positions (2) and (3), for which there are abundant textual sources, (1) must be gleaned from a few of Wittgenstein's letters, of which only that of January, 1913, is really helpful. My presentation of (1) is essentially a reconstruction, based on this letter, but often going beyond anything explicitly stated there. Nevertheless, nothing in my formulation of (1) is the result of mere guesswork, but consists rather in placing Wittgenstein's remarks in that historical context which we can reasonably assume provides the background for the development of his own thought—the context in this case being provided by the work of Russell, Wittgenstein's teacher and colleague. I begin by briefly recapitulating the view of the relation between universals and particulars held by Russell prior to his retraction of the view that universals could be logical subjects.

If we suppose that 'Socrates is mortal' is an elementary proposition of the subject-predicate form, then, according to Russell, both 'Socrates' and 'mortality' are names of objects, a particular and a universal, respectively. In this proposition, only 'Socrates' names an individual, but in a different proposition 'mortality' could also name an individual if it were to occur in this proposition as logical subject. Of the two names, only 'Socrates' is a proper name, since it can only occur as naming an individual, whereas 'mortality' can occur either as naming an individual or as naming an object in its predicative capacity.

Against this view, Wittgenstein feels that 'Socrates' and 'mortality', in their occurrence in the proposition 'Socrates is mortal', both name individuals and are indeed both proper names. By this view, Wittgenstein is not maintaining that 'mortality' is here functioning as a logical subject, let alone that it can only occur as the subject of a proposition. On the contrary, his view is that 'mortality' can only occur predicatively and never as subject, the different syntactic functions of 'Socrates' and 'mortality' being ensured by a difference in logical type of their respective objects. He nevertheless prefers to regard both 'Socrates' and 'mortality' as proper names (and presumably, therefore, the named objects as individuals) because he does not see the difference in syntactic function of the two names as reflecting a fundamental difference in the kind of object named.

This is in contrast to Russell, who reserves the expression 'proper name' for names of objects which can only occur as subjects, because he wants to distinguish such objects, i.e., particulars, from universals in virtue of a peculiar characteristic which he supposes to belong solely to the latter kind of object. This is the characteristic of being a constituent of a proposition in such a way as to bring together the other constituents of the proposition so as to constitute a *unity* rather than a mere aggregate, an ability which Russell attributes to the constituent in its predicative or relational role, a role which he sees as the unique province of universals. The difference between a unity and an aggregate is most easily illustrated by considering a relational proposition, e.g., 'John loves Mary'. If we suppose this to be an elementary proposition of two terms and a relation, represented by the three names 'John', 'loving', and 'Mary', then the proposition itself is not just a list of these names, but a unification of them into one proposition, where 'loving' actually functions relationally to relate 'John' to 'Mary' and furthermore to relate them in a specific direction, i.e., where the love is said to proceed from John to Mary and is not said to proceed from Mary to John.[2] In *Problems of Philosophy* Russell speaks of this relational function of relations as that of uniting, or 'knitting together', the terms between which the relation holds into one complex whole and giving this complex a specific sense, or direction.[3] Likewise, in the proposition 'Socrates is mortal', assuming it to be of the subject-predicate form, the predicative function of 'mortality' performs this same job of combining the two names into a propositional unity, which is, however, not quite so obvious as in a relational proposition, since in a subject-predicate proposition, containing as it does only one term, no problem about the 'direction' of such a proposition arises. Nevertheless, it too is not a mere list of the names 'Socrates' and 'mortality', but is a unity for which Russell feels the predicative constituent is responsible.

A consequence of Russell's view is that analysis is always in some measure a falsification, since predicative and relational constituents retain their unifying function only while they are actually combined with the other constituents in the proposition. As he says in *Principles of Mathematics*, "...analysis gives us the truth, and nothing but the truth, yet it can never give us the whole truth."[4] Wittgenstein avoids this difficulty—and in so doing minimizes the difference between universals and particulars—by attributing the unifying power, not to the predicative or relational constituents in the proposition, but rather to a special copula, which is introduced only for this purpose and is not an additional constituent. Thus, 'Socrates is mortal' is analyzed into the two constituents Socrates and mortality, and the completely general proposition—though at this time Wittgenstein thought of it as a name rather than as a proposition—'$(\exists x, y)\varepsilon_1(x, y)$', where '$\varepsilon_1$' represents the unifying copula and where the proposition as a whole represents that aspect of the original proposition which constitutes its unity, in abstraction from the particular content which is unified. The subscript to the copula is presumably meant to indicate that the copula is predicative, i.e., that it combines two constituents, since Wittgenstein writes the relational proposition 'aRb' as '$\varepsilon_2(a, R, b)$', where the changed subscript presumably means that the copula is here doing its combining work in two places, between a and R and between R and b. This analysis, which allows us to isolate all the constituents of a proposition and treat them simply as things, none of which have a special unifying role, removes the outstanding rationale for recognizing two kinds of names, one kind for particulars and the other kind for universals, and Wittgenstein therefore regards both 'Socrates' and 'mortality' as proper names. At the same time, he does not want a method of analysis which makes it look as if 'Mortality is Socrates' makes sense, which he seems to be in danger of permitting if both 'Socrates' and 'mortality' are proper names of things. His strategy, accordingly, is to affirm that 'Mortality is Socrates' is nonsense—though not because 'Socrates' is given a syntactic role which names of particulars are incapable of fulfilling because of the absence of a certain capacity in such objects which is possessed by other objects, viz., universals, and which allows universals but not particulars to act predicatively and relationally—but rather because universals and particulars are simply objects of different logical types. This strategy ensures that 'Socrates' can never occur as a predicate or relation, but it also means that, by the same token, 'mortality' can never occur as subject, and that propositions in which it superficially occurs as the grammatical subject must be capable of further analysis which shows that it is not the true logical subject.

While the pre-Wittgensteinian Russell may or may not also have held that particulars and universals were always of different logical types—an interpretive issue which the previous chapter left without a definitive resolution—the type-difference between particulars and universals posited by Wittgenstein is in any case distinguished from any version of Russell's position by Wittgenstein's assumption that this type-difference automatically assigns to the particular the role of logical subject, and to the universal the role of predicate or relation. Since, on this view, universals cannot be logical subjects, there is no longer any need to posit the peculiar capacity of universals which allows them to perform the two-fold role demanded by Russell's account. This concludes my exposition of (1).

By January of 1913, Wittgenstein has come to a conclusion which requires the abandonment of (1) and which sets in motion a train of thought whose culmination in the *Tractatus* has been widely misunderstood to be what I have called a kind of nominalism. Though, as I shall subsequently argue, the mature position of the *Tractatus*, viz., (3), is clearly realistic, including as it does properties and relations among objects, the intermediate position we are now about to consider appears—on the basis of some of Wittgenstein's statements in (2)—to embrace an extreme version of nominalism. Even here, however, appearances are deceiving, and we shall see that (2) amounts to no more than the claim that symbols for properties and relations are radically different from symbols for things (particulars)—which I express by saying that the former are dependent, and the latter independent, symbols—a claim which falls far short of impugning the ontological status of universals. I proceed now with an account of (2), beginning with

Wittgenstein's reason for abandoning (1).

As we have seen, (1) depends on the assumption that things are of different types to explain the restrictions which must be placed on the syntactic roles of the names of these things so as to prevent nonsensical formulations such as 'Mortality is Socrates'. By January of 1913, Wittgenstein has become convinced that things, i.e., the simple objects represented by proper names, cannot be of different types. He does not give reasons for his change of heart—perhaps the invocation of types to differentiate simple objects just looks suspiciously *ad hoc*—but, in any case, the consequence of his rejection of this solution is that he must find some other way to ensure that nonsensical formulations remain illegitimate. His new solution is to attribute differences in the syntactic roles of symbols for particulars and symbols for universals, not to differences in the type of objects but to differences in the kinds of symbols themselves. Only symbols for particulars are now considered proper names; symbols for universals, on the other hand, are viewed as having a distinctive form which renders impossible, by the nature of the symbols themselves, the substitution of one kind of symbol for another. For example, 'Socrates is mortal' is analyzed into the proper name 'Socrates' and the form '($\exists$x) x is mortal', or generally into 'x' and '($\exists$x)ϕx'. A relational proposition such as 'John loves Mary' is analyzed into 'John', 'Mary', and '($\exists$x, y)R(x, y)'. On this analysis, properties and relations are no longer represented by symbols which have meaning in isolation, as do the names of particulars; rather, the symbols for universals manage to symbolize at all only by symbolizing the whole form of the proposition in which such properties or relations are represented.

This way of characterizing the difference between kinds of symbols, as stated in the letter of January, 1913, remains essentially the same in the notes dictated to Moore in April, 1914 and in the "Notes on Logic" of September, 1914. The one change is that the former regards '($\exists$x)ϕx' and '($\exists$x, y)R(x, y)' as simple symbols, indeed, as names—only not names of things, but names of forms. By the time of the "Notes on Logic," however, Wittgenstein has amended his position to allow that symbols such as those above are not names, since it makes sense to negate these symbols, while it makes no sense to negate a name. These symbols are now conceived to perform their role, not by being names of forms, but by being forms themselves.[5] In other words, these symbols are facts, which symbolize by corresponding with facts, or at least possible facts, in reality. Thus, what symbolizes in 'ϕx' or in 'R(x, y)' —alternatively written as 'xRy'—is not 'ϕ' or 'R', conceived as a name, but rather the fact that 'ϕ' is to the left of a name-form (i.e., a variable in the place of a proper name) or the fact that 'R' is between the name-forms 'x' and 'y'. Such, in essence, is position (2). What can we conclude from all this about the ontological status of properties and relations?

The answer is: (a) Wittgenstein, who has no metaphysical axe to grind, is quite willing to adopt a nominalistic attitude, and thus to view words like 'mortality' as having to do only with the form of a proposition and not with its content, as long as this strategy succeeds in rendering impossible the substitution of one kind of symbol for another, or at least makes this impossible in a perspicuous logical symbolism; (b) nevertheless, the view he actually advances cannot be regarded as nominalistic, even though he has no qualms about so conceiving it, since it does not really expunge the symbolic content from words like 'loving' and 'mortality' (or—in the logical symbolism—from letters like 'ϕ' and 'R'). Rather, the most we can say about such words (or letters)[6] is that their way of having a content is different from the way proper names have a content, since the former kind of symbol, unlike the latter, has a representative capacity only in the context of a proposition. This is all that Wittgenstein need claim to provide for the difference in the two kinds of symbols, and, in the last analysis, this is all that he does claim. I shall now elaborate on both parts of this answer.

(a) It is clear that the demands of logic shape Wittgenstein's metaphysics and not vice-versa.[7] The most striking illustration of this is in the letter of 1913, where, to accomodate his rejection of the notion of type-differences among things, he moves at one stroke from a full-fledged realism to a view which regards properties and relations as mere copulae, i.e., as taking over the unifying role that in (1) had been given its own special symbol 'ε'. Actually, Wittgenstein's willingness, for the sake of a solution to his logical difficulties, to give up any claim to an ontological status for properties and relations, extends even further than a concession that words such as 'mortality' or 'loving' symbolize only the form of a proposition and not its content, since, by regarding '$(\exists x)\phi x$' and '$(\exists x)xRy$' as themselves names of forms, i.e., as simple, un-analyzable symbols, Wittgenstein implicitly allows the symbolic role of 'ϕ' and 'R' to be reduced to the level of, e.g., the letter 'c' in the name 'Socrates'. That is to say, 'ϕ' and 'R' are left with no integrity as individual symbols at all. Even when he later retracts this extreme view and admits that, e.g., '$(\exists x, y)xRy$' retains the complexity of the proposition whose form is here symbolized, so that there is once again an opportunity to view 'R' as in some sense a separable symbolizing component, he feels content to attribute the bare minimum of symbolic integrity to the letter 'R' by speaking at times as if its only role is to occur between 'x' and 'y' in order that the arrangement as a whole might constitute a symbolizing fact, without any suggestion that 'R' has any other symbolic role at all. Thus, in the notes dictated to Moore we find the blunt assertion: "...[T]hat 'R' stands between 'a' and 'b' expresses a relation."[8] Yet all of this shows, not an antipathy towards realism, but merely Wittgenstein's willingness to adopt whatever ontology his logical arguments suggest to be appropriate, and it is this same dispassion towards ontological issues that facilitates his re-affirmation of realism, once he becomes aware that the nominalist flavor which pervades his statement of (2) is not warranted by his own arguments.

(b) The basis for denying that (2) is nominalistic is quite simple.[9] If we consider, e.g., the form '$(\exists x, y)xRy$', where 'R' is constant, the reason Wittgenstein cannot be said to have successfully contended that 'R' symbolizes no content, and instead only helps to symbolize a form, is that 'R', in addition to contributing to the symbolization of a form, by being between 'x' and 'y', tells us something else about any particulars which would be represented by 'x' and 'y'; viz., we are told that these particulars are related by the relation symbolized by 'R' rather than the relation symbolized, say, by 'S'. That is, both 'xRy' and 'xSy'—or 'aRb' and 'aSb', where 'a' and 'b' are constants—exhibit the same form; if they nevertheless say something different, as they surely do, this is because 'R' and 'S' symbolize different contents, i.e., stand for different relations.

This is such an obvious point to be made against a nominalist interpretation of (2) that it might be supposed to have missed the subtlety of Wittgenstein's position. But let us consider the alternatives. Any account of Wittgenstein's position that is advanced will have to allow for a difference between 'aRb' and 'aSb'. If my interpretation of (2) is mistaken, and 'R' and 'S' do not symbolize different contents, so that the difference between the two propositions is not to be explained by saying that 'R' and 'S' stand for different universals, then Wittgenstein is presumably left only the option of saying that 'R' and 'S' are used only to differentiate the *forms* of the two propositions, i.e., the manner in which the names are arranged in the propositions so as to reflect a corresponding (possible) configuration of particulars in reality.

I can think of two ways in which one might try to follow up this line of reasoning. The first way—which to my knowledge has not had any advocates but is nevertheless at least a remotely possible way of construing some of Wittgenstein's remarks—is to say that 'aRb' and 'aSb' are different propositions, but not because 'R' and 'S' symbolize different contents; rather, since what symbolizes in each proposition, other than proper names, is the fact that the symbols are in such-and-such an arrangement, 'aRb' and 'aSb' say something different because the propositional signs constitute different facts—the first fact being that 'a' and 'b' are in a certain relation to the letter 'R' and the second fact being that 'a' and 'b' are in this same relation to the letter 'S'. Therefore, we need not suppose that 'R' and 'S' symbolize contents to account for 'aRb' and 'aSb' symbolizing different facts; the propositional signs themselves provide all the differences that we need.

Whatever slight merit this interpretation may have is far outweighed by its obvious difficulties, and we can attribute it to Wittgenstein only at the cost of admitting the utter untenability of his position. That is, conceding that the difference between 'R' and 'S' as letters is sufficient to distinguish the propositional signs 'aRb' and 'aSb' as facts, it is hard to see how this difference alone in the two facts is supposed to symbolize a difference in the configuration of the actual particulars. In other words, if 'aRb' and 'aSb' are to symbolize different (possible) configurations of particulars, the symbolic role of 'R' and 'S' must be greater than their mere occurrence as letters between the symbols 'a' and 'b'; if such a difference were enough to constitute a symbolization of different propositional forms, as would have to be the case if 'aRb' and 'aSb' were of different forms merely in virtue of the difference between 'R' and 'S' as letters, then 'aRb' and 'cRd' would also be of different forms, in virtue of the different letters comprising these two propositional signs. The difficulties of this interpretation lead us to consider a second interpretation, which grants that 'R' and 'S' have a symbolic role over and above their occurrence as different letters in propositional signs, and it is to this latter interpretation that I now turn.

This second interpretation, unlike the first, has a number of adherents,[10] though as an interpretation of the *Tractatus* itself, and not just of (2), since (2) and (3) are not distinguished by other commentators. The passage of central importance for this interpretation is 3.1432 of the *Tractatus*, which says:

> Not: "The complex sign 'aRb' says that a stands in the relation R to b",
> but: That 'a' stands in a certain relation to 'b' says that aRb.

The crux of this passage is taken to be that Wittgenstein omits mention of the letter 'R' in discussing the relation of 'a' to 'b', which in turn is taken to mean that in a logically perspicuous symbolism 'R' would be superfluous, so that the configuration of particulars could be fully symbolized by a corresponding arrangement of names. For example, 'aRb', 'aSb', and 'aTb' might be equivalent to 'ab', 'ba', and '$\frac{a}{b}$', respectively. On this view, unlike the first interpretation, 'R', 'S', and 'T' have a symbolic role in addition to their occurrence as letters, but this is not the role of standing for universals; rather, it is the role of being a shorthand indication of the way 'a' and 'b' would be arranged in the perspicuous notation. Thus, the 'R' in 'aRb' tells us that 'a' is to the left and adjacent to 'b', and so on.

Admittedly, Wittgenstein's silence about the place of 'R' in the symbolizing fact might encourage the view that 'R' does not help constitute this fact, but this in itself is hardly evidence for a nominalistic interpretation of the *Tractatus*. We can account for the nominalistic tone of 3.1432 by considering the source from which the passage is lifted nearly *ver-*

batim, viz., the "Notes on Logic,"[11] whose nominalistic tone we can acknowledge without having to conclude that it is this same tone that Wittgenstein wants to preserve in 3.1432. Rather, the context of 3.1432 suggests that Wittgenstein is utilizing his earlier remark (as, indeed, the whole *Tractatus* substantially consists in a re-arrangement and re-working of such earlier remarks) only to emphasize that a propositional sign is a fact as opposed to a complex name. That is, according to Wittgenstein's decimal notation, 3.1432 is a comment on 3.143, and this latter passage is concerned only to make the point that a propositional sign is a fact, not a name; this is also the context of the remark in the "Notes on Logic" which corresponds to 3.1432. On my interpretation, then, the purpose of 3.1432 is only to contrast symbolizing facts with names, and the nominalist tone of this passage—which could have been avoided altogether had Wittgenstein specified that the relation in which 'a' stands to 'b' consists in their respective relations to 'R'—is in any case minimized by the realization that the status of 'R' as a name is implied in many other contexts in the *Tractatus*. My subsequent account of (3), by providing independent grounds for supposing that the *Tractatus* regards 'R' as the name of an object, will by implication bear out my interpretation of 3.1432. What I want to consider now, however, is why the popular interpretation of the *Tractatus*, based on 3.1432, is not the right interpretation even of (2), whose ostensible nominalism makes such an interpretation at least *prima facie* plausible for this earlier position.

The reason for rejecting such an interpretation for (2) is that there is no suggestion in any of the textual sources of (2) that a letter like 'R' would disappear in a logically perspicuous symbolism; in fact, there are clear statements to the contrary. Thus, in the notes to Moore we find:

> When we say of a proposition of [the] form 'aRb' that what symbolizes is that 'R' is between 'a' and 'b', it must be remembered that in fact the proposition is capable of further analysis because a, R, and b are not simples. But what seems certain is that when we have analysed it we shall in the end come to propositions of the same form in respect of the fact that they do consist in one thing being between two others.... [T]hough we don't know any unanalyzable propositions of this kind, yet we can understand what is meant by a proposition of the form $(\exists x,y,R)xRy$ (which is

unanalyzable…and *unanalyzable* proposition = one in which only fundamental symbols = ones not capable of definition, occur)….[12]

From this passage we can conclude, first, that 'R' is not theoretically superfluous and, secondly, that the form of the proposition is really that in
which all the letters, including 'R', are apparent variables, so that 'aRb'
and 'aSb', where the constants 'R' and 'S' take the place of the apparent
variable, are propositions of the same form, which they could not be if
'R' and 'S' were shorthand indications of different arrangements of 'a'
and 'b'.

If, as seems the undeniable conclusion, we must admit that 'R'—
where it is a constant in a proposition such as 'aRb'—symbolizes a
specific relation, and does so precisely in virtue of being that letter and
no other, how do we explain the passage from the "Notes on Logic" corresponding to 3.1432, in which the omission of 'R' from the description
of the symbolizing fact appears deliberate? The answer is that 'R' is not
mentioned because, unlike 'a' and 'b', 'R' is not considered to stand for
anything in isolation; if, instead of saying that 'a' stands in a certain relation to 'b', Wittgenstein had said that 'a' and 'b' stand in a certain relation to each other by standing in a certain relation to 'R', he might thereby have fostered the misimpression, by treating 'R' in isolation, that 'R'
was a symbol just like 'a' and 'b'—and, as we have seen, Wittgenstein is
insistent that it is not 'R' that symbolizes a relation, but rather *that* 'R' is
between 'a' and 'b'. So, even though the symbolizing fact includes 'R'
just as much as it does 'a' and 'b', Wittgenstein does not mention 'R' in
his description of the fact in order to avoid any possible confusion. Unfortunately, as the history of Wittgensteinian exegesis has borne out, his
innocent remark has occasioned little else but confusion, a confusion
which I hope my own account has done something to dispel.

To sum up: despite appearances, (2) is not nominalistic. We are
misled in this direction by Wittgenstein's exaggeration of the difference
in the symbolic role of proper names, on the one hand, and words for
properties and relations, on the other. When he says that "…in 'aRb', 'R'
is *not* a symbol, but *that* 'R' is between one name and another symbolizes…,"[13] he is justified only in saying that 'R' is not an *independent*

symbol. Matters are only obscured by the suggestion that 'R' is not a symbol at all; 'R' and 'S' can very well serve by themselves to tell us that a different relation is being symbolized in each case, even though neither 'R' nor 'S' fully exercises its symbolic function except in the context of a proposition or a propositional schema.

It is obvious, then, that Wittgenstein's intention to establish a radical dichotomy between proper names and words for properties and relations—the former kind of symbol having to do only with the content, and the latter only with the form of a proposition—cannot be realized within (2) itself, which allows at most a distinction between symbols which concern only a content and symbols which concern both a content and a form. Wittgenstein's eventual realization of this marks his transition from (2) to (3), where he once again acknowledges that both particulars and universals constitute the content of a proposition, i.e., both are included among objects, and that the symbols of both universals and of particulars are names of these objects. We might suppose that, despite this re-assimilation of universals and their symbols with particulars and their symbols under the general heading 'object and name', there remains at least the difference between those names involved only in symbolizing a content and those which help symbolize a form as well. But even this one remaining rationale for distinguishing between kinds of symbols is eliminated by Wittgenstein's admission that names of particulars, just as names of universals, symbolize a form as well as a content—i.e., names of both kinds of objects are dependent symbols. With this admission, the false dichotomy between symbols which are names and those which are forms is totally repudiated, and Wittgenstein thereby arrives at his definitive view of the nature of names and objects—or at least the view which prevails throughout the *Tractatus* and is not again to be revised until 1929. It is to an exposition of (3), the mature position of the early Wittgenstein, that I now turn.

From the time of the notes to Moore in April, 1914, in which Wittgenstein unreservedly embraces (2), until the first entry in the *Notebooks* on August 22 of the same year, we have no record of his development. We can only say that his willingness to embrace nominalism probably continues throughout this time, since the first passages which indicate a disaffection with (2)—or at least with his uncritically nominalistic conception of it—do not appear until the end of September, 1914, when his views on the status of properties and relations begin a metamorphosis which, some weeks later, issues in the definitive position of (3), viz., that universals are objects on a par with particulars. I shall now examine this transformation, recorded primarily in pp. 6-27 of the *Notebooks*, beginning with Wittgenstein's discussion of the problem of true and false propositions, where his desire to retreat from nominalism first becomes manifest. The gist of this discussion, paraphrased and quoted (where such paraphrases and quotations will be cited by dates rather than by page references, in order to show the chronological development of Wittgenstein's thought), is as follows:

The proposition, which is one fact (*Sachverhalt*), is a logical representation of its meaning (*Bedeutung*), which is another fact, only if there is a correlation between the components of both facts. Besides the correlation of names and things named, "...it is clear that a correlation of relations too takes place somehow" (25.9.14). In this respect, a proposition is like a picture. Both the proposition 'A is fencing with B' and the picture of A fencing with B are able to express a sense independent of their truth or falsity, which means that they are both able to represent the relation of fencing (29.9.14). But if A and B are not actually fencing, and the picture nevertheless portrays them as fencing, the picture represents a relation that does not exist (30.9.14).

> How is that possible? Now once more it looks as if all relations must be logical in order for their existence to be guaranteed by that of the sign (30.9.14).

From this last remark we may conclude that Wittgenstein is tending towards the view that relations have some kind of ontological content, and is driven back to the view that symbols for relations represent no content—i.e., that they are merely 'logical', merely copulae[14]—only by the consideration that if the relational component in a false proposition has no correlative component in reality, then neither can any such content be represented in a true proposition, since the truth or falsity of the proposition is irrelevant to its sense. We may also gather that the ontological status Wittgenstein would be willing to give to relations, were it not for the difficulty raised by false propositions, is something less than the status of particulars, in the sense that particulars exist on their own, while Wittgenstein apparently feels that relations cannot exist apart from the existence of particulars in these relations. Thus, e.g., if A is not fencing with B, then the relation of fencing, with respect to A and B, does not exist. I say 'with respect to A and B', because C and D may very well be fencing, so that the relation exists between them, though not between A and B. In this view, the existence or non-existence of a relation is always with respect to specific particulars, even though the relation itself can be represented in the abstract, viz., in a propositional schema, where the other symbols are all variables (4.10.14) or in a picture whose figures standing in this relation themselves represent no specific individuals (30.9.14).

In any case, the question as to how Wittgenstein would view the status of relations appears moot, since the problem of finding a correlative component in reality for the relational component of a proposition forces his concession that relations might just be 'logical' after all. This concession, however, is only temporary, for we find him a few days later again mulling over the possibility that there is a correlation of relational components, only to be discouraged once more by even further difficulties. Thus:

> If there were such a thing as an immediate correlation of relations, the question would be: How are the things that stand in these relations correlated with one another in this case: Is there such a thing as a direct correlation of relations without consideration of their *direction*? Are we misled into assuming "relations between relations" merely through the apparent analogy between the expressions: "relations between things" and "relations between relations"? (9.10.14)

This passage shows that he regards a correlation between relational components, assuming it were possible, to be between two contents only. That is, if 'aRb' is the proposition, the relational component of the proposition to be correlated with its counterpart in reality would be 'R' *simpliciter*, and since this isolation of 'R' from the propositional sign as a whole would destroy the representation of the sense (i.e., direction) of the relation, Wittgenstein once again concludes that perhaps the whole attempt to correlate relations is misconceived, having received its impetus only by a misleading grammatical analogy. Yet he feels that this conclusion, too, is unsatisfactory, as is any conclusion which undertakes—after the fact, as it were—to settle the question concerning the *possibility* of relations existing, since logic must decide this possibility for us from the start. As he says: "The question about the possibility of existence propositions does not come in the middle but at the very first beginning of logic..." (9.10.14), and he sees his previous attempts to deal with the question about the status of relations from the vantage-point of the 'middle' of the inquiry as a "fundamental mistake" (9.10.14).

It is this observation which spurs him on to the final solution of the problem, though by a circuitous route. Thus, as another illustration of the theme that questions of logic must be decided from the beginning, he considers the axiom of infinity, and says that there can be no logical problem, in connection with the proposition which states that an infinite number of things exist, which is not already solved in the proposition stating that one thing exists—since, presumably, no further *logical* difference is reflected in the number of things we assert to exist.[15] From this he is led to a discussion of infinite numbers (11.10.14), and then to a consideration of the definitions of cardinal numbers generally, "...in order to understand the real sense of propositions like the Axiom of Infinity" (12.10.14). Wittgenstein then moves on to a consideratioon of the proposition: 'There is a class with only one member', which he symbolizes as '$(\exists\phi)\therefore(\exists x):\phi x:\phi y.\phi z.\supset_{y,z} y=z$'. That is, he expresses what is meant here by 'one', by saying that there is a property which some thing uniquely possesses. It is clear from this that, in addition to particulars, universals are subject to existential quantification.[16] As he rhetorically puts the matter,

> [c]an we speak of numbers if there are only things? I.e. if for example the world only consisted of one thing and of nothing else, could we say that there was ONE thing? (13.10.14)

His conclusion is that it is likely that "...we can only talk of 1 if there is a material functions which is satisfied only by one argument" (13.10.14). As we have seen, in his notes to Moore Wittgenstein had already admitted that relations can be thus generalized, viz., in the form '(∃x, y, R)xRy', but the implication of this possibility of turning 'R' into an apparent variable had obviously not struck him at the time. Now, however, he sees that if 'φ' can be turned into an apparent variable, then, when 'φ' is constant, it must symbolize some specific content. Hence, by 15.10.14 we find him maintaining that 'φ' and 'a' are both elements of the proposition 'φa' which relate to their respective meanings (*Bedeutungen*) in reality. There is no doubt that '*Bedeutung*' as here employed carries the full weight of 'ontological content', since he also speaks on 15.10 of the elements of a proposition being correlated with objects.[17] Of perhaps even greater significance in the entry of 15.10 is Wittgenstein's recognition that '(∃x,φ)' contains a plurality of forms—presumably, though he does not explicitly say, a function-form and an argument-form—an admission no doubt brought on by the realization that both components are generalizable independently of each other and must therefore be regarded as separate units regarding both content and form.

By 15.10, then, Wittgenstein's notes contain the essentials of position (3): both universals and particulars are included among objects, and the symbols for both kinds of objects represent a form as well as a content. If his remarks at this stage are little more than hints and allusions he soon becomes more specific. By 17.10.14 he says that in a description of the world by means of completely general propositions, we would need the proposition '(∃φ)(ψ)ψ=φ'—supposing there were only one property in the world—to identify that property, and he explicitly calls the property an object. Numerous subsequent remarks throughout the *Notebooks* show that he continues to use the term 'object' to include universals, the most patent example being his statement on 16.6.15 that relations and properties are objects.

Regarding the question of form and content, he says on 1.11.14 that

[t]he logical form of the proposition must already be given by the forms

> of its component parts.... In the form of the subject and of the predicate there already lies the possibility of the subject-predicate proposition....

That he continues to regard all components of a proposition as having a form is confirmed in the remark of 20.6.15, where he says that we find in the theorems of mathematical physics "...neither things nor functions nor relations nor any other logical forms of object!"[18]

Wittgenstein's allusion here to various logical forms serves to remind us of an important point: in spite of the main thrust of (3), which is to re-assimilate universals with particulars as being equally objects, he nevertheless wants to preserve some distinction between the two, if only a difference in the logical form of these two kinds of objects, as is manifest in the different syntactic roles of their respective symbols. Even with respect to differences in logical form, however, there is no emphasis on the distinction between universals and particulars, since within these categories themselves there are objects of various forms. Among universals, the most obvious example would be the difference in form of any of those which function relationally. But even particulars, all of which seem to have at least that aspect of form in common which permits them to occur only as logical subjects of a proposition (i.e., only as subjects in a subject-predicate proposition, or as terms in a relational proposition), can nevertheless differ in over-all logical form. Thus:

> If, e.g., I call some rod "A", and a ball "B", I can say that A is leaning against the wall, but not B. Here the internal nature of A and B comes into view.... "The watch is *sitting* on the table" is senseless! (22.6.15)

That the substitution of the name of one particular for the name of another can turn a proposition into nonsense shows that the syntactic roles of these names differ, i.e., that the particulars have different logical forms. Still, the occurrence of particulars only as subjects and the occurrence of universals only predicatively and relationally does mark a basic distinction, and Wittgenstein's desire to acknowledge this distinction between universals and particulars, coupled with his desire to stress their common nature as objects, creates a minor tension whose main result is a fluctuation in the use of the expressions 'name' and 'thing', depending on whether he is thinking of the difference between universals and particulars or is thinking of their similarities. That is, he sometimes speaks as if only particulars are things and have names, while at other times he uses both expressions in connection with universals as well. So, e.g., by 17.10.14, he has admitted that objects include universals, but he still feels compelled at this time to qualify his characterization of completely general propositions by saying that we describe such propositions "...without using any name or any other denoting sign...," where the phrase 'any other denoting sign' presumably alludes to symbols for universals.[19] By 22.10.14 this distinction between names and other denoting signs seems to have been abandoned, since Wittgenstein now contrasts names only with the logical, non-arbitrary features of representation in a proposition, which suggests that the symbols which are arbitrarily stipulated to stand for universals are names as well. On 28.10.14 he says that

> [w]hat the pseudo-proposition "There are n things" tries to express shows
> in language by the presence of n proper names with different meanings.

This suggests, first, that the distinction between universals and particulars is not reflected in a distinction between names and other denoting signs, but between different kinds of names, where one kind has the qualification 'proper'; second, that 'thing' is synonymous with 'particular', since presumably only particulars have 'proper' names.

By 3.11.14 the treatment of both symbols for universals and symbols for particulars as names of objects is re-inforced, when he says that "[t]he arbitrary correlation of sign and thing signified..." occurs in the elementary proposition "...by means of names...," where the context makes clear that by 'things signified' he is including all the components of a fact, universals as well as particulars. This quotation also shows his widening use of the expression 'thing' to cover both kinds of components rather than just particulars, a practice which is continued in his remark on 4.11.14 that

> [o]ne name is representative of one thing, another of another thing, and
> they themselves are connected; in this way the whole images the situation—like a *tableau vivant*.

On 21.1.15 we again find him using the expression 'thing' in the narrower sense, i.e., in contrast with properties and relations as different species of which objects are the genus, a use of the expression which reoccurs on 31.5.15, when he says that

> [n]ames are necessary for an assertion that *this* thing possesses *that* property and so on. They link the propositional form with quite definite objects.[20]

On 16.6.15 he once again uses the expression 'name' in the narrow sense, in speaking of a proposition as containing "...names, relations, etc....," though by 17.6.15 he again speaks of mentioning a property by name ("...*müsste ich sie namentlich anführen* ..."), a use of 'name' which is reconfirmed on 21.6.15. To complicate matters further, on 22.6.15 he uses the expression 'object' itself in a narrow sense, in speaking of the fact expressed by the proposition 'The watch is lying on the table' as one in which two objects are in a relation. That universals are not being denied status as objects in the wide sense is obvious from the context, where there is no indication that any drastic reversal in outlook has taken place from only the day before, when he had spoken of the property mortality as an object. Also, when the *Notebooks* resume nearly a year later (the entry of 22.6.15 marks the end of the second notebook and the entries of the third notebook begin on 15.4.16), he again explicitly uses 'object' in the wide sense—for example, on 9.7.16 he says that "[t]he proposition fa speaks of particular objects..."—so that the differentiation of objects and relations on 22.6.15 clearly does not portend a return to nominalism.

I have illustrated Wittgenstein's fluctuating terminology at length to make the point that even when he restricts the expressions 'thing', 'name', and even 'object' to particulars, there is no suggestion that relations and properties are not themselves entities. Particulars and universals continue to stand on equal footing as objects, in the wide sense, so that the use of 'thing', 'name', or 'object' in the narrow sense can be intended to do no more than call attention to the distinctive status of particulars as logical subjects. What makes our recognition of this fluctuating terminology in the *Notebooks*, and a proper assessment of its significance, especially important is that we thereby establish a precedent for explaining comparable passages in the *Tractatus*, which gives us a reason for denying that such passages support a nominalist interpretation of the *Tractatus*, despite any prominence they may give to particulars by the narrow use of these expressions.

Before moving on to an examination of the *Tractatus* itself, I want to consider two more points in connection with the development of (3) in the *Notebooks*. The first point concerns the status of relational components in false propositions, a problem which initially provides a stumbling-block for Wittgenstein's acceptance of these components as symbols of correlative components in reality, but which is simply shoved aside when he realizes that symbols for universals must represent contents in order for us to have something from which to abstract when such symbols are made into apparent variables. He does not entirely forget about this problem, however; within a few weeks of this decisive development, which we placed at 17.10.14, he again addresses himself to the problem of the false proposition, though now with one important difference: whereas he had previously characterized a false proposition in terms of the non-existence of a correlative relational component in reality, he now characterizes such a proposition in terms of the non-existence of *connections* between objects in reality. Thus:

> But when I say: the connection of the propositional components must be possible for the represented things—does this not contain the whole problem? How can a non-existent connection between objects be possible? "The connection must be possible" means: The proposition and the components of the situation must stand in a particular relation. Then in order for a proposition to present a situation it is only necessary for its component parts to represent those of the situation and for the former to stand in a connection which is possible for the latter (5.11.14).

On this account, the falsity of the proposition 'A is fencing with B' is due, not to the non-existence of a component, but only to the non-existence of a certain connection, or configuration, of existent components. Even if A is not configured with B in the relation of fencing, the components themselves—including fencing—exist nonetheless, so that false propositions give rise to no problems concerning relational contents.

With this account of false propositions, Wittgenstein finally disposes of the one obstacle that had prevented him from according ontological status to relations.

The second point I want to consider, though not directly concerned with the question of the status of universals, is relevant to our appraisal of the *Notebooks* as a source for understanding the *Tractatus*. On 18.10.14 Wittgenstein remarks: "Roughly speaking: before any proposition can make sense at all the *logical* constants must have meaning (*Bedeutung*)." Anscombe translates '*Bedeutung*' here as 'reference' to emphasize that the word is being used in the technical Fregean sense of 'what the word stands for', from which she concludes that

> ...there is a great contrast between his ideas at this stage of the *Notebooks* and those of the *Tractatus*, where he denies that logical constants or sentences have 'Bedeutung'.[21]

If Wittgenstein's views at 18.10.14 are at the relatively crude stage of development that Anscombe would have us believe, this casts suspicion on contemporaneous passages stating that universals are objects. Might not such passages reflect an equally primitive hypostatization, all such errors being corrected by the vastly more sophisticated *Tractatus*? The fact is, however, that in the passage in question Wittgenstein is obviously not maintaining the naive view, attributed to him by Anscombe, that logical constants have reference. He is on record as objecting to this naive view as far back as 22.6.12, where, in a letter to Russell, he says:

> ...[W]hatever may turn out to be the proper explanation of apparent variables, its consequences *must* be that there are *no logical* constants. Logic must turn out to be a *totally* different kind than any other science.[22]

So, right from the beginning of Wittgenstein's philosophical development, he sees a problem in the view that symbols like '∨', '⊃', and '∼' stand for objects, in the way that names do, and one of his preoccupations from then on is to give an explanation of the nature of logical symbols which does not suppose that these symbols refer to special 'logical' objects. The view of the *Tractatus* that the inter-definability of

'∨', '⊃', etc., shows that they are not symbols for objects (5.42) has already received expression in the "Notes on Logic,"[23] and his view that we could say that the one logical constant would be what all propositions have in common (5.47) has already been worked out in the notes to Moore, where Wittgenstein says that

> ...in order to introduce so-called "logical constants" properly, you must introduce the general notion of all possible combinations of them = the general form of a proposition.[24]

Therefore, by the time Wittgenstein makes his remark in the *Notebooks* about the '*Bedeutung*' of logical constants, it is clear that he is using this term in a wide, non-technical sense, an interpretation which is supported by the qualifying preface, viz., 'Roughly speaking', as well as by everything else that he has ever said on the subject, including the remark made only a week later, on 25.10.14, when he says: "With the logical constants one need never ask whether they exist, for they can even *vanish*!" (where he is presumably alluding to their inter-definability, in which, for example, '⊃' vanishes when 'p ⊃ q' becomes 'p ∨ ~q').

As for Anscombe's other charge—viz., that the *Notebooks* allow, but the *Tractatus* denies, a '*Bedeutung*' to proposition—it is true that in the *Tractatus* '*Bedeutung*' is used only in connection with objects (except in 5.31, where '*Bedeutung*' is used in a wide, non-technical sense); this terminological restriction, however, is not intended to repudiate the notion that a proposition can stand for something, but only to emphasize that the relation of a name to that for which it stands—viz., the object—is different from the relation of a proposition to that for which *it* stands—viz., the fact—since the proposition succeeds in having something for which it stands only when it is true. Hence, Anscombe's remark about the 'great contrast' between the *Notebooks* and the *Tractatus* with regard to this question of the '*Bedeutung*' of logical constants and propositions is totally without foundation.

This example illustrates the danger of treating Wittgenstein's remarks in isolation and merely at face-value, instead of trying to fit them into their historical context. My own exegetical approach has been to attempt to provide just such a background for understanding the ontology of the *Tractatus*. The results of this approach can be briefly recapitulated: we have seen that the initial realism of (1) is brought into question in (2) by Wittgenstein's realization that symbols for universals cannot perform their function apart from the context of a proposition, which he takes as a reason for distinguishing symbols into those dealing exclusively with contents and those dealing exclusively with forms. (3) is his realization that this dichotomy is unwarranted, since symbols for universals concern a content as well as a form, and symbols for particulars concern as form as well as a content.[25]

Now, my contention is that the ontology of the *Tractatus* neither reverts to the professed nominalism of (2), nor moves on to a new nominalistic position beyond (3), but is simply a statement of (3) itself. If I am right in my assessment of the importance of the conclusions of (3) in providing a definitive solution to the problems which had plagued Wittgenstein nearly through the end of 1914, we should expect to find these conclusions prominently displayed in the *Tractatus*. In fact, this is precisely what we find. The middle of the very first page of the text through the beginning of the third page, from 2.01 to 2.02, is devoted exclusively to setting out the radical idea that objects are essentially dependent, in that they are not merely a content but also a form.[26] Thus, after telling us that a state of affairs is a combination (*Verbindung*) of objects (2.01), the first thing Wittgenstein wants to tell us about objects is that it is essential to an object to be able to be a constituent of a state of affairs (2.011), which he immediately supplements by saying that

> [i]n logic nothing is accidental: if a thing *can* occur in a state of affairs, the possibility of the state of affairs must be written into the thing itself (2.012).

These passages make clear from the start that objects are not the sort of self-subsistent entities that Russell—or Wittgenstein in (1) and (2)— had assumed them to be. The nature of this dependence of objects is then elaborated in the following passages, which are comments on 2.012:

> If I can think of objects combined in states of affairs, I cannot think of them excluded from the *possibility* of such combinations (2.0121).
> Things are independent in so far as they can occur in all *possible* situa-

tions, but this form of independence is a form of connection with states of affairs, a form of dependence. (It is impossible for words to appear in two different roles: by themselves, and in propositions.) (2.0122)

If I know an object I also know all its possible occurrences in states of affairs. (Every one of these possibilities must be part of the nature of the object.) (2.0123)

The key passage here for our purposes is 2.0122, which explicitly articulates this notion of dependence, saying in effect that the dependence of objects—which consists in their ability to occur only in the context of a state of affairs—has its parallel in the dependence of symbols, which have meaning only in the context of a proposition (this point about symbols being made again at 3.3). He concludes this crucial section by specifically identifying that aspect of an object which makes for its dependence as the object's *form* (2.0141).

Now, although it could be argued that this doctrine of the dependence of objects does not by itself show that properties and relations are regarded as objects, I have shown that in the *Notebooks* this strategy of extending the notion of form to particulars coincides with the admission of content to universals, and facilitates the re-assimilation of universals with particulars. Under these circumstances, it would be remarkable, to say the least, if Wittgenstein were to retain this sophisticated and ingenious outlook originally developed to bridge the gap between universals and particulars, only to throw away the fruits of this solution for a re-affirmation of nominalism.

This is strong circumstantial evidence in favor of the view that the *Tractatus* includes universals among objects. Many commentators, nevertheless, have adopted the view that the *Tractatus* holds that properties and relations are merely the way in which particulars are arranged—i.e., that particulars are the only objects and that properties and relations are their configuration—and they generally defend this view in a manner which suggests that there are little or no textual grounds in the *Tractatus* itself for any other interpretation. Keyt, for example, admits that the *Notebooks* treat universals as objects, but then says "...I can find no passage in the *Tractatus* that either says or implies this."[27] Pitcher is only slightly more generous in conceding that one passage in the *Tractatus*,

4.123, has the appearance of advocating the position that universals are included among objects, though Pitcher argues that even this appearance is misleading, and he concludes:

> Everything else [Wittgenstein] says in the *Tractatus* seems to me to require that objects be particulars, that they not include universals.[28]

These are bold claims, and although not all proponents of a nominalistic interpretation go to this extreme—for example, Müller admits that quite a few passages at least superficially (though, as it turns out, not ultimately) lend themselves to a realist interpretation[29]—a widely held view is that the textual evidence is, at any rate, preponderantly weighted in favor of nominalism. If this opinion were anywhere near being correct, my own argument would have to rest largely on the circumstantial evidence already given (assuming that we have set aside, as I am presently doing, Lee's revealing account of Wittgenstein's own explanation of 2.01). In fact, however, not only the circumstantial evidence, but also the textual evidence definitely supports a realistic interpetation of the *Tractatus* and poses insuperable difficulties for the view that universals are merely configurations of objects and not objects themselves. The next two chapters will be taken up with an examination of just such textual evidence.

CHAPTER THREE

ARGUMENTS FOR A REALISTIC
INTERPRETATION

The first textual evidence which I offer in favor of a realistic interpretation of the *Tractatus* concerns those passages in which Wittgenstein says that a state of affairs is composed of objects (2.01, 2.0272), or—to make the same point at the level of language—that an elementary proposition consists of names (4.22). The use of the plural implies that in a proposition of the subject-predicate form, e.g., 'f(a)', both 'f' and 'a' are names,[1] each of which symbolizes an object—a property and a particular, respectively. If an opponent of the realistic interpretation concedes this implication, he can evade its consequences only by maintaining that according to the *Tractatus* there are no propositions of the subject-predicate form, and that propositions which seem to concern only one particular are really relational propositions concerning two or more particulars. This view, advocated notably by Anscombe, is given a concise statement by another advocate, Pitcher:

> Wittgenstein could perfectly well have held that an object's having a property is not a matter of its being configured with a universal, but rather of its being configured with other simple particulars. He could have maintained, for instance, that to say that *a* is red is not to say that *a* is configured with the universal "redness", but rather to say that *a* is configured with *b*, *c*, and *d*—all simple particulars—in a certain way.[2]

On this view, the 'f' in 'f(a)' has the dual-purpose of representing the three particulars b, c, and d, as well as representing the configuration of these particulars. This supposition, viz., that the symbol for a property in an ostensibly subject-predicate proposition can represent particulars other than the one explicitly named in the argument-place, is probably one reason why Anscombe feels no need to confine the role of the symbol for a relation, in a proposition such as 'aRb' which is ostensibly relational, to that of symbolizing the configuration only of the explicitly named objects a and b. Like the 'f' in 'f(a)', the 'R' in 'aRb' might equally well represent other particulars in addition to the configuration of all of them, so that while

> ...the objects a and b occur 'in the sense' of the proposition 'aRb'...50 or 1000 or an infinity of other objects may occur in that sense as well.[3]

This interpretation of the *Tractatus*, however, which allows that symbols for functions also covertly represent particulars, cannot plausibly be maintained. First of all, the idea that a proposition such as 'f(a)' might really symbolize a configuration of the particulars a, b, c, and d is wholly alien to Wittgenstein's desire that his symbolic language be perspicuous. If, for example, we consider his meticulous effort to capture in his symbolism, without recourse to the to the sign of identity, what we mean by saying 'Only one x satisfies f( )'—his rendering being '$(\exists x)fx:\sim(\exists x, y)fx.fy$'—the whole spirit of this pains-taking enterprise would seem to be mocked if he really means, but neglects to mention, that the one particular satisfying this function is of course joined by the three other particulars (or whatever number) symbolized by 'f' itself. That Wittgenstein could attribute any such symbolic role to 'f' is extremely unlikely in light of his claim that a proposition is a *picture*, with the same logical multiplicity as the state of affairs it represents. Granted, we could learn to use this one poor symbol 'f' to express the fact that, besides the particular represented in the argument-place, there are three other particulars—b, c, and d—configured thus and so, but if the picture theory amounts to no more than this, it seems a gratuitous gesture to bother dividing a proposition into function and argument at all. Why not symbolize the whole proposition by a single letter?

Even supposing that we could reconcile such a symbolic role for 'f' with Wittgenstein's desire for a perspicuous symbolism, there is the problem of explaining the unique status of the one particular which happens to be the argument to this function. If 'f(a)' symbolizes a configuration of a, b, c, and d, what is the symbolic import of regarding one of these particulars as the argument rather than any of the others? We might suppose that there is no intrinsic difference between a and the other particulars, so that 'f(a)' could be equivalent to some other proposition 'g(b)', where 'g' symbolizes a, c, and d, in addition to symbolizing the same configuration of all four particulars—the only difference between 'f(a)' and 'g(b)' being the manner in which the responsibility for symbolizing the four particulars is divided up between the function-sign and the argument-sign. If, however, we deny any special symbolic import to the explicit occurrence of a particular in the argument-place, and say that the same particular could just as well have been symbolized by a function-sign, we remove any reason for the distinction of propositions of the form '$\phi(x)$' from those of the form '$\phi(x, y)$'; i.e., propositions of either form would supposedly symbolize a configuration of more than one particular, so there can be no point at all in differentiating these two forms, as Wittgenstein does in 4.24, unless the explicit mention in the argument-place of *two* particulars, in the one case, and of only *one* particular, in the other, reflects some special feature of the particulars so honored. The *Tractatus* offers no clue as to what this special feature might be, which is not really surprising, since neither is there anywhere a suggestion that function-signs can represent particulars at all. The whole problem is a bogus one, easily dissolved by the recognition that a subject-predicate proposition represents two and only two objects, the function-sign standing for a universal and the argument-sign standing for a particular.

Difficulties in the nominalistic account of functions do not end here. The view which attributes to the function-sign the dual-purpose of representing particulars *and* their configuration has the additional curious consequence that, except for particulars explicitly represented in the argument-place, we cannot generalize the particulars without generalizing the configuration. Thus, if 'f(a)' represents a configuration of a, b, c, and d, the symbolism does not permit a representation of this specific configuration apart from a representation of these specific particulars, except for the particular represented by the letter 'a', which can be replaced by an apparent variable while 'f' remains constant. If we try to generalize the remaining three particulars by turning 'f' into an apparent variable, we thereby abstract from the specific configuration as well. But surely the most elementary prerequisite of Wittgenstein's symbolism is that it should be able to represent a constant configuration without representing any specific particular. For this reason, he could not have tolerated a symbolism giving this dual-role to function-signs, and that he *does* refer, without qualms, to propositions of the form 'ϕ(x)' shows that 'ϕ' cannot be intended to designate both the configuration and particulars in the configuration. At best, 'ϕ' symbolizes a configuration, but since only one particular can be symbolized in 'ϕ(x)', we are led to conclude that 'ϕ' designates neither any particular nor a configuration, but rather designates a property, i.e., an object which is a universal.

This problem, it is true, need arise only for propositions of the form 'ϕ(x)', since in propositions which are overtly relational, i.e., which have two or more argument-places, we can suppose that the function-sign is concerned solely with representing the configuration and that all the particulars occur explicitly as arguments. So, at least for propositions of the form 'ϕ(x, y,...n)', the particulars can be generalized while the configuration remains constant. But even if we confine ourselves to relational propositions, there remains a further problem for the view that function-signs represent configurations of particulars, viz., the problem of explaining the nature of the form-content distinction as such. That is, if, in the proposition 'R(a, b)', 'a' and 'b' represent the content and 'R' represents the form,[4] then the form, in this sense, would still seem to have some kind of content. Suppose, for example, 'R(a, b)' expresses the fact that a is to the right of b, and 'S(a, b)' expresses the fact that a is to the left of b. Must we not say that 'R' and 'S' thereby represent different contents, just as surely as these letters would if they were conceded to have the status of names? The form of a proposition is what remains when we abstract from the content by turning constants into variables, and from this it should be obvious that a function-sign cannot be regarded by Wittgenstein as representing a form, since he allows that function-signs, too, can be turned from constants into variables, which implies that such signs represent a content no less than do signs for particulars. Surely, the form of a state of affairs is mirrored by the form of the proposition and not represented by its own individual symbol, so that the same form continues to be represented whether the function-sign remains constant or is turned into an apparent variable.

It is Wittgenstein's consideration of this topic, viz., the possibility of generalizing function-signs, which provides the context for a remark in the *Tractatus* which clearly implies that function-signs are names of objects. In 5.526 he says that

> [w]e can describe the world completely by means of fully generalized propositions, i.e. without first correlating any name with a particular object.
>
> Then, in order to arrive at the customary mode of expression, we simply need to add, after an expression like, 'There is one and only one x such that...', the words, 'and that x is a'.

The second paragraph, which shows the replacement of an apparent variable by a name only for the case of 'a', a letter customarily used to represent an argument (i.e., a particular), is slightly misleading, because the point of talking about completely generalized propositions—as is made clear by 5.5261 as well as by the comparable discussion of completely generalized propositions in the *Notebooks*[5]—is that in such propositions even the function is generalized. Thus, we can describe the world not merely through propositions such as '$(\exists x)fx$' or '$(x)fx$' (these being the examples just previously given in 5.521 of propositions embodying generality), where the function remains constant, but, as 5.5261 shows, we can describe the world even through propositions such as '$(\exists x, \phi)\phi x$', in which all constants are generalized. The point, then, of the statement in 5.526 that the description of the world can take place 'without first correlating any name with a particular object' is surely to stress that even those objects which are universals, and thus represented by function-signs, can be represented by apparent variables rather than by constants. It is instructive to compare 5.526 to the passage which is its counterpart in the *Notebooks*:

> Yes, the world could be completely described by completely general propositions, and hence without using any names or any other denoting signs. And in order to arrive at ordinary language one would only need to introduce names, etc. by saying, after an '$(\exists x)$', "and this x is A" and so on. (17.10.14)

In this passage, the expressions 'other denoting signs' and 'etc.' are meant to cover the case where functions are generalized, since at this stage of the *Notebooks* Wittgenstein is not yet ready to accord function-signs the status of names (even though such signs are admitted to represent objects), a scruple which our examination of the *Notebooks* has shown him to abandon soon afterwards. By the time the *Tractatus* is written, he fully accepts function-signs as being names; hence, in 5.526 the qualifying expressions found in the comparable passage in the *Notebooks* are no longer needed. We may conclude, then, that 5.526 constitutes incontrovertible evidence—about as straightforward as one could ever hope to glean from the cryptic prose of the *Tractatus*—that objects include universals.

I want now to examine some passages which show that Wittgenstein regards universals as objects by showing how he proceeds to effect their re-assimilation with particulars. A common view is that even if we grant that universals and particulars are both species of objects, they are at any rate quite different kinds of objects, and commentators have used this view to support a nominalistic interpretation of the *Tractatus* by arguing that, if Wittgenstein had meant by 'objects' things as radically distinct as universals and particulars, he would have said so.[6] To be sure, I hope to have shown in my previous arguments that he does say, or at least clearly imply, that universals are included among objects, but in any case such an objection to the realist interpretation misses the point, which is that he wants to show that universals and particulars are not radically distinct. I have suggested that this re-assimilation is achieved by Wittgenstein's view that all objects have both form and content, so that the different syntactic roles enjoyed by the names 'Socrates' and 'mortality', supposing for purposes of illustration that they are names of simple objects, can be explained at the most comprehensive level simply by saying that the objects represented by these names have different forms, this being an explanation which covers not only the difference between universals and particulars but also differences between objects within each category. On this account, a division of objects into universals and particulars ceases to be of much significance, except perhaps to distinguish those objects whose forms share the common characteristic of permitting such objects to occur only as logical subjects from those objects whose forms determine that such objects occur predicatively or relationally. It might be said, however, that even apart from their syntactic roles there is another respect in which universals and particulars differ radically, which is that while at least some particulars are locatable in space and all particulars are locatable in time—unless we want to make an exception for instants themselves—universals would seem to exist in a world apart, outside of space and time. Russell, in *Problems of Philosophy*, expresses the difference as follows:

> The 'idea' *justice* is not identical with anything that is just: it is something other than particular things, which particular things partake of. Not being particular, it cannot itself exist in the world of sense. Moreover it is not fleeting or changeable like the things of sense: it is eternally itself, immutable and indestructible.[7]

Russell feels the difference between objects which exist in time and those which exist outside of time to be sufficiently great that he prefers to say that objects of the latter kind, viz., universals, do not exist at all; rather, they subsist, or have being. Thus, universals and particulars comprise, as it were, two distinct worlds:

> The world of being is unchangeable, rigid, exact.... The world of existence is fleeting, vague, without sharp boundaries, without any clear plan or arrangement....[8]

Such a bifurcation of universals and particulars, as proposed by Russell, is indeed an obstacle to the programme for their mutual re-assimilation. Therefore, given my contention that this is Wittgenstein's programme, it is not surprising to find that the *Tractatus* addresses itself to this problem, and hardly more surprising that the language in which Wittgenstein's own solution is framed shows that he probably has Russell's views as expressed in *Problems of Philosophy* specifically in mind, since we know that Wittgenstein was familiar with this work, and indeed had strong negative feelings about it.[9] Thus, against the view that universals are immutable and particulars are fleeting and changeable, Wittgenstein says that

52

[t]he permanent (*Feste*), the existent (*Bestehende*), and the object are one (2.027).

The object is what is permanent, existent; the configuration is what is changing, unstable (2.0271).

In other words, Russell's characterization of universals is extended by Wittgenstein to universals and particulars alike. That is, not only universals, but particulars as well, are outside of space and time.

To see how this is possible, we need only consider Wittgenstein's remark that objects are colorless (2.0232), for in this respect a particular's status of having a spatial and temporal location is on a par with its status of being colored. Suppose, then, that there is a state of affairs in which a particular, which we will call 'John', is red. Now, according to 2.0231 there is a sense in which we can say that John is colorless. This seemingly enigmatic remark becomes readily understandable if we look at 2.0231, which says:

The substance of the world *can* only determine a form, and not any material properties. For these material properties are represented only by propositions, formed only by the configuration of objects.

In other words, our acquaintance with John does not include knowledge of John's redness, which is after all only an external property which John could cease to have without ceasing to be John. What we do know, as included in John's form, is that John is the sort of object that must have a color, though which one is something that can only be determined by extending our knowledge beyond the single object John, with its possibilities of configuration with other objects, to the state of affairs in which John is actually configured with redness. Since John and redness are two separate objects, each having its own form and content,[10] obviously neither content is part of the other, and so John is in a sense colorless; at most, it is part of John's nature to be required to be configured with some color or other and to be able to be configured specifically with redness as one of the options. Applying what has been said about color to space and time, if John is a spatial and temporal object (and if it is the former, it must be the latter as well), this means that John's form requires that it be configured with some spatial point and some temporal instant (or series of points and instants as its existence continues), though which specific point and instant this should be is external to John's nature and is determined only by the actual configuration of objects. In this sense, just as John is colorless, so is John outside of space and time.

Therefore, when Wittgenstein characterizes objects as being permanent or unalterable, he does not mean that they continue to exist unchanged throughout every moment of time, but rather that even if an object should exist only for the briefest temporal span, it is eternal in the sense that whatever relation it has to any particular time is external to its own nature. This is not to deny that there may also be objects which are eternal in the sense of persisting throughout every moment of time—and Wittgenstein may well have thought that the material points of physics were just such objects[11]—but the permanence which he attributes to objects generally, in 2.027, is of a different, more fundamental kind. By this strategy, then, the basis for distinguishing between universals and particulars as radically different kinds of objects is removed.

Although I think that my account of Wittgenstein's strategy for dealing with space and time does provide evidence that he regards universals as objects, by showing that his programme is indeed to assimilate universals with particulars and, if anything, to model the latter on the former, I admit that the account, as it stands, begs the question insofar as it relies on the example of color to illustrate the strategy of separating a spatial and temporal object from the points and instants with which it can be configured. It would be desirable if independent evidence could be found for this treatment of space and time; such evidence would not only make possible an explanation of Wittgenstein's assimilation of particulars with universals without presupposing that colors are objects, but would in addition confirm that this interpretation of his remark about colorless objects is correct, since we have reason to suppose that his treatment of color parallels his treatment of space and time, given that space, time, and color (being colored) are grouped together in 2.0251 as being forms of objects. The one difference will be that while those objects which are capable of being configured with a particular in virtue of its spatial and temporal form will themselves be (or at least function as) particulars, viz., points and instants, those objects capable of such a configuration in virtue of the particular's form of coloredness will be universals, viz., colors. Therefore, the task at hand is to produce evidence for supposing that an object's spatial and temporal form amounts to its configurability with points and instants. This evidence, I think, can be found in 2.0121:

> Just as we are unable to think of spatial objects outside of space, or temporal objects outside of time, so it is that we can think of *no* object apart from the possibility of its combination with others.

Clearly, the reference to space and time is here intended as a specific illustration of the general notion of an object's form, i.e., its possibility of combining with other objects, from which we can only conclude that just such a possibility of combination with other objects is indicated by saying that the object is spatial or temporal. What could these other objects be, in the case of spatial and temporal objects, if not points and instants?[12]

It is instructive to compare my interpretation of Wittgenstein's views on space and time with the following passages from *Principles of Mathematics*:

> Among terms which appear to exist, there are...four great classes: (1) instants, (2) points, (3) terms which occupy instants but not points, (4) terms which occupy both points and instants.[13]

> Change is due, ultimately, to the fact that many terms have relations to some parts of time which they do not have to others. But every term is eternal, timeless, and immutable; the relations it may have to parts of time are equally immutable. It is merely the fact that different terms are related to different times that makes the difference between what exists at one time and what exists at another. And though a term may cease to exist, it cannot cease to be....[14]

From these passages we may reasonably conclude that Wittgenstein's treatment of space and time in relation to particulars which are in space and time directs itself against Russell's position in *Problems of Philosophy* by adopting the viewpoint of Russell's earlier work.[15]

The influence of *Principles of Mathematics* on the *Tractatus* is also apparent in the related problem of the individuation of objects. According to the former, an object's properties or relations to other objects, including its location in space and time, cannot ultimately serve to differentiate one object from another object, because the properties and relations of this object are external to its essential nature and are, indeed, objects in their own right. Russell is thus forced to say that "...any two simple terms simply differ immediately—they are two, and this is the sum total of their differences."[16] This notion that there is no basis for distinguishing objects apart from their being different is taken over by Wittgenstein, with one modification: even when we consider an object apart from its external properties, Wittgenstein recognizes that there are still internal properties which can distinguish this object from others, so that the necessity of appealing solely to the 'immediate difference' of two objects as two arises only when these objects have the same internal properties, i.e., are of the same logical form. Thus:

> Two objects of the same logical form are—apart from their external properties—distinguished from one another only in that they are different (2.0233).

Principles of Mathematics, therefore, has evidently left its mark on Wittgenstein's discussion of objects in the *Tractatus*, presumably extending to a comparable treatment of points and instants. A simple identification of the two views, however, would be a mistake, because Wittgenstein also has had the benefit of reading *Our Knowledge of the External World*,[17] in which Russell follows Whitehead in regarding points and instants as logical constructions rather than as simple objects in their own right. So Wittgenstein at least has been exposed to this way of thinking about space and time, and he probably has this development in mind when, in the *Notebooks*, he says: "A singular logical manipulation, the *personification* of time!" This is followed almost immediately by the remark: "Can we regard a part of space as a thing? In a certain sense we obviously always do this when we talk of spatial things."[18] The first remark is admittedly cryptic, but, taken in conjunction with the second remark, the general theme likely concerns the status of points and instants as entities. I take the 'personification' of time to be that process whereby instants are given the appearance of being genuine entities,

56

though they are really only logical constructions defined in terms of
events,[19] which is why Wittgenstein calls this personification a 'logical
manipulation'. What is not clear is whether, in calling this a *singular*
(*eigentümlich*) logical manipulation, he means to suggest with a touch of
irony that instants cannot really be defined in this way at all, and that
they just *are* simple objects, or whether he admits that instants are logical constructions and is simply struck by the peculiarity of this process.

The intent of the second remark is also unclear, in that we cannot be
sure whether the phrase 'in a certain sense' is meant to suggest that parts
of space—presumably, spatial points—though treated as things, are really logical constructions, or whether he regards points as genuine objects
and inserts the qualifying phrase only to allow that there are other contexts in which it would be odd to regard parts of space themselves as
things, but that this is nevertheless the proper way to regard them when
considering their relation to spatial objects. So, although these remarks
about space and time are quite likely prompted by his reading of *Our
Knowledge of the External World*, in which the status of points and instants as entities is questioned, we cannot tell from these remarks
whether or not Wittgenstein himself is willing to admit that points and
instants are possibly just constructions.

A clue towards determining Wittgenstein's own outlook is perhaps
provided by a passage in the *Notebooks*, following these first remarks by
about a month, in which he says:

> If a point in space does not exist, then its co-ordinates do not exist either,
> and if the co-ordinates exist then the point exists too. That is how it is in
> logic (21.6.15).

This passage suggests that he may have regarded a point as a complex
object constructed out of its co-ordinates, an interpretation supported by
the context, which is a discussion of the functioning of complex objects
as simples. He might be saying, then, that points 'exist' in the sense that
logic compels us to say, of any complex, that it exists when its parts are
appropriately assembled, even though this existence of the complex is
really nothing over and above the existence of its parts (in their appropriate configuration)—in this case the existence of a spatial point

being nothing more than the existence of its co-ordinates. Such a view of the nature of the complexity of points—if this is indeed Wittgenstein's view (and we should not be too hasty to suppose that he seriously holds the admittedly peculiar view that co-ordinates exist as constituent objects)—is at any rate far different from Russell's view in *Our Knowledge of the External World* of the nature of this complexity. Russell defines a spatial point "...as a certain class of spatial objects, namely all those. which would naturally be said to contain the point...,"[20] i.e., "...all the objects which enclose members of a given punctual enclosure-series."[21] This requires, "...to prevent trivial exceptions...,"[22] that "...there are to be instances of enclosure, i.e. there really are to be objects of which one encloses the other."[23] All of this implies (and indeed Russell explicitly adopts the view[24]) that space is relative to spatial objects; without such objects there would be no points, and therefore no space. Wittgenstein, on the other hand, seems to treat space as being absolute, depending on no spatial object for its own existence, but rather, like a graph, requiring only its co-ordinates to define any spatial point. That he regards space as absolute is supported in the *Tractatus* by 2.013:

> Each thing is, as it were, in a space of possible states of affairs. I can think of this space as being empty, but I cannot think of the thing without the space.

This assertion that space[25] could be thought of as empty—which implies that it is logically possible that space could *be* empty—is incompatible with Russell's definition of spatial points in *Our Knowledge of the External World* and shows that if Wittgenstein does go beyond Russell's earlier view of *Principles of Mathematics*, in which points are straightforwardly regarded as simple objects, the kind of complexity Wittgenstein allows points to have leaves his conception of space much closer to this earlier, absolutistic view than is Russell's own subsequent, relativistic view. We may conclude, at any rate, that Wittgenstein does not hesitate to treat spatial points, for all practical purposes, as though they were objects in their own right. Even if he might concede that, in the last analysis, such an attitude towards spatial points reflects a hypostatization, this is a hypostatization in which he nevertheless seems to be willing to indulge.[26]

There is one passage in the *Tractatus* which could be taken to be evidence against my claim that spatial points are treated as objects. This is the remark that "[a] spatial point is an argument-place" (2.0131). If this passage is construed as a remark about the manner in which spatial points are represented in the symbolism, then we would have to say that points are not being treated here as objects, because an object (i.e., an object which is a particular) is represented as an argument which fills an argument-place, and not as this argument-place itself, which is only a set of parentheses and/or a variable indicating where the argument is to appear. Black does construe 2.0131 in this way, and he concludes:

> Since space is a form of objects...we may infer that 'space' alludes to a 'formal concept'.... Thus 2.0131a expresses an internal 'feature'...of spatial facts. In a satisfactory notation, this internal feature would be *shown* by an internal property of the sign used—perhaps by the occurrence in it of a (three-dimensional) variable. When we talk about a 'spatial point' (or a 'position') we are not referring to a thing, but rather to a certain common internal feature of propositions 'about' that position.[27]

Black's interpretation, however, is untenable. He fails to appreciate that the form of an object, though itself internal to the object, essentially involves the configuration of this object with other objects, which cannot themselves be represented merely by an internal feature of the symbolism; hence, in attempting to characterize spatial points as just such internal features—the spatial object being regarded as the argument and the spatial point as the argument-place—he neglects to tell us which objects are those able to be configured with a spatial object in virtue of its form, if these objects are other than spatial points themselves. Furthermore, the view that a spatial point is an argument-place means that there is no difference in spatial points, since one blank argument-place is the same as any other, unless we want to adopt Black's *ad hoc* solution that the spatial object itself carries the burden of indicating its own spatial position, in which case spatial points are rendered completely superfluous. Also, supposing that the spatial form of an object *were* symbolized merely by the argument-place, how would, say, the object's temporal form be symbolized—by the same blank argument-place or, if by something else, what?

The obscurities into which we are led by Black's interpretation constitute a good case for supposing that Wittgenstein is not, in 2.0131, using the expression 'argument-place' in the usual sense of designating an internal feature of the symbolism. A plausible alternative interpretation is that he is using the expression 'place' in the sense of 'spatial position', and 'argument' in the sense of 'particular', so that to say that a spatial point is an argument-place is simply to say that it is a position occupiable (but not necessarily occupied) by a spatial particular. This interpretation is borne out by the context. The passage in question actually occurs in 2.0131 as a parenthetical remark, so that the entire paragraph reads: "A spatial object must be situated in infinite space. (A spatial-point is an argument-place.)" That is, a specific point is one of an infinite number of places that a spatial object may occupy.[28] 2.0131, in turn, is a comment on 2.013, which articulates the notion of an object being in a 'space' of possible states of affairs—this being another expression for the object's possibilities of configuration with other objects—so that the overall context favors my claim that spatial points, or places,[29] are not internal features of the symbolism, but are themselves objects (at least according to the treatment they receive in 2.0131) which are configurable with spatial objects so as to comprise states of affairs. And, of course, if the relation of a spatial object to spatial points is an illustration of the theme of the configurability of one object with others, then the other examples discussed in 2.0131—the relation of a patch in the visual field to color-space, a sound to pitch-space, or an object of the sense of touch to hardness-space—imply that colors, pitches, and hardnesses are objects as well.

So, to sum up the results of our examination of the status of spatial points, we can say that the form of a spatial object is its internal property of being able to combine with spatial points, which are themselves objects. By parity of treatment, we can assume that temporal objects have the form of being configurable with those objects which are instants; this renders temporal objects themselves 'timeless' and thus provides for the assimilation of particulars with universals. Finally, given that similar treatment should be accorded to color, since 2.0251 groups together space, time, and color as forms of objects (and from 2.0131 we see that

pitch and hardness could also be included as such forms), we may conclude that objects of this latter form are configured with colors which,
like points and instants, are themselves objects, though universals rather
than particulars. Therefore, a proper understanding of Wittgenstein's
views on space and time confirms, from two different directions, a realistic interpretation of the *Tractatus*.

I turn next to a group of passages which provides evidence that
universals are included among objects by the contrast made between
them and so-called 'logical constants'. First, there is 4.0312:

> The possibility of propositions is based on the principle of the repre-
> sentation of objects by signs. My fundamental idea is that the 'logical
> constants' do not represent anything; that the *logic* of facts permits no
> such representation.

Now, the objection made here to the reification of logical constants is
relatively mild compared to the view that *no sign*, other than the sign for
a particular, represents an object. Therefore, if Wittgenstein actually held
this more extreme view, we would expect him to say so here, rather than
to place exclusive emphasis on the milder view; that he does not do this
is an indication that the intended contrast is between logical constants
and all other signs—including function-signs as well as argument-
signs—which, as long as they are primitive signs (*Urzeichen*), are all
names of objects.

That this is Wittgenstein's intention is subsequently confirmed in his
extended discussion of logical constants starting at 5.4. In 5.42 and
5.461, taken together, we see that logical constants such as '∨' and '⊃'
are only pseudo-relations, as opposed to real relations such as right and
left, and that, since logical constants are inter-definable, only the signs
for real relations are primitive (*Urzeichen*).

Now, a case could be made for saying that Wittgenstein uses the expression 'primitive sign' synonymously with 'name',[30] which would
show directly that the intended contrast is one between logical constants
and other signs, all of which are names. Even apart from this consideration, his intent is made clear in 5.44:

> Truth-functions are not material functions.... The proposition '~~p' is not

about negation, as if negation were an object; to be sure, however, the possibility of negation is already contained in affirmation.

And if there were an object called '~', '~~p' would have to say something other than what 'p' says. For the one proposition would then be about ~, and the other would not.

Here the assertion that truth-functions are not material functions is explained by a statement to the effect that '~' is not the name of an object, which would be a pointless illustration unless the sign for a material function were such a name.

Wittgenstein's discussion of logical constants gives additional evidence that not all objects represented by primitive signs are particulars by implying that some primitive signs stand for *concepts*, which, if regarded as objects at all—and the context shows that he does so regard them—must be considered to be universals rather than particulars. The relevant passages here are 5.45 and 5.451:

> If there are primitive logical signs, a correct logic must make clear their relation (*Stellung*) to one another and justify their existence (5.45).
>
> If logic has primitive concepts (*Grundbegriffe*), they must be independent of one another. If a primitive concept is introduced, it must be introduced in all the combinations in which it ever occurs....
>
> (In short, Frege's remarks about introducing signs by means of definitions...also apply, *mutatis mutandis*, to the introduction of primitive signs.) (5.451)

If there *were* logical *Urzeichen*, they would stand for logical objects—as is shown by 5.4, 5.42, and 5.44—so the fact that Wittgenstein elaborates upon the supposition that there *are* such primitive signs by supposing that logic has primitive *concepts* shows that he is willing to include concepts among objects. Also, the remark that concepts must be introduced in all combinations in which they can occur echoes the discussion in the 2.01's concerning the logical form of objects, which gives us a further reason to suppose that he regards concepts as objects. As it turns out, of course, logical constants are not primitive signs and so are not signs for concepts, but we are left with the impression that he does include concepts among the *Bedeutungen* of primitive signs.

The realistic interpretation of concepts is confirmed by 4.126, in which Wittgenstein criticizes the 'old' logic—undoubtedly that of Frege and Russell—only for regarding formal concepts as concepts proper (*eigentliche Begriffe*), which implies that he is in general accord with Frege's and Russell's treatment of concepts proper. Since their treatment is realistic, we may conclude that Wittgenstein's is realistic as well; if his treatment were nominalistic, and thus a striking departure from Frege and Russell, the relatively mild criticism advanced in 4.126 of the old logic would be a puzzling understatement.

This is not to say that, apart from Wittgenstein's distinction between formal concepts and concepts proper, his own view of the nature of concepts proper is in complete accord with the views of Frege and Russell, nor even that Frege and Russell are themselves in complete accord with one another, though the *Tractatus* admittedly does underplay those differences which exist between the three, as when, in 4.126 and 4.1272, Wittgenstein implies that in representing concepts proper by means of functions he is merely following Frege and Russell. What Wittgenstein means by saying that he represents concepts proper by functions is innocent enough; supposing that 'John is red' is a proposition of the subject-predicate form, then he is saying only that this proposition can be symbolized as 'f(a)', where the argument-sign represents John and the function-sign represents the concept, or property, of redness.[31] This manner of symbolizing the proposition follows the practice of Frege and Russell, and to this extent all three views are the same. Wittgenstein, however, obscures an important difference between Frege and Russell concerning the relation of concepts to functions. As far as Frege is concerned, it is strictly inaccurate to say that concepts are represented by functions, because concepts *are* a species of function, viz., those functions of one argument-place whose value is always a truth-value. Concepts, then, are represented by *expressions* for just those kinds of function, i.e., by function-signs and not by functions themselves.

Russell, unlike Frege, regards concepts as capable of assuming the role of logical subject in a proposition (or at least he assumes this until persuaded otherwise by Wittgenstein), which they could not do if they were themselves 'unsaturated' or incomplete, as functions would have to be if they were entities. Since concepts cannot be functions and there is no reason to assume that propositions somehow involve entities such as functions in addition to concepts, functions are relegated to the status of merely a symbolic device—provided that we discount those few carelessly-worded passages in *Principia* which seem to impute to functions an ontological status—enabling us to represent a proposition in abstraction from some specific part of its content. Unlike the sign for a complete proposition, which, if the proposition is true, has as its ontological counterpart the appropriate complex of objects and concepts in reality, a propositional function, which is merely the schema which remains when part of the content of a proposition is abstracted, has no 'schematic' ontological counterpart. Thus, the distinction between sign and thing signified, with respect to functions, is inapplicable, so that insofar as the notation of *Principia* can be said to provide for the representation of concepts at all,[32] there can be no scruple against assigning the symbolic role to functions themselves rather than to function-signs, since both amount to the same thing.

Wittgenstein agrees with Frege against Russell in allowing that not just symbols but also the entities they represent are, as it were, 'unsaturated', so that we might also expect Wittgenstein to follow Frege in distinguishing between functions and function-signs. Ironically, however, Wittgenstein's extension of the feature of unsaturatedness to *all* objects, and not just to concepts (and relations, if we want to distinguish between functions with one argument-place and those with more than one), drives him instead towards Russell's view that functions are a symbolic device rather than a kind of object. That is, if all entities are unsaturated, the main point in speaking about functions will be to distinguish those signs which overtly symbolize the unsaturatedness of the object they represent—by containing within them an empty set of parentheses, or one filled only with a variable, which shows where another sign may be inserted—from those signs which make no such overt display but which are nevertheless equally unsaturated, i.e., dependent symbols in the sense of 2.0211. The former we call function-signs and the latter argument-signs. We may, of course, continue to observe the function/argument distinction at the level of ontology in addition to the corresponding distinction between function-signs and argument-signs at the level of symbolism (and I have indeed done so in my exposition of Wittgenstein's views), as long as we recognize that, by the criterion of unsaturatedness, entities which we call arguments could be called functions as well, so that if we continue to distinguish between them, this is only to express their different syntactic roles, a difference illustrated at the level of symbolism by confining overt unsaturatedness to those signs which behave predicatively or relationally, i.e., function-signs. Of course, since we also have other distinctions to mark the different syntactic roles of entities (or, rather, of the names which represent them)— e.g., the distinction between thing and property, or between object and concept (where the terms 'thing' and 'object' are used here in the narrow sense of 'logical subject', as opposed to the wide sense in which concepts and relations are things, or objects, as well)—the function/argument distinction has its particular usefulness primarily at the level of symbolism rather than at the level of ontology. It is therefore understandable that Wittgenstein should slur over Frege's distinction between functions and function-signs in expressing his own position as being that concepts are represented by functions, though Wittgenstein is still being careless in attributing this view to Frege himself. In any case, whatever differences may exist between the views of Frege, Russell, and Wittgenstein regarding the nature of concepts and their relation to functions, the important point for our purposes is that Wittgenstein does follow Frege and Russell in regarding concepts as objects.[33]

A striking confirmation of Wittgenstein's realistic interpretation of concepts is found in Appendix A of Waismann's *Ludwig Wittgenstein and the Vienna Circle*. In this appendix, consisting of material based on Waismann's conversations with Wittgenstein which Waismann put in writing (and which is thus evidentially on a par with Lee's notes, considered in isolation, but which provides confirmation of Lee's account, as the latter also provides for Waismann's, when both are considered together), we find Wittgenstein taking pains to prevent the sort of misunderstanding of his position that has nevertheless become prevalent in the nominalistic interpretation of the *Tractatus*, a misunderstanding epitomized in the following passage of Anscombe's:

What...has become of Frege's 'concepts' in Wittgenstein's theory? They seem to have disappeared entirely; actually, however, instead of making concepts or universals into a kind of objects...Wittgenstein made the gulf between concepts and objects much greater than Frege ever made it. So far as concerns the content of a functional expression, that will consist in the objects covered by it. But in respect of having argument-places, concepts go over entirely into logical forms. In the 'completely analysed proposition'...the Fregean 'concept', the thing with holes in it, has become simply the logical form.[34]

In the section of Appendix A of Waismann's notes appropriately titled "Concept and Form," Wittgenstein expressly sets out to combat this conflation of concepts with forms. Thus:

The form of a proposition is produced by abstracting from the meaning of the words, by turning them into variables. A subject-predicate proposition has a different form from that of a relational proposition, a symmetrical relational proposition a different form from one which is assymetrical. The state of affairs is a combination of things. The things are represented in the proposition by signs, but the form of the state of affairs is not; it is shown by the form of the proposition. A concept must be explained, the form of a proposition shows itself. The form is not describable, for the description portrays the form. To have a form means to be a picture, to think or to speak means to picture. Concepts are expressed through signs. The form, the propositional-picture, shows itself. The form is not a generalization and not a common property of a class of propositions. Symmetry and assymetry show themselves in the propositions, are contained in the description—they are not properties like yellow and hard, which are expressed through a propositional-function as names.[35]

Unless we quite arbitrarily assume that the realistic position expressed in this passage reflects a complete departure from view of the *Tractatus*—an assumption which is not merely implausible but is utterly gratuitous when we consider that this passage in other respects, e.g., concerning the state of affairs as a combination of things, or the proposition as a picture of this state of affairs, faithfully embodies the outlook of the *Tractatus*—we can only conclude that this passage decisively confirms that the *Tractatus* includes concepts, or properties, among objects.

In addition to this passage from "Concept and Form," there are a number of other passages in Wittgenstein's own post-*Tractatus* writings that at least indirectly confirm the realistic interpretation of the *Tractatus*, in that their intense concern to combat this sort of realism suggests that they are intended as a repudiation of a position held earlier by Wittgenstein himself. A number of these passages will be discussed subsequently, especially in Chapter Six. For now I will confine myself to examining only those few passages which are especially noteworthy. In *Philosophical Grammar*, Wittgenstein observes that

> [o]ne can, quite understandably, speak of *combinations of colors with shapes* (for instance, the colors red and blue with the shapes of different figures or bodies. And here is the root of the ill-chosen expression: the fact is a complex of objects. That a man is sick here becomes compared with the putting together of two things, of which one would be the man and the other would be sickness.[36]

Although the *Tractatus* nowhere contains precisely the phrase 'the fact is a complex of objects', other remarks—e.g., 2.01—are sufficiently close that we can reasonably assume that the *Tractatus* is the subject of criticism. If this assumption is correct, then the implication is that the attribution of a property to a thing is indeed treated in the *Tractatus* as the configuration of two entities, one of them being of a predicative nature.

In an article entitled "Complex and Fact," written in 1931 and published as an appendix both to *Philosophical Remarks* and *Philosopical Grammar*, this same concern to distinguish between facts and complexes issues in the following series of remarks:

> To say that a red circle *consists of* redness and circularity, or is a complex of these constituents, is a misuse of these words and is misleading....
>
> It is likewise misleading to say that the fact that this circle is red (that I am weary) is a complex of the constituents red and circle (of me and weariness).
>
> The house is also not a complex out of bricks and their spatial relations. That is, this also goes against the correct use of words. Also, the chain consists of its members, not of them and their spatial relations. The fact that these members are so combined 'consists' of nothing at all.[37]

Since the denial that a fact 'consists' in anything is clearly aimed at the

Tractatus (e.g., 2.05, 2.14, 2.141), which confirms that the *Tractatus* is the subject of criticism here, the obvious implication once again is that properties and relations are regarded in the *Tractatus* as configurable objects.

It would be possible to cite further passages, both from the *Tractatus* and from the later writings, that lend support to the realist interpretation, but none would be as decisive as those already cited; anyway, what is needed now is not more evidence supporting this interpretation, but an examination of the counter-arguments, since the popularity of the nominalistic interpretation of the *Tractatus* shows that there must after all be *some* passages in the *Tractatus* which at least ostensibly favor such an interpretation. Before the realistic interpretation can be regarded as conclusively established, these counter-arguments will have to be met.

CHAPTER FOUR

ARGUMENTS AGAINST A REALISTIC
INTERPRETATION

Great weight is given to a number of passages in the *Tractatus* which use the expressions 'thing', 'object', and 'name' in a manner plainly suggesting that only particulars are being considered as things, or symbols for particulars as names, and therefore implying that objects do not include universals. The most frequently cited passage of this sort is 4.24:

> Names are the simple symbols: I indicate them by single letters ('x', 'y', 'z').
>
> I write an elementary proposition as a function of names, in the form: 'fx', '$\phi(x, y)$', etc.

Here names seem to be restricted to argument-signs and to be opposed to functions (or, rather, function-signs, if we want to maintain a distinction here between the level of ontology and of symbolism), leading many commentators to suppose that function-signs are not names and therefore do not represent objects.[1] Just as 4.24 restricts names to argument-signs, 4.1211 restricts objects to what are represented by argument-signs:

> Thus one proposition 'fa' shows that the object a occurs in its sense, two propositions 'fa' and 'ga' show that the same object is mentioned in both of them.

A comparable use of the expressions 'object' and 'thing' is found in 5.5301, 5.5352, and 5.553. These passages have been generally regarded as compelling evidence of Wittgenstein's nominalism, and a realistic interpretation of the *Tractatus* must take them into account. In fact, the compatibility of these passages with realism is easily shown. We need only assume that Wittgenstein here means to contrast entities, or their symbols, which function as logical subjects, with those entities, or their symbols, which function predicatively or relationally; in order to emphasize this contrast, he restricts the expressions 'object', 'thing', and 'name' to this first kind of entity or its symbol, and calls the other kinds of entities 'properties', 'concepts', or 'relations', and calls their symbols 'functions' or 'function-signs'. That properties or relations are not objects in this narrow sense would then be perfectly compatible with their being objects in the wide sense of constituting the meanings of primitive signs; in this same wide sense, the signs themselves, whether function-signs or argument-signs, would all be names.

Granted that the assumption that Wittgenstein uses 'object', etc., in both a narrow and a wide sense enables us to reconcile passages such as 4.24 with a realistic interpretation of the *Tractatus*, are there any grounds for making this assumption? Clearly, there are such grounds; the precedent for the use of these terms in both a narrow and a wide sense has been established in the *Notebooks*, as has been shown by our examination of these writings in Chapter Two. Further confirmation is found in the *Proto-Tractatus*, which is more explicit than the *Tractatus* in this matter. Thus, corresponding to 4.24 of the *Tractatus* are the following passages of the *Proto-Tractatus*:

> In what follows I indicate names of objects (*Gegenstandsnamen*) by the letters x, y, z, u, v, w (4.2211).
> Generally in what follows I indicate elementary propositions by the letters p, q, r, s, t, or else (like Frege) I write them as functions of their objects in the form '$\phi(x)$', '$\psi(x, y)$', etc. (4.2212)

The expression '*Gegenstandsnamen*' is pleonastic, unless Wittgenstein is using '*Gegenstand*' in the narrow sense, and, on one occasion (*Proto-Tractatus* 4.102273) he uses the expression 'names of concepts' (*Begriffsnamen*) as well, which reinforces the supposition that the expression '*Gegenstandsnamen*' is intended to single out names of one kind of entity among others, viz., names of objects as opposed to names of concepts. Furthermore, that the restriction of the term 'object' in this context to those entities represented by argument-signs is not to be taken as an endorsement of nominalism is shown by Wittgenstein's explicit comparison of his view of elementary propositions with that of Frege, who also contrasts functions and objects, while maintaining that functions are entities in their own right.

Unfortunately, the version of these passages which ultimately appears as 4.24 of the *Tractatus* has been revised in a way which obscures its original pro-realist intent. '*Gegenstandsnamen*' has been changed to 'Namen', reference to Frege has been omitted, and the Fregean distinction between functions and objects—which is a distinction between kinds of entities and thus which implies that functions do have ontological status—has been replaced by the distinction between functions and names, a distinction which is no better than neutral as far as providing evidence in favor of realism. Whatever prompted these revisions, we can see from the *Proto-Tractatus* that it was not Wittgenstein's original intent to deny that function-signs symbolize objects, in the wide sense, and unless one is prepared to contend that the change from the text of the *Proto-Tractatus* to that of the *Tractatus* marks the change from realism to nominalism—a gratuitous suggestion, given that the *Proto-Tractatus* and the *Tractatus* are otherwise much too similar to allow the supposition that they maintain radically different ontologies —the only possible conclusion is that, like *Proto-Tractatus* 4.2211 and 4.2212, 4.24 of the *Tractatus* does not advocate nominalism, though it preserves its compatibility with realism by using 'name', rather than 'object', in the narrow sense.

Admittedly, Wittgenstein's casual employment of these key terms opens the door to a great deal of confusion—as is shown by the many commentators who are unaware of the two senses of 'object', etc., and who therefore take passages like 4.24 to be compelling evidence against the realist interpretation—but, given the assiduously cultivated obscurity of the *Tractatus*, Wittgenstein's nonchalance in a matter of this importance is not really too surprising. We are, after all, warned in the preface to the *Tractatus* that he has not written a text-book and that the book might be understood only by someone who has had thoughts along the same or similar lines; such a reader would not be misled by a few isolated passages, or rather by what might superficially be taken as their intent. Of course, with the benefit of exposure for well over half a century, the *Tractatus* has become accessible to the general philosophical public, and for the sake of all concerned we can only regret that Wittgenstein was not more careful in his employment of key terms. Still, I hope to have shown that his terminological carelessness does not prevent his realistic ontology from clearly emerging, as long as we have the patience to fit together the pieces of the puzzle.

Of those passages other than 4.24 whose nominalistic appearance is accounted for by our recognition of Wittgenstein's fluctuating terminology, 5.553 deserves mention as a special case because questions are also raised here about the use of the expression 'individual'. It is the first sentence of 5.553, in which Wittgenstein is characterizing a position of Russell's, that concerns us. He observes that "Russell said that there were simple relations between different numbers of things (individuals)." Müller takes this passage as implying that relations are not things, an interpretation confirmed, he thinks, by Wittgenstein's identification of things with individuals.[2] Now, even if we contend in opposition to Müller that the contrast is between relations and things only in the narrow sense of 'thing', so that in the wide sense relations are things as well, there remains the problem of explaining the parenthetical reference to individuals, since, on my interpretation of what Wittgenstein means by 'individual', relations are included among individuals rather than contrasted with them. To solve this problem we must look to the context in which 5.553 appears.

From 5.55 to 5.6 the discussion concerns the possibiity of investigating and classifying logical forms. In *Our Knowledge of the External World*, which is clearly the Russellian text to which 5.553 alludes, Russell holds that "...the first business of logic..." is "...a classification of the logical forms of facts...."[3] According to Russell, a prime example of such classification is the determination of whether there are relations of more than two terms, which he cautions us against confusing with the issue of whether a two-termed relation can relate more than two different terms in the sense in which this relation is a constituent of two different facts, as when a man is the son of his father as well as a son of his mother. Thus:

When we say that there are relations of more than two terms, we mean that there are single facts consisting of a single relation and more than two things.... [T]he facts I am speaking of have no facts among their constituents, but only things and relations. For example, when A is jealous of B on account of C, there is only one fact, involving three people; there are not two instances of jealousy, but only one. It is in such cases that I speak of a relation of three terms, where the simplest possible fact in which the relation occurs is one involving three things in addition to the relation. And the same applies to relations of four terms or five or any other number. All such relations must be admitted in our inventory of the logical forms of facts: two facts involving the same number of things have the same form, and two which involve different numbers of things have different forms.[4]

From this passage we can see that Wittgenstein's parenthetical reference to individuals in 5.553 is simply the expression of Russell's requirement that the classification be of relations as constituents of single facts, i.e., relations which have only simple things (individuals) and not complexes as their terms, since complexes would themselves be further facts and so would violate the requirement that the relational facts to be considered are *single* facts (i.e., atomic facts, states of affairs). Hence, the introduction of the expression 'individuals' in 5.553 bears only on the distinction between a thing's being simple or complex, and not on its being a particular or a universal, so that 5.553 does not constitute counter-evidence to my claim that Wittgenstein includes universals among individuals.[5]

Thus far I have been arguing that the distinction between a wide and narrow sense of 'object' enables us to reconcile some seemingly nominalistic passages with a realist interpretation. Interestingly, proponents of a nominalist interpretation, though showing no awareness that Wittgenstein is operating with such a distinction, at least as I have drawn it, have on occasion allowed for a different distinction between a narrow and a wide sense of 'object', and they have appealed to this distinction in interpreting a particular passage in the *Tractatus* in a way favorable to nominalism. The passage in question is 4.123:

A property is internal if it is unthinkable that its object does not possess it.
(This blue color and that one stand in the internal relation of lighter and darker *eo ipso*. It is unthinkable that *these* two objects should not stand in this relation.)

(Here the shifting use of the word 'object' corresponds to the shifting use of the words 'property' and 'relation'.)

Just as 'darker' is an internal relation between two colors, and not a relation proper, likewise—so runs the argument—the colors themselves are not objects proper; talk of the shifting use of 'object' is meant to warn us that properties are objects only in a wide sense, i.e., only in a loose way of speaking.[6]

My view, on the other hand, is that we can make more sense out of this passage by supposing that the shift here is not between a wide and narrow use of 'object', but rather a shift between talk of objects proper (in the narrow sense)—which are the bearers of genuine properties, i.e., which fall under real (*eigentlich*) concepts, or which are related to one another by genuine, external relations (these properties and relations themselves being objects proper, in the wide sense)—and those so-called 'objects' which fall under formal concepts, or are related by internal relations. Another example of this same shifting use of 'object' occurs shortly afterward, in 4.126, where Wittgenstein says:

> That something falls under a formal concept as one of its objects cannot be expressed by means of a proposition. Instead it is shown by the sign of this object itself. (A name shows that it signifies an object, a sign for a number that it signifies a number, etc.)

In other words, both names and number-signs are signs of objects in the sense that what each of them represents falls under a formal concept, but only names represent objects proper, i.e., entities capable of falling under real concepts.[7] The shifting use of 'object', therefore, is only a shift *within* what I have called the narrow sense of that expression, the sense in which objects are contrasted with predicative entities (i.e., concepts, properties) as their subjects and with relational entities as their terms. The shift within this narrow sense is between objects proper, which are qualified by external properties and related by external relations, and what we may call 'formal' objects, which are qualified by internal properties and related by internal relations. To say, then, that A is darker than B (where A and B are two shades of blue) is to treat A and B as two terms of a relation, but just as the relation is in this case internal, so likewise, are A and B objects (in the narrow sense) only in the formal sense of being terms of an internal relation. So the shift in 4.123 is only between proper and formal objects, which corresponds to a shift between external and internal relations. No doubt Wittgenstein could have expressed himself here more clearly—and 4.123 involves the additional complication that there is not even the possibility that colors, which are predicative, could be objects proper, in the narrow sense, which makes the warning about the shifting use of 'object' almost superfluous, as it would not have been had the example concerned particulars rather than colors—but when all is sorted out 4.123 says nothing which impugns the ontological status of properties as objects (in the wide sense of being predicative entities).

With this discussion of 4.123 I conclude the examination of those passages whose nominalistic appearance depends either upon the failure to distinguish between a wide and narrow sense of the expressions 'object', 'thing', and 'name', or upon the failure to make a judicious use of such a distinction. Of the remaining arguments against the realistic interpretation, most have already been either explicitly or implicitly answered in the course of my exposition of that interpretation, so that the majority of such arguments need be dealt with here only briefly.

First, there is the argument that external properties cannot be objects because they are configurations. That is, we know that formal, or internal, properties are obviously not objects, because we cannot represent them as we do objects; neither, however, can material, or external, properties be objects, because, according to 2.0231, material properties are first formed by the *configuration* of objects. Therefore, no properties are objects.[8]

The answer to this argument is that, while it is true that formal (or internal) properties are not objects, the notion that material (or external) properties are only configurations of objects, rather than themselves objects, is based on a misunderstanding of 2.0231. As I have argued, what requires the configuration of objects is the *attribution* of the property to the particular, since, apart from this configuration, the particular cannot be said to have the property, which is, after all, external to the particular's nature, unlike the form of the particular, which is internal.

This account satisfactorily explains 2.0231, while allowing that both particulars and material properties are objects, and, as we have seen, such an account is overwhelmingly confirmed by independent evidence.

Next, there are those arguments which simply assume that properties and relations are configurations of objects, and which then argue from this assumption that properties and relations cannot be objects as well. The main argument along these lines is the infinite regress argument. According to Copi, if properties were objects, then 2.0231

> ...would assert material properties to be first formed by the configuration of material properties, themselves first formed by the configuration of material properties, and so on.[9]

Pitcher puts the same argument for relations:

> If relations were objects, then when two or more particulars were configured so as to form a state of affairs, the configuration—i.e., the relation amongst the particulars—would be another object, over and above the particulars. But then we would be lost in an infinite regress, for if the configuration of two or more particulars were an object, then presumably the configuration of the particulars and the first configuration would also be an object, and the configuration of the particulars and the first and second configurations would also be an object, and so on ad infinitum.[10]

Needless to say, these infinite regress arguments are generated in the first place only by assuming that properties and relations are configurations of objects. Once we reject this assumption—as being based on a misunderstanding of 2.0231 as well as being a failure to understand that the way objects are configured constitutes the structure (or form, depending on whether or not we specify which objects are in configuration), not the content, of a state of affairs, and therefore concerns only *internal*, and not *external*, properties—the possibility of an infinite regress vanishes.

The assumption that relations are configurations of objects is also behind Müller's argument that if no objects stand in a certain relation, then that relation does not exist and is therefore not part of the substance of the world, i.e., it is not an object.[11] We have already seen that Wittgenstein, in the *Notebooks*, has raised the problem of the status of relations in false propositions and eventually dealt with it by holding that a false (relational) proposition happens to represent a non-existent configuration of an existent relation with existent particulars. That is, the relation is not the configuration of particulars, but is itself an object in this configuration. So Müller's objection fails.

Other miscellaneous arguments advanced, as far as I know, only by Müller include the following:

> When, according to 3.314, "the variable name too" can be regarded as a propositional variable, what other expressions could be "transformed" into variables (3.315)? It can be a question only of functions, which therefore are not names and yet indicate "a form and a content" (3.31).[12]

Leaving aside the problem of what Müller thinks 'content' means here, given his view that a function-sign represents the *structure* of a state of affairs,[13] he is wrong in supposing that the only possible contrast is between names and functions (or function-signs). The contrast might also be intended to be between *names*, which represent simples, and *expressions*, which may be treated as representing simples by being able to be turned into variables, etc., but which may nevertheless represent complexes.[14] Even if Wittgenstein does intend the contrast to be between names and function-signs, this need not be taken as implying more than that function-signs are not names in the narrow sense. That function-signs are names in the wide sense has been more than amply demonstrated.

Another of Müller's objections is that the objects referred to in 2.02251—where space, time, and color are given as forms of objects—can only be particulars, since universals are not at a specific place, etc.[15] What Müller says here is true, but irrelevant. Granted that the objects referred to in 2.0251 are particulars, this does not exclude the possibility of there being other objects which are universals, and, as I have argued, to say that space, time, and color are forms of objects is to say that such objects can be configured with other objects—which, in the case of objects having the form of being colored, will be universals, viz., colors.

Müller also argues that 4.013, which says that the pictorial character of a proposition is not destroyed by apparent irregularities in the notation, implies that function-signs are not really names because the parallel between the example given by 4.013 of such an apparent irregularity, viz., the use of accidentals (sharps and flats) in a musical score, and propositions of the form 'f(x)' is "...only too obvious."[16] That is, sharps and flats do not stand for notes, but have a representational role only by being to the left of a note, and the same thing can be said for function-signs.

The answer to this argument is that, while it is true that function-signs symbolize only by being to the left of argument-signs, it is equally true that argument-signs symbolize only by being to the right of function-signs, which is a consequence of Wittgenstein's view that all names are dependent symbols. This similarity between function-signs and accidentals, then, cannot count against function-signs having the status of names; furthermore, in other respects the parallel between function-signs and accidentals is lacking, since only the latter can claim to be notational irregularities. In sum, there is no reason to suppose that 4.013, with its example of sharps and flats, intends any parallel to be drawn to function-signs at all, let alone that it wants to show that function-signs are not names.

I consider next two more arguments of Copi's. In the first argument, Copi rightly points out that 2.022 and 2.023 together imply that the objects which constitute the substance of the world must be the same in all possible worlds and so cannot be contingent. He then contends that Wittgenstein's claim in 6.1233 that we could think of a world in which the axiom of reducibility does not hold—which is equivalent to the claim that we could think of a world in which certain properties which are assumed to exist in virtue of the axiom of reducibility do not exist—shows that Wittgenstein regards the existence of properties as contingent. Therefore, since objects are not contingent, properties cannot be objects.[17]

In response to this argument, I should first point out that Copi is on precarious ground in trying to build any kind of argument around Wittgenstein's attitude towards the axiom of reducibility, because Wittgenstein's attitude in not all that clear. Copi's assumption—which admittedly seems to be borne out by 6.1232 and 6.1233—is that Wittgenstein regards the axiom of reducibility as a contingent proposition, so that, were this proposition false, there would be at least one higher-order function for which there was no formally equivalent predicative function. But surely the whole thrust of Wittgenstein's distinction between functions and operations (5.25)—only the latter of which is involved in building up all other propositions as truth-functions of elementary propositions (5.3) or in building up anything like the Russellian hierarchy of orders or types (5.252)—is to do away with the need for higher-order functions entirely. The only propositional functions required by the *Tractatus* are those which take particulars as arguments and which, when completed, constitute elementary propositions.[18]

If I am right about this, it is hard to see what Wittgenstein would have in mind in suggesting that the axiom of reducibility was a contingent proposition. Even if we ignore this difficulty, however, and grant that the axiom of reducibility is indeed a contingent proposition which asserts that a certain predicative function exists, Copi is still mistaken in supposing that the falsity of this proposition, and hence the non-existence of a predicative function of the requisite character as specified by the axiom of reducibility, shows that the existence of such functions, or properties, is contingent. For Wittgenstein, the contingency of a proposition concerns only the configuration of objects and not objects themselves. Whether the objects named in a proposition are or are not in a certain configuration is contingent, but the existence of these objects themselves is guaranteed by the very meaningfulness of their names and so cannot be contingent. Even when, by making an existential generalization, we assert the existence of an object without naming it and thus without presupposing its existence, the existence of the object in this case as well is not contingent. That is, we are only claiming that there is an object answering a certain description; if our assertion is false, this again shows only that a certain configuration does not exist. For example, the falsity of '$(\exists x)$ x is red' would show only that no particular happens to be configured with redness, but not that the number of particulars themselves is less than it otherwise might have been.[19] Similarly, the falsity of a proposition such as '$(\exists \phi)\phi b$', where the function is generalized, would show only that the object b was not configured with any properties (which would be the case, e.g., if b were to be found only as a term in various relations), and not that those properties which do exist are contingent. These same considerations would apply to the existential claim put forth in the axiom of reducibility, were this axiom conceded to be a contingent proposition. The falsity of this proposition would show only that no predicative function happened to be configured with other objects in the manner specified in the proposition; it would not show, as Copi claims, that properties themselves are contingent. Therefore, this argument of Copi's can be dismissed.

In his second argument, Copi observes that 6.3751 shows that color-predications are not elementary propositions, since two different color-predications can be mutually incompatible, whereas elementary propositions are always compatible. He assumes that if any properties were simple objects, colors would be, and since 6.3751 shows that colors are not simple objects, therefore no properties are such objects.[20] Edwin Allaire, another defender of a realistic interpretation of the *Tractatus*, examines this objection at length,[21] so I will confine myself to a few remarks. Copi's conclusion does not follow, because his assumption is not shared by Wittgenstein. To be sure, the *Tractatus* treats colors as if they were simple objects just as it treats spatial points as if they were objects. At the same time, Wittgenstein's view that elementary propositions are mutually independent requires that colors be regarded as complex, and the common-sense view that colors are simple must therefore give way to this requirement. We should note that Wittgenstein had already acknowledged the possibility of incompatible color-predications in the patently realistic *Notebooks*, where he speaks of an incompatibility in the structures of the two objects (i.e., complex objects) red and green (16.8.16), and where the complexity of colors does not count against properties being objects, but rather counts against colors being (simple) properties (11.9.16). We can easily see, therefore, that 6.3751 provides no evidence against the view that Wittgenstein regards properties as objects.

Finally, I shall consider four arguments advanced by Keyt. The first argument concerns the metaphor of logical space:

In this metaphor an existent atomic fact is the analogue of a material point; a possible atomic fact, of a geometrical point; and an object, of the reference of a co-ordinate of a point. In analytic geometry a point may be indicated by writing three numerals in a certain relation, for example, by writing "(3, 2, 1)". Similarly an atomic fact may be indicated by writing names in a certain relation.... Now if Wittgenstein held that in every atomic fact one object must be a quality or a relation, then in the metaphor a point should be indicated not by three co-ordinates but by two co-ordinates and the sign of a function....[22]

As should be obvious from my previous discussion of logical space, the difficulty which Keyt poses for realism arises only because he has the analogues wrong. Thus, a material point, or spatial object, has as its analogue, not an existent state of affairs, but an object in logical space. A geometrical, or spatial, point has as its analogue, not a possible state of affairs, but any of those objects the totality of which constitutes the logical space of the object in this space, just as space proper is constituted by the totality of spatial points within which the spatial object is situated. As far as states of affairs are concerned, there is no question of an *analogue* between space proper and logical space; in either case, states of affairs in the usual sense result when the object in space is configured with one of the objects which together constitute that space. Since, on this account, objects in logical space are not the analogue of co-ordinates, Keyt's objection that a function-sign is the wrong kind of sign to be a co-ordinate loses its force.

Keyt's other three arguments concern the 'chain' simile of 2.03. The first argument is that the notion that "...objects hang together like the links of a chain..." (2.03), suggests that objects are all fundamentally alike. Therefore, objects cannot include both universals and particulars, since these are fundamentally unlike one another. The answer to this argument is that, for Wittgenstein, particulars and universals *are* fundamentally alike, as I have shown, and 2.03 can therefore be no evidence against realism on this account.

Keyt's second argument is that a relation is of a higher type than its terms, so that a relation cannot be an object in the chain, since all such objects are surely of the same type.[24] This argument fails to see that, not only in the *Tractatus*, but even in the earlier transition from (1) to (2), one of Wittgenstein's main objectives has been to render the theory of types superfluous. There is no need in the *Tractatus* for a type-distinction to ensure that we do not try to give relations a syntactic role appropriate only to particulars, since the proper syntactic role for each kind of object is 'written into' the object itself, in virtue of the object's logical form. Hence, particulars, properties, and relations, differing as they do both in form and in content, nevertheless stand on equal footing as objects.

Keyt's third argument is that if we include relations among objects, the chain-simile breaks down, because a three-termed relation is more like a key-ring that holds three keys than it is like the link in a chain, which is connected at best with only two other links.[25] This argument, to be sure, is evidence for the truism that similes, when pressed, tend to break down, but there is no reason to suppose that Wittgenstein himself intends the simile to extend this far. Surely the point is that, just like the links of a chain, objects in a state of affairs fit into one another directly, without the need of some connecting 'cement' such as the copula which Wittgenstein had originally postulated in position (1). The fact that a chain-link connects with two links while a relation may connect itself with three—or twenty—terms is, for the point of the simile, irrelevant.

2.03, then, is in no way incompatible with realism; on the contrary, this passage is quite likely intended to support realism, particularly against the Bradleyian charge that the admission of relational entities leads to an infinite regress. Whether or not Wittgenstein ever read Bradley, we can presume that he was acquainted with at least that famous paragraph from *Appearance and Reality* (since it is quoted by Russell in *Our Knowledge of the External World,* which Wittgenstein did read) in which Bradley argues that if a relation is to be anything to its terms, it must itself bear a relation to these terms, with the result that

> ...we are hurried off into the eddy of a hopeless process, since we are forced to go on finding new relations without end. The links are united by a link, and this bond of union is a link which also has two ends; and these require each a fresh link to connect them with the old.[26]

Bradley assumes that the linking of a relation with one of its terms requires, *per impossible*, an infinite number of intermediate links. This conception of the way a relation manages to link itself to a term treats the link as something external to the nature and function of the relation itself. If we take instead the Fregean approach and allow relations themselves to perform this linking role by supposing that, apart from their actual performance of this role, relations are merely incomplete, unsaturated entities, we eliminate the need for postulating intermediate links. In other words, on Bradley's view, for a relation to be something to its terms, it must be more than it is in itself apart from connection with its terms, and this 'something extra' can only be another, intermediate relation. For Frege, on the other hand, a relation is only fully what it is in the act of being saturated by its terms, thereby relating them. Apart from this state of saturation, the relation retains its identity as a distinctive entity, but only in a kind of privative status, so that when the saturation does come about, it is more as though a potential relation were actualized than that something extra is added to what was already a self-sufficient, independent entity.

Wittgenstein, as we have seen, adopts the Fregean approach, though modifying it to include not only relations, but their terms as well, among unsaturated entities. So, while in Frege's conception, a relation might be appropriately compared to a board with a number of holes into which fit corresponding pegs, the relating of the pegs being accomplished by their being plugged into the holes, the chain-simile of 2.03 is more appropriate for Wittgenstein, since each link must be entered into, or 'saturated' as it were, by another link in order to be part of the chain (whereas for Frege the status of the pegs, at least, would seem to remain essentially the same whether or not they were plugged in). I would contend, then, that the chain-simile is carefully chosen by Wittgenstein and is probably meant to illustrate his modified Fregean response to Bradley.[27]

That this should be the nature of Wittgenstein's answer to Bradley will no doubt disappoint those who suppose that one of the most ingenious accomplishments of the *Tractatus* lies in getting rid of relations altogether—or at least in retaining them in a way which avoids criticisms such as Bradley's—by the doctrine that relations are only shown, and not said, by language in its properly analyzed form. Of course, if Wittgenstein's view *were* that we avoid trouble by employing a symbolism which completely excludes relation-words, thereby depriving Bradley of a way of formulating his objection to relations, this would still leave unclear the ontological status of relations. I have called such an interpretation of the *Tractatus* 'nominalistic' for the sake of convenience, but such a view is not nominalistic in any ordinary sense. It is not that relations themselves are held to be a 'linguistic fiction', on this interpretation; ordinary, unanalyzed language misleads us only in supposing that we represent relations in the same way that we do particulars—viz., according to the name-object treatment—but that we do somehow represent relations—viz., by their being shown in a perspicuous language—is not denied. So the question remains as to what it is that is being represented. If a relation is not an object, does it nevertheless have a kind of content? Or is it perhaps a kind of contentless, structural entity? And in either case, supposing that we can even make sense of these options, to what extent has a realist ontology of some sort thereby been avoided, if at all?

There is the further problem, again supposing that the view that relations are shown rather than said were indeed Wittgenstein's, that whatever gains might be had in being able to answer Bradley in a way that avoids treating relations as objects would seem to be at least partially offset by the incredible complexity of any supposedly perspicuous symbolism which attempted to carry out the programme of showing different relations by means of the various spatial arrangements of names of particulars. Now, it is no doubt true that a symbolism which renders 'aRb' as 'ab', 'aSb' as 'ba', and so on, is in some sense as perspicuous as the symbolism it replaces, but we need little imagination to see that the obstacles in developing such a symbolism to handle more than a few two- or three-place relations would be formidable—the prospect is even ludicrous. I concede, however, that the bizarreness of the programme of 'showing' relations by scattering symbols all over a page does not by itself show that Wittgenstein could not have held this view; one could argue, I suppose, that Wittgenstein's concern is solely with the possibility, and not the practicality, of this sort of symbolism, since his programme stems entirely from *a priori* considerations which demand this 'showing' capability of the symbolism as a logical requirement. Fortunately, there is no need to pursue these speculations, at least as they bear on the views of the *Tractatus* itself, for we already have ample evidence that the doctrine of showing is by no means intended to do away with relations or properties as named objects. Wittgenstein is not, with his doctrine of showing, trying to avoid the difficulties posed by Bradley, and therefore the peculiarities of this nominalist version of the doctrine need not concern us further.

This concludes the survey of the various arguments in favor of a nominalistic interpretation of the *Tractatus*. All such arguments have been shown to be based upon misunderstandings, and none poses a serious challenge to the realist interpretation. I submit, therefore, that the realism of the *Tractatus* has been conclusively established.

CHAPTER FIVE

WITTGENSTEIN'S MODERATE REALISM

Wittgenstein's attack on Platonism in his later philosophy is well known. As he says in the *Blue Book*, we have a primitive, too simple idea of the structure of language when we suppose that

> ...*properties* are *ingredients* of the things which have the properties; e.g. that beauty is an ingredient of all beautiful things as alcohol is of beer and wine, and that we therefore could have pure beauty, unadulterated by anything that is beautiful.[1]

What has not been commonly appreciated is that the view of properties as ingredients, capable of existence apart from the things in which they are 'contained', is precisely Wittgenstein's own earlier position in the *Tractatus*.[2] The importance of appreciating this is that if we do not, and instead assume that this attack on Platonism is just part of a generally anti-realist attitude prevalent in the *Tractatus* as well, we will overlook the possibility that Wittgenstein's attack is not against realism as such, but only against a Platonic realism, in which properties are held to exist separately from things which have these properties. There is, of course, another version of realism, put forward most notably by Aristotle, in which properties really exist, though only in things as their common qualities and not apart from these things. Now, there can be no doubt that a major thrust of Wittgenstein's later philosophy is not just against Platonic realism, but against an uncritical realism as such. The criticism of "[t]he tendency to look for something in common to all the entities which we commonly subsume under a general term..."[3] applies both to Platonic and Aristotelian realism. The issue, however, is not whether Wittgenstein rejects the Aristotelian account of the use of most general terms—for he clearly does—but whether he rejects such an account for all general terms. My contention is that Wittgenstein does in fact acknowledge that some general words are names of non-particular objects, i.e., universals, and that he is therefore an Aristotelian realist to at least a limited extent. All other commentators, so far as I am aware, agree that the later Wittgenstein is not a realist of any sort, though there is some disagreement among them concerning the nature of his attack upon realism. In this chapter, I shall examine the views of various commentators and defend my own interpretation against theirs.

I begin by considering the view of Bambrough, who thinks that Wittgenstein is opposed to any version of realism and that this opposition is based on his doctrine of family-resemblances. Bambrough cites #66-67 of the *Philosophical Investigations*—in which Wittgenstein says that the general term 'game' is applied to its various instances, not on the basis of some element common to them all, but rather on the basis of a network of similarities which serve to form a family of cases—and then argues that what holds for the general term 'game' holds for all general terms. Thus, Bambrough contends against Ayer that Wittgenstein does not in this example mean to contrast a complicated concept like 'game'[4] with a simple concept like 'red', because the observation that there is no essential element common to all instances of games applies equally well to all instances of red things. To show that this is Wittgenstein's own view, Bambrough cites two passages. The first is from the *Brown Book*, where Wittgenstein poses the rhetorical question: "Could you tell me what is in common between a light red and a dark red?"[5]—the implication being that there need be nothing in common. The second is #73 of the *Investigations*, where Wittgenstein again asks: "Which shade is the 'sample in my mind' of the color green—the sample of what is common to all shades of green?—with the same implication as before.[6]

In fairness to Ayer, it should be said that if Bambrough's conclusion were correct, Ayer would be no less correct in supposing that 'game' and 'red' differ markedly in that the former term does not, while the latter term does, mark 'a simple and straightforward resemblance' between the things to which the word is applied, because Ayer's position is itself non-essentialist. That is, for Ayer the difference between 'game' and 'red' is not that the latter term names a common quality of its instances while the former does not, but only that the resemblance between red things is more straightforward than the resemblance between games. So Bambrough's disagreement with Ayer is not over the account of the difference between 'game' and 'red', but only over the question of whether the point of *Investigations* #66-67 is to emphasize the contrast between complicated and simple concepts; Bambrough thinks it is not.

Bambrough's argument is really directed, not against Ayer, but against a defender of the view that at least some general terms are applied to their instances in virtue of the presence of a common element in these instances. Leaving aside for the moment the question of Wittgenstein's own intentions, can we say that the two passages cited by Bambrough are sufficient to refute the defender of a moderate realism, provided he accepts their implication? Clearly, I would contend, they are not. The realist can readily accept that different shades of red are all called 'red' only because they resemble one another and not because they possess a common quality. It is not the general term 'red', but the general term for a specific shade of red, e.g., 'fire-engine red', which provides a better example for the realist. Different things which are fire-engine red do not merely resemble one another, as something light red resembles something dark red; rather, they each possess a quality common to them all.

Surely, if I cut three handkerchiefs from a piece of uniformly dyed cloth, it would be a strained use of language to say that the three handkerchiefs *resembled* one another in respect of their color, or that their colors were quite *similar*. Rather, we would say that they have the *same* color. In fact, our linguistic practices tend to lean in the opposite direction: in most contexts we would call different shades of a color the same color when, strictly speaking, there would be only similar colors, so that in the context under consideration, where the purpose is to make the most precise discrimination possible with respect to observed differences of color, we would say that the color of the handkerchiefs is *exactly* or *precisely* the same, to distinguish the cases where there was no observable difference of color at all from those cases where there were at least slight differences.[7]

It could be objected that I have assumed that the three handkerchiefs are cut from a uniformly dyed piece of cloth, which ensures that the observable differences between the handkerchiefs with respect to color will be nil, but that in fact no general term, even one ostensibly standing for a specific shade of color, ever actually names just precisely one shade, because even if the three handkerchiefs have precisely the same shade of color, it is nevertheless not in virtue of having this specific color-quality, and no other, that they are called 'fire-engine red' or whatever, since they might have varied slightly in color and still properly be called 'fire-engine red'.

While this criticism is, from a certain perspective, a just one, it is not fatally damaging, for once we admit that two or more things can have precisely the same color, the way has been cleared in principle for the recognition of such common qualities, even though in practice we may not be equipped to make such precise distinctions with the general terms at our disposal, where—at least in their normal use—such a degree of precision would be irrelevant. Paint stores, on the other hand, might have occasion to use general terms for naming specific shades of color with the requisite degree of precision, a feat they could easily manage by utilizing a color-chart and stressing that, in applying a color-name to a patch of paint, no observable difference from the sample in the color-chart corresponding to that name was to be permitted. Nothing in principle, then, prevents this degree of rigor from being in force, and this is all that we need to counter Bambrough's claim that realism cannot possibly be true because there cannot be any general terms that name common elements. My argument is that there could be, and even very well may be, such general terms. Besides specific shades of color, other likely candidates for the status of common elements nameable by general terms would be specific tastes, smells, textures, etc.—in short, specific sensible qualities.

If it is granted that Bambrough's all-out attack on realism is at least *prima facie* unconvincing, the question then becomes: is Bambrough's position, nevertheless, also Wittgenstein's? The answer, I submit, is that Wittgenstein does not try to dispose of all universals, in Bambrough's fashion, but rather that he is content to maintain a limited realism in which at least specific sense-qualities such as shades of color are regarded as common elements of the things they qualify. I will attempt to make the argument only for colors, if for no other reason than that those remarks of Wittgenstein's which can be cited as positive textual evidence for his realism are themselves almost invariably concerned with the topic of color. What other kinds of universals he would acknowledge, if any, I am not prepared to say, although a good case could also be made for shapes, since the topics of color and shape are frequently discussed together in a way that suggests that Wittgenstein treats colors and shapes on a par as the most obvious examples of qualities common to many particulars. In any case, since the common view is that the later Wittgenstein is, for one profound reason or another, opposed to realism *in principle*, and not just in practice, my argument that he admits the existence of at least one kind of universal will be sufficient to show that the common view is mistaken.

Before citing my positive evidence, I want first to rebut Bambrough's claim that Wittgenstein intends the family-resemblance treatment for all concepts. The invitation of *Investigations* #66 for us to 'look and see' if there is a common element, an essence, of all games in virtue of which they are called 'games' shows that the issue is not to be determined by general, *a priori* considerations, as Bambrough supposes, but is rather to be determined by seeing how, in each case, the general term in question actually operates, the implication being that some general terms may very well name common elements. Furthermore, in the course of arguing that there is no common element of gamehood, Wittgenstein makes clear that he is not attacking the notion of a common element as such, for, in denying that there is a common element in all instances of games in virtue of which they are games, he admits that various kinds of games might have common elements. Thus: "Look for example at board-games... Now pass to card-games.... [M]any common features drop out, and others appear" (#66). So, within the concept 'game', there are various sub-concepts such as 'board-game', 'card-game', 'ball-game', etc., and though the general term 'game' is not applied in virtue of the presence of a common element, we can by no means conclude that the general terms 'board-game', 'ball-game', etc., follow suit. On the contrary, 'board-game' is presumably applied to all its instances in virtue of their having in common that they are all played on a board, 'ball-game' is applied to those games which involve the use of a ball, and so on.

Of course, it could be contended that the same family-resemblance treatment could be extended in turn to 'board', 'ball', and generally to any purportedly common element; this, however, would be to go beyond anything that is actually said or implied in the text. The emphasis of Wittgenstein's attack in #66 is not against an essentialist account of the use of concepts generally, but rather is directed against the simplistic attitude which advocates the essentialist account not only for a sub-concept of some more inclusive concept (e.g., a species-concept, such as 'board-game', of the genus-concept 'game'), where such an account might be perfectly proper, but also extends this essentialist account to the more inclusive concept as well. Thus, the term 'board-game' may be applied in virtue of its instances having a common element, but the mistake is in supposing that what holds for 'board-game' also holds for 'game'.

An exact parallel can be drawn in this respect between Wittgenstein's discussion of the concept 'game' and the concept 'number'. The general term 'number', we are told in #67, is applied to all its instances, not in virtue of their possessing a common element, but rather in virtue of all these instances having various resemblances. At the same time, the sub-concepts 'cardinal number', 'rational number', 'real number', etc., admit of an essentialist account, as their genus-concept 'number' does not. Wittgenstein implies this in his response to the hypothetical interlocutor who tries to make a case for the essentialist account of the genus-concept 'number' by saying that what is common to the various kinds of numbers in virtue of which the general term 'number' applies to them all is "...the disjunction of their common properties (*Gemeinsamkeiten*)..." (#67). Wittgenstein's reply here is that the interlocutor is only

> ...playing with words. One might as well say: 'Something runs through the whole thread—namely the continuous overlapping of those fibres'.

Now, such a reply would be completely inappropriate if Wittgenstein were attacking the assumption that common elements existed even within various kinds of numbers. Surely he is admitting that such common elements do exist in connection with the sub-concepts, his point being that it is a sophistic trick which tries to do for the genus-concept 'number' what can be genuinely and helpfully done for the species-concepts 'cardinal number', 'rational number', etc., viz., to give an account of the use of the term by reference to an essential feature or group of features belonging to all of the instances to which the term is applied. Obviously, then, Wittgenstein intends the family-resemblance account only for some concepts and not for others; such an account cannot, therefore, be regarded as the key to a *general* solution of the 'problem of universals', as Bambrough supposes, and certainly cannot be used to show that sensible qualities such as specific shades of color are not universals.

Of course, from the fact that board-games have boards as their common quality, it does not follow that the concept 'board' is a universal, for it is possible—as previously suggested—that 'board' is a family-resemblance concept in its own right; alternatively, 'board', though not itself a family-resemblance concept, is definable in terms of simpler concepts, which themselves may or may not be family-resemblance concepts. The issue, though, is whether there can be common qualities which are neither family-resemblance concepts themselves nor are further definable by simpler concepts of either sort. Colors, I have argued, are plausible candidates for just such concepts (where, when I speak of 'color' in this context, it should be understood to mean 'specific shade of color').

Positive evidence that Wittgenstein, too, would allow that different particular things can have a color as their common quality is found in *Investigations* #72. I will first put this passage in its proper setting so that its full import may be understood. In #71, Wittgenstein is defending the appropriateness—indeed, the necessity—of explaining certain concepts such as 'game' by giving various examples of games rather than by formulating a general definition which will apply to all examples. In the case of the concept 'game', the absence of any element common to all games in virtue of which they are called 'games' makes any general definition impossible, or at least unwieldy and useless, unless we concede—as Wittgenstein apparently does not—that there is a sufficiently small core of properties to allow, as something more substantial than an *ad hoc* exercise, a general disjunctive definition of 'game' along the lines of that suggested in #67 for 'number'. Also, and perhaps the more decisive reason for our being confined here to giving examples rather than a general definition, the concept 'game' has 'blurred edges' or, to use Waismann's expression, is 'open-textured'—i.e., we do not give the concept 'game' a strict boundary which provides us with a procedure for deciding of everything whether or not it is a game—and this shows, not only that we must be content with explaining the concept 'game' by giving examples, but furthermore that there is not even such a thing here as enumerating all the examples. We must be content to describe various games and to add: "This *and similar* things are called 'games'" (#69), where the phrase 'and similar things' cannot be more precisely filled in. Thus, when I point out to someone examples of games in the hope of bringing him to understand what games are, I am not using an indirect method which could be replaced by the direct method of isolating the essential element of gamehood and directing his attention to that alone, in abstraction from the particular examples. There is not even a possibility of enumerating *all* the relevant examples and thereby achieving a comprehensive, if not an essentialist, account of the concept 'game', for this concept has 'blurred edges'. Rather, it is the nature of the case that I can only give particular examples and hope that they are understood in the relevant way. That this kind of explanation can be misunderstood does not make it inferior to an essentialist account, since "...any general explanation can be misunderstood too" (#71). The upshot of #71, then, is that certain concepts are legitimately and solely explained by the giving of particular examples.

Now, the implication of #71, and the point that #72 proceeds to discuss, is that there is more than one way that examples could be involved in the explanation of a concept. That is, #71 says that, in explaining to someone what a game is by giving examples,

> I do not...mean by this that he is supposed to see in those examples that common thing which I—for some reason—was unable to express.... Here giving examples is not an *indirect* means of explaining—in default of a better.... The point is that *this* is how we play the game (I mean the language-game with the word "game".)

This suggests that, while giving examples is as direct a means as one could have for explaining the concept 'game', there are other concepts in which the giving of examples *would* be merely an indirect means of explanation, capable of being replaced by a more direct one, presumably one in which the common element in the examples could be *directly* pointed out. That Wittgenstein believes there can be both indirect and direct explanations of concepts by means of giving examples is confirmed by #72, since the purpose of this passage is to illustrate these different kinds of explanations. The passage itself is as follows:

> *Seeing what is common.* Suppose I show someone various multi-coloured pictures, and say: "The colour you see in all these is called 'yellow ochre'".—This is a definition, and the other will get to understand it by looking for and seeing what is common to the pictures. Then he can look *at*, can point *to*, the common thing.
>
> Compare with this a case in which I show him figures of different shapes all painted the same colour, and say: "What these have in common is called 'yellow ochre'".
>
> And compare this case: "The colour that is common to all these is what I call 'blue'".

Three different cases are being considered here. The first case is obviously intended as an illustration of an indirect explanation which could be replaced by a direct one. Instead of explaining the concept 'yellow ochre' by saying that it is the color common to all the pictures, the instructor could directly display this quality common to all the examples by using a color-chart or by pointing to the color as it is found on one or more of the pictures. The second case is also an illustration of an indirect explanation, slightly different from the first in that the instructee is not told what kind of common element he is looking for, and he must determine by a process of elimination that it is the color and not, e.g., the shape, whereas in the first case the instructee knows what kind of common quality he is looking for, and the process of elimination is confined to the task of picking out the correct color among others. Since the same concept is being explained in the second case as in the first, the second kind of indirect explanation could be replaced by the same direct explanation that could replace the first explanation. The third case is significantly different from the other two. Here, I take the point to be that various samples of different shades of blue could not be dispensed with in favor of a direct display of their common quality of blueness, because there is no such common quality to be found. We call these various samples 'blue', not in virtue of a quality they commonly share, but in virtue of resemblances which they bear to one another. The concept 'blue' is, in this respect, like the concept 'game', both such concepts being contrasted with a concept like 'yellow ochre', where the general term stands for a common quality that can be directly displayed.[8]

In #73 Wittgenstein does go on to say that even a concept like 'green' or 'blue' could be explained by a single color-sample, but such a color-sample would not be a direct display of the color-quality blue or green, as would a color-sample of yellow-ochre (assuming that 'yellow ochre' is here regarded as the name of a specific shade of color), because the former sort of sample would have a different kind of application than the latter, representing a whole range of color-qualities rather than one specific color-quality. The notion that it is the *use* to which a sample is put that determines whether it is a specific sample of pure green[9] or a general sample representing many different shades of green, rather than some intrinsic difference in the two samples—since the same sample could be used for either purpose—shows that even a specific sample acts as a direct display of a certain color only in the context in which we treat the sample accordingly. Apart from this context of human activity, the sample is 'dead', i.e., it has no intrinsic force to compel us to see it as a specific sample, just as the act of pointing has no intrinsic power to establish which object is being singled out. Still, we do successfully single out objects or common qualities by pointing, just as we use specific color-samples, and so the distinction between concepts like 'blue' and 'green', on the one hand, and 'yellow ochre', on the other, remains a legitimate and—for our purposes—a crucial one.

In Wittgenstein's *Remarks on Colour*, a late work which discusses in detail a variety of themes concerning color, he makes a number of observations bearing on the issue of sameness of color which show that the account I have given so far, though not fundamentally inaccurate, is nevertheless simplistic and requires qualification. I have been speaking as if the notion that two things could have the same color as a common quality is, for Wittgenstein, unproblematic. The sorts of examples previously discussed, such as comparing two pieces of cloth, or a patch of paint with the sample in a color-chart, seem straightforward enough, and we might be tempted to conclude from a consideration of these examples alone that we understand what 'sameness of color' means generally. In *Remarks on Colour*, however, Wittgenstein contends that whether it even makes sense to say of two colored things that they are of the same color depends upon what two things we are comparing. Thus,

> [o]ur colour concepts sometimes relate to substances (Snow is white), sometimes to surfaces (this table is brown), sometimes to the illumination (in the reddish evening light), sometimes to transparent bodies. And isn't there also an application to a place in the visual field, logically independent of a spatial context? (III, #255)

The suggestion is that whereas two things within one of these categories might be compared for sameness of color, we might well lack a method of comparison for making such a judgement of two objects falling under different categories. Hence, Wittgenstein is led to say that "...we have not *one* but several related concepts of the sameness of colours..." (III, #251), and elsewhere, that our concept of sameness of color is "indeterminate" (I, #56). The subtleties and complexities involved in this issue, however, do not serve to undermine the conclusion I have been concerned to establish, which is that Wittgenstein allows that there are cases—the discussion of #72 of the *Investigations* being one such example—of two things having a common quality. Even if we cannot unproblematically compare the color of a pile of snow with the color of the crest of a wave, or the color of either of these with the color of a baseball, we can say of two piles of snow, or of a baseball and a tablecloth, that they are exactly the same shade of white, or whatever.[10] We may conclude our examination of #72 and neighboring passages, then, with the assurance that there is clear evidence that Wittgenstein acknowledges one case of a quality common to many instances, viz., a specific shade of color, and to this extent at least, he gives an implicit endorsement to Aristotelian realism.

There is, however, another interpretation of Wittgenstein, advanced by Kennick, which also purports to show that Wittgenstein is not a realist, but for reasons quite different from those proposed by Bambrough. I shall now show that Kennick's arguments succeed no better than Bambrough's. Kennick's position can be summarized as follows:

The passages in the *Philosophical Investigations* on family-resemblances are not an attack on realism, but on essentialism. These two positions should be kept distinct, but they are confused because there is a realist as well as an essentialist interpretation of the doctrine that 'if two or more things are univocally called by the same name, they must have something in common'. On the essentialist interpretation, this doctrine is simply an implicit definition of 'univocity'—not an argument for universals—and it can be rejected, as Wittgenstein does in the passages on family-resemblances, by arguing that a word can be univocally applied to things that merely resemble one another in certain ways. In order, however, for Wittgenstein's rejection of this doctrine to be considered as a rejection of realism, we must add to this doctrine the realist assumption that

> ...a general name, univocally applied...names, denotes, stands for, or designates one thing, the same and identical in each case, which is other than the thing of which it is predicated.[11]

Now, since one can be an essentialist without granting this additional assumption of realism—(Kennick thinks that Socrates, if we accept Aristotle's testimony, was such an essentialist)—there is no reason to assume that in the passages on family-resemblances Wittgenstein is doing more than attacking essentialism. Admittedly, he challenges this additional assumption of the realist as well, but he does so in the course of his attack on the name-object theory of meaning, which occurs in a quite separate context from the discussion of family-resemblances; in short, although Wittgenstein attacks both essentialism and realism, his two attacks ought to be kept distinct. The ammunition for the latter attack consists in various strategies designed to undermine that picture of language in which the meaning of a word is regarded as detachable from the word in the way that the bearer of a proper name is detachable from his name. These strategies include, first, the denial that the bearer of a name is the same as the meaning of the name (*Investigations*, #40); second, the denial that properties are ingredients of things (*Blue Book*, p. 17); third, the admonition against looking for a substance answering to every substantive (*Blue Book*, pp. 1 and 5); fourth, and perhaps most importantly, the injunction to speak of the use of a word, rather than its meaning, wherever we can (*Investigations*, #43). If we think of meaning as use,

> ...we may no longer be inclined to say that every general term (primitive predicate) must denote something. For we are not inclined to think of the use of a word as an entity corresponding to the word, any more than we are inclined to think of the use of a hammer as an entity corresponding to the hammer.
>
> What, then, do Wittgenstein's reminders add up to? Apparently to the claim that being the meaning of a general word or primitive predicate is *not* being something corresponding to the word, and hence something the word stands for or denotes in addition to the things to which it may be applied or of which it may be predicated.[12]

In response to Kennick, I would say, first, that it is doubtful that a clear-cut distinction between essentialism and realism can be maintained. Presumably even Kennick would admit that realism implies essentialism—i.e., that the universal named by a general term is the common element, or essence, of those instances to which, and in virtue of which, the general term is applied—so the only question is whether essentialism implies realism. Kennick cites Socrates as an example of a non-realist essentialist, i.e., as one who holds that every general term must be definable in terms of a conjunction of properties which collectively constitute the general term's essence, but who does not suppose that this essence is a thing which is named, denoted, etc., by the general term. Now, I do not understand on what basis Kennick can claim that Socrates denied that there are such things as virtue and knowledge, other than that Socrates may not have held that these things (i.e., properties) exist apart from their instances in a separate realm of Platonic Forms, the source for this latter doctrine being that of Socrates' most prominent student rather than Socrates himself. No doubt Kennick is right in supposing that essentialism does not imply a Platonic realism, but the issue ought to be whether Socrates or anyone else can be an essentialist without being to any extent any kind of realist. Even if some sophisticated argument could be produced showing that essentialism does not imply realism, the *prima facie* connection between the two, at any rate, is sufficiently intimate that the burden of proof is on Kennick to show that Wittgenstein does not regard an attack on one as an attack on the other. As it is, I can see no reason to deny that Wittgenstein, in the passages on family-resemblances, conceives himself to be attacking both positions, to the extent that he is attacking either one, and therefore Bambrough cannot be faulted for regarding these passages as having a bearing on the problem of universals. Bambrough's mistake, as we have seen, is to assume that the family-resemblance account is intended for *all* general terms, but at least those general terms for which the account is correct are thereby shown not to be names of universals, and to this extent the family-resemblance doctrine does help to undermine an uncritical realism.

If there is any truth to Kennick's claim that the target of the doctrine of family-resemblances is essentialism rather than realism, it is that Wittgenstein undoubtedly recognizes that an uncritical essentialist is not necessarily an uncritical realist—indeed, this is an accurate description of Wittgenstein's own earlier position in the *Tractatus*, in which only the ultimate residue of analysis—the simple objects—are given ontological status as universals or particulars, even while the analysis is carried out on the basis of essentialist assumptions concerning the way complexes are defined by simples. Thus, an essentialist could, and probably would, give an account of the concept 'game' without supposing that 'game' is itself the name of a universal. Even the essential properties of a game would not necessarily be thought of as universals, provided that they could be defined by means of still simpler properties, and so on. Only at the point where this analysis could go no further and we arrived at primitive general terms would the essentialist have to acknowledge universals corresponding to these terms. So, while not agreeing with Kennick that the doctrine of family-resemblances does not bear on the problem of universals at all, I concede that the doctrine is much more concerned to combat an uncritical essentialism than an uncritical realism.

Leaving aside the question of Kennick's correctness in playing down the relevance of the family-resemblance doctrine to the problem of universals, the more important issue for our purposes is his claim that Wittgenstein produces other grounds for rejecting realism. If Kennick is right, then, no matter what we conclude about the family-resemblance issue, my interpretation of Wittgenstein is wrong. In fact, however, the compatibility of Wittgenstein's attack on the name-object theory of meaning with his endorsement of a moderate realism is easily shown. Of the four strategies cited by Kennick as being intended to discredit the view that a word is related to its meaning as a proper name is related to its bearer, the second—viz., that properties are not ingredients capable of existence apart from the things they qualify—and the third—viz., that there is not a substance corresponding to every substantive—are plainly compatible with a limited Aristotelian realism. The second strategy attacks only Platonic realism, and the third strategy is compatible not only with a moderate Aristotelianism, but even with a moderate Platonism. The two remaining strategies, which constitute an explicit attack on the name-object theory of meaning, first, by denying that the meaning of a name is the bearer of the name, and secondly, by urging that we think of the meaning of a word as the word's use, are of no particular help to Kennick either; if the identification of meaning with use is sufficient to justify our doing away with universals, since they do not constitute the meaning of general terms, then, by parity of reasoning, we also ought to be able to do away with the bearers of proper names, since they do not constitute the meaning of proper names. It is presumably to mitigate the force of this parallel that Kennick says, alluding to #43 of the *Investigations*, that "...the meaning of a word can *sometimes* be explained by pointing to its bearer ...but not always...,"[13] the implication being that the bearers of proper names can be relevant to the meanings of these names, and that the meanings of general terms, on the contrary, involve no such reference to bearers or objects. But this is simply to beg the question. Even if the injunction to think of a word's meaning as its use, rather than as an object corresponding to the word, is intended to eliminate the postulation of all sorts of superfluous entities in some realm of meaning, nothing in this injunction runs counter to the position that the meanings of some general terms are explained by reference to universals, and, as we have seen, the evidence clearly indicates that Wittgenstein regards at least the names of specific shades of color to be explained in just this way. There is no basis, then, for regarding the meaning-is-use doctrine as an attack against realism in general.

There is one other line of argument against my interpretation of Wittgenstein to which Kennick briefly alludes in a footnote,[14] only to dismiss it as being uncharacteristic of Wittgenstein's usual strategy, but which I believe deserves more serious consideration than the arguments preferred by Kennick himself. This is the argument that Wittgenstein's rejection of realism is shown by his insistence on the difference in function between general words and proper names. Kennick cites only one page reference in the *Brown Book* as evidence for this kind of approach, but there are other passages which could have been cited as well, not only in the *Brown Book*, but also in the *Investigations*. That words have various functions is indeed an important and recurring theme in Wittgenstein's later philosophy, and if there is any reason at all to believe that the sounding of this theme is intended to dispel the notion that any general words are names of universals, then my interpretation faces a serious, even insurmountable, difficulty. It is, therefore, crucial for me to show that there is no basis for supposing that Wittgenstein regards this theme as incompatible with realism, and I think that this can be shown, even though a superficial reading of certain passages might suggest otherwise. Let us first consider the passage to which Kennick refers:

> Our use of expressions like "names of numbers", "names of colours", "names of materials", "names of nations" may spring from two different sources. One is that we might imagine the functions of proper names, numerals, words for colours, etc., to be much more alike than they actually are. If we do so we are tempted to think that the function of every word is more or less like the function of a proper name of a person, or such generic names as "table", "chair", "door", etc. The second source is this, that if we see how fundamentally different the functions of such words as "table", "chair", etc., are from those of proper names, and how different from either the functions of, say, the names of colours, we see no reason why we shouldn't speak of names of numbers or names of directions

either, not by way of saying some such thing as "numbers and directions are just different forms of objects", but rather by way of stressing the analogy which lies in the lack of analogy between the functions of the words "chair" and "Jack" on the one hand, and "east" and "Jack" on the other hand.[15]

An initially plausible reading of this passage is that if we are to speak of colors, etc., as having names, such 'names', at any rate, do not have objects corresponding to them. That is, the reason it is unenlightening to say that numbers and directions are different forms of objects from chairs and tables is because the former are not really objects at all.

It seems to me, on the other hand, that Wittgenstein is not concerned in this passage to deny that numbers and directions are objects; he may indeed want to deny this, but his point here is only that it is, in any case, an unhelpful explanation of the difference in function of various names to say merely that the names refer to different kinds of objects, as if such an explanation could be sufficient by itself. In other words, he is trying to get away from the simplistic doctrine, characteristic of his own earlier philosophy, which says that to know the function of a name is simply to be acquainted with the object named. Even if numbers and directions *were* objects, the difference between the function of names of numbers or of directions from the function of names of pieces of furniture would not be explained by saying that numbers, directions, etc., are just different forms of objects, for we would also have to know how these objects were involved in the use of these names, and the nature of this involvement can only be discovered by looking beyond the objects to the linguistic practice itself.

Let us apply both interpretations—the anti-realist one as well as my own—to another passage from the *Brown Book* just a few pages prior to the one we have been examining, where Wittgenstein is discussing the difference between the demonstrative teaching of names of kinds of building blocks, of names of numerals, and of proper names. He says:

This difference does not lie...in the act of pointing and pronouncing the word or in any mental act (meaning?) accompanying it, but in the role which the demonstration (pointing and pronouncing) plays in the whole training and in the use which is made of it in the practice of communication by means of this language.

He then goes on to say that

> [o]ne might think that the difference could be described by saying that in the different cases we point to different kinds of objects. But suppose I point with my hand to a blue jersey. How does pointing to its colour differ from pointing to its shape?[16]

Clearly, he feels that the answer to this last question will go some way towards showing why the description in terms of 'different kinds of objects' is unsatisfactory; but what, we may ask, could be the purpose of this question if he were trying to discredit realism? Is he rhetorically suggesting that since shapes and colors are not objects, we cannot really point to one or the other, and that the description of the demonstrative teaching of these other names in terms of pointing to different kinds of objects fails for the same reason, viz., because there are no objects to be pointed to in these other cases as well? Surely, his argument is not that we cannot point to colors or shapes of things—for we certainly can—but rather that there is no characteristic mental act of meaning the color or the shape which must accompany this act of pointing to one or the other. The difference between pointing to the color and the shape, "...one might say, does not lie in the act of demonstration, but rather in the surrounding of that act in the use of the language."[17]

Obviously, then, colors and shapes are not chosen as examples because they have an especially dubious ontological status, but rather because the implausibility of regarding an ostensive definition as the primitive linguistic datum from which all subsequent explanations concerning the use of a word must flow, is in their case especially evident. That is, we might suppose that pointing to a color or a shape would have to be a mental act, since a physical act of pointing with one's finger would not by itself serve to draw attention to the shape of a thing as opposed to its color, or *vice versa*, but since there is no characteristic mental act of pointing either, we are led to acknowledge the importance of the linguistic practices which surround the act of demonstratively teaching the names of colors and shapes. Thus, in the case of explaining the difference in function between names of colors and names of shapes, the inadequacy of the bare act of pointing to a thing, apart from a wider context of linguistic practice, is apparent, and it is this inadequacy that Wittgenstein means to expose in his criticism of the proposed description of the differences in other sorts of demonstrative teaching.

There is one other passage in the *Brown Book* that might be interpreted as going along with an anti-realist interpretation of the passage cited by Kennick, in which Wittgenstein says that

> ...we can draw a distinction between observing, attending to, the shape of the sample and attending to its colour. But, attending to the colour can't be described as looking at a thing which is connected with the sample, rather, as looking at the sample in a peculiar way.[18]

Wittgenstein might be thought to be saying here that the color of an object is not itself an object connected with the object which it qualifies, and this—if the phrase 'is connected with' is taken widely enough to include the 'connection' of objects with their inherent qualities—could be taken as an attack on both the Platonic and Aristotelian versions of realism. But it is plain from the context that the 'thing' which is called into question is not the color of the sample, but rather the sense-impression which is supposed to be directly seen in the course of attending to the color. Thus he continues:

> When we obey the order, "Observe the colour...", what we do is to open our eyes to colour. "Observe the colour..." doesn't mean "See the colour you see". The order, "Look at so and so", is of the kind, "Turn your head in this direction"; what you will see when you do so does not enter this order. By attending, looking, you produce the impression; you can't look at the impression.[19]

His point is that attending to an object's color and then to its shape supposedly result in different visual experiences, but because these experiences are themselves brought about by the process of attending, they cannot really be 'things' which we point to with our attention. As he says in the course of the same discussion, if I suppose myself to be attending to an inner 'feeling',

> ...I don't point to the feeling by attending to it. Rather, attending to the feeling means producing or modifying it. (On the other hand, observing a chair does not mean producing or modifying the chair.)[20]

That it is the status of one's supposedly private sense-impression of color, and not the status of the color itself, that is the source of Wittgenstein's concern is seen by his treatment of the same subject in #275-276 of the *Investigations*, where colors are regarded as objective, public qualities, and only the status of color-impressions is called into question. Wittgenstein's mature position on the relation between colors and color-impressions is itself problematic, and I will defer a consideration of the issues it raises until Chapter Eight. For now it is sufficient to point out that he does want to preserve the publicity of colors, and thus to classify them together with chairs, rather than with feelings, with respect to their being possible objects of attention. I conclude that nothing said in the *Brown Book* about the topic of observing color is intended to impugn the ontological status of colors themselves, and so cannot be taken as supporting an anti-realist interpretation of the passage cited by Kennick.

My strategy so far has been to contend that those passages in the *Brown Book* which seem to be explaining the difference in function of various words by denying that certain words do name objects are not really making any such denial. Still, the text of the *Investigations*— which is, after all, our main concern—leaves no doubt that Wittgenstein does regard the name-object account to be gratuitous and misleading as an explanation of the function of many words. To cite the most famous (or notorious) example, words expressing sensations are not names of inner, private objects; rather, in their second- and third-person uses, such words allude to a combination of behavior and circumstances, while in their first-person use, such words do not name or describe anything at all, and are in this respect like 'ouch' or 'hurrah'. Again, words like 'expecting', 'wishing', 'hoping', 'believing', etc., are not names of inner objects, i.e., specific mental states, but are family-resemblance words which characterize a complex blend of a wide variety of behavior and dispositions to behave, as manifested in many different kinds of circumstances. Indeed, from the very first paragraph of the *Investigations*, Wittgenstein sets out to combat what he takes to be the Augustinian view of language, in which all words are treated as names of objects, and I have yet to determine the extent of this attack. Is he denying that any general words are names of objects, or is his attack consistent with the admission that some general words name universals? With a view towards answering this question, I shall now examine the main drift of the argument in the first few pages of the *Investigations*.

So that we may from the beginning avoid confusion, it should be clear that the question is not whether Wittgenstein admits that any words other than proper names are names of objects, in some sense or other, since he obviously does admit this. Thus, in #1 and #2, general terms like 'chair', 'slab', etc., are given as the prime examples of words for which the name-object account is appropriate. The fact that Wittgenstein allows that different particular things can be given the generic name 'chair', however, does not commit him to the existence of the universal Chairness, for reasons we have already considered in our discussion of concepts such as 'game' or 'board': 'chair' is probably a family-resemblance concept, and even if not, it would seem to be definable in terms of simpler properties. The question I am concerned to answer is whether Wittgenstein allows that the name-object account holds in any case where the object is itself a universal.

Evidence that he does make such an allowance can be found at the very beginning of the *Investigations*, in #1. Here, he tries to combat the tendency to characterize all words as having the same kind of function by giving us an example of a language-game where the different functions of various words is obvious. Thus:

> I send someone shopping. I give him a slip marked "five red apples". He takes the slip to the shopkeeper, who opens the drawer marked "apples"; then he looks up the word "red" in a table and finds a colour sample opposite it; then he says the series of cardinal numbers—I assume that he knows them by heart—up to the word "five" and for each number he takes an apple of the same colour as the sample out of the drawer.—It is in this and similar ways that one operates with words.—"But how does he know where and how he is to look up the word 'red' and what is he to do with the word 'five'?—Well, I assume that he *acts* as I have described. Explanations come to an end somewhere.—But what is the meaning of the word "five"?—No such thing was in question here, only how the word "five" is used.

Now, it might be thought that Wittgenstein's explanation of the functions of these three words, by stressing what we do with the words and how we use them as we use instruments or tools for various jobs, is in the case of each word meant to undercut the idea that the word names an object. But this cannot be the general moral that he intends to draw, since 'apple' (or 'apples') is the kind of word for which the name-object account is correct, i.e., it is a generic name on a par with 'chair' or 'slab'. Wittgenstein is thus making the more subtle point that even where a word names an object, the meaning of the word is not identified with the named object, but is instead the use to which the name is put. Even if 'five', 'red', and 'apples' were all names of objects, this would not affect the main point, which is that the functions of the three words differ markedly. That he does not, however, regard all three words as names of objects is indicated by the question: "But what is the meaning of the word 'five'?" and the answer: "No such thing was in question here, only how the word 'five' is used." Wittgenstein is not here saying that he has not given the meaning of the word 'five' by describing its use, but only that he has not satisfied the requirement of a primitive theory of meaning, i.e., his explanation of the meaning has not alluded to any object designated by the word 'five'. So, while allusion to an object may be relevant to the explanation of the meaning of a word, it need not be; such an allusion is evidently relevant in explaining the meaning of 'apples', but irrelevant in explaining the meaning of 'five'.

We come now to the crucial question: Is 'red', in this respect, like 'apples' or like 'five'? Wittgenstein provides the answer by restricting the rhetorical charge—viz., that his description of the use of these words has failed to give the meaning—to the case of the word 'five'. That is, the hypothetical interlocutor who complains that Wittgenstein's account has not given the meaning of 'five' makes no comparable complaint about 'apples' or 'red', the implication being that at least the explanation of the use of these two words involves an allusion to the appropriate objects, viz., the apples in the drawer and the color of the color-sample, respectively. Judging by the question that the interlocutor is allowed to pose concerning the use of the word 'red'—viz., where and how are we to look up the word?—Wittgenstein apparently feels that his explanation of the use of 'red' presents a problem to the traditionalist, not in failing to allude to an object, but only in supposing that the connection between name and object is made in this case by the utilization of a color-chart, where the shopkeeper's ability to use this chart is left unexplained. Had Wittgenstein felt that an additional problem existed as to whether the color-qualities shown by the color-chart were legitimate objects, he likely would have found a way to raise rhetorical doubts on this score as well, so that he could have the opportunity of sweeping aside such troubles by giving the same response for 'red' as he does for 'five', viz., that we need not suppose that the word names an object in order for it to have meaning. As he does not avail himself of this opportunity, we have good reason to suppose that he has no qualms about regarding color-qualities as objects.

The next few pages of the *Investigations* are mainly concerned with spelling out more explicitly the nature of Wittgenstein's departure from a simplistic name-object theory of meaning. The language-game described in #2, consisting of the four words 'block', 'pillar', 'slab', and 'beam', which are names of four different kinds of building-stones, is offered as an example of a language "... for which the description given by Augustine is right" (#2).[21] Shortly thereafter, Wittgenstein describes an expanded version of language-game (2) in order to show that the Augustinian account, which is appropriate enough for the simpler language-game, no longer applies here, where words with functions radically different from that of 'slab' and 'brick' have been introduced. Thus:

> Besides the four words "block", "pillar", etc., let it contain a series of words used as the shopkeeper in (1) used the numerals (it can be the series of letters of the alphabet); further, let there be two words, which may as well be "there" and "this" (because this roughly indicates their purpose), that are used in connexion with a pointing gesture; and finally a number of colour samples. A gives an order like: "d—slab—there". At the same time he shews the assistant a colour sample, and when he says "there" he points to a place on the building site. From the stock of slabs B takes one for each letter of the alphabet up to "d", of the same colour as the sample, and brings them to the place indicated by A.—On other occasions A gives the order "this—there". At "this" he points to a building stone. And so on (#8).

Then, to the Augustinian's question: "What do the words of this language signify?" Wittgenstein replies: "What is supposed to show what they signify if not the kind of use they have? And we have already described that" (#10).

In saying that what the word signifies is shown by its use, Wittgenstein is stressing two points: first, even where a word does straightforwardly name an object, it could still be misleading to say that the word signifies the object, if this were taken to mean that the function of the name is thereby given. As he says:

> Of course, one can reduce the description of the use of the word "slab" to the statement that this word signifies this object. This will be done when, for example, it is merely a matter of removing the mistaken idea that the word "slab" refers to the type of building-stone that we in fact call a "block"—but the kind of *'referring'* this is, that is to say the use of these words for the rest, is already known (#10).

Secondly, by seeing that the meaning of a word amounts to no more and no less than its use, we feel no need to deny dogmatically that signs like 'a', 'b', etc., signify numbers. As Wittgenstein shows, there are contexts in which saying some such thing would be perfectly proper, as

> ...when, for example, this removes the mistaken idea that "a", "b", "c", play the part actually played in language by "block", "slab", "pillar". And one can also say that "c" means this number and not that one; when for example this serves to explain that the letters are to be used in the order a, b, c, d, etc. and not in the order a, b, d, c (#10).

We can comfortably admit that 'a', 'b', etc., can be said to signify numbers, and know that we are not thereby committing ourselves to an ontology of numbers in the way that we are committing ourselves when we acknowledge the existence of slabs and bricks, because the general concession abput words signifying objects finally amounts to no more than that these various signs are *used* thus and so, where the appropriateness of the name-object characterization will depend on the context. So, while Wittgenstein does not dogmatically deny the correctness of the assertion that number-words signify numbers, he does suggest that assimilating the description of the use of number-words to that of words like 'brick' can be seriously misleading, because the words themselves are used in quite different ways. Wittgenstein's answer, then, to the question: "Do the signs 'a', 'b', etc., signify numbers?" can best be given by a remark made in *Investigations* #79 in another connection:

> Say what you choose, so long as it does not prevent you from seeing the facts. (And when you see them there is a good deal that you will not say.)

What can we conclude from all this about the ontological status of colors? As far as Wittgenstein's discussion of language-game (8) is concerned, we can conclude nothing at all directly, for this language-game does not even include color-words. He is anxious to make the point, for reasons which will become clear in the next chapter, that color-samples themselves can be regarded as instruments of language, i.e., as the means of representation rather than that which is represented (#50), and so he uses the occasion of his description of language-game (8) to make color-samples do the job of color-words.

Still, there is in this discussion at least some evidence supporting my earlier contention that a word whose function differs from that of a word like 'brick', which can be straightforwardly regarded as the name of an object, is not on the basis of this difference necessarily assumed by Wittgenstein *not* to be the name of an object. As the following example suggests, there is also the possibility that this word names an object as well, and that the word differs from 'brick' only in the kind of name it is, i.e., the way it relates to its object.

Thus, after suggesting that a number-word is not *really* the name of an object—or, at any rate, that to speak of numbers as objects is not to commit ourself to the existence of curious entities—Wittgenstein illustrates his point by comparing different kinds of words to different kinds of tools, and says: "The functions of words are as diverse as the functions of these objects. (And in both cases there are similarities.)" (#11) The remark about 'similarities' is meant to indicate that the differences between the functions of various words is not always so extreme as that between a word like 'brick' and a number-word, which suggests that the scope of the application of the name-object account of language is not to be settled by studying two kinds of examples. Even if a number word is not the name of an object, other kinds of words may well be such names, even though they, too, differ from words like 'brick'.

That there are different kinds[22] of significative functions among words, in addition to words whose function is not to signify any object at all, is again implied in #14:

> Imagine someone's saying: "All tools serve to modify something. Thus the hammer modifies the position of the nail, the saw the shape of the board, and so on."—And what is modified by the rule, the glue-pot, the nails?—"Our knowledge of a thing's length, the temperature of the glue, and the solidity of the box."—Would anything be gained by this assimilation of expressions?—

The implication is not only that it is misleading to say of certain tools that they modify something, but also that at least two different kinds of tools *can* appropriately be said to modify something. Since the analogy is between a tool modifying something and a word signifying something, we can conclude that the significative function, likewise, is not the exclusive prerogative of one kind of word. Applying this analogy of tools to the words of the language-game described in #1, we can say that 'apples' and 'red' are like the hammer and the saw, while 'five' is like, e.g., the glue-pot.

We can see from Wittgenstein's discussions of these various language-games that there is no basis for concluding that no general words serve to name non-particular objects. Considering the emphasis placed on the multiplicity of functions of words, we are on precarious ground in attributing to Wittgenstein *any* position characterizing general words as a class. It is only as a protest against this tendency to over-simplify, and not as the advocacy of some simplistic view of his own, that we should take Wittgenstein's comment in #26:

> One thinks that learning language consists in giving names to objects. Viz, to human beings, to shapes, to colours, to pains, to moods, to numbers, etc. To repeat—naming is something like attaching a label to a thing. One can say that this is preparatory to the use of a word. But *what* is it a preparation *for*?

And the answer to this question will not be determined by some neat, pre-conceived idea such as that only publicly observable particulars qualify as objects. Rather, each case will be judged on its own merits, and if it turns out that there are no objects such as pains (as Wittgenstein does subsequently contend), then this conclusion is determined, not in advance, but by the same procedure of carefully weighing linguistic facts[23] which shows, for example, that human beings are indeed properly considered to be objects named by the generic term 'human being' (*Mensch*), a procedure which could also be used to show that a good case can be made for saying that colors are non-particular objects. And, as I have contended on other grounds, Wittgenstein definitely goes some way towards making this case.

To sum up the results of our examination, we have found nothing in Wittgenstein's later writings incompatible with a limited Aristotelian realism, and some passages which can reasonably be taken to imply that this is his position. Still, it must be admitted that at no place in the later writings does he go out of his way to claim this position as his own. There are, I think, chiefly two reasons for this. The remainder of this chapter will concern itself with the first reason, and the second reason will be discussed in the following chapter.

The first reason for the lack of an open proclamation of realism is that Wittgenstein conceives himself to have developed a method of treating philosophical problems which transcends the traditional approach of affirming or denying specific positions. The long-standing disputes between metaphysicians of different persuasions, which are viewed as disagreements about the nature of reality and are thought to be decidable by quasi-scientific methods, are viewed by Wittgenstein as no substantive disagreements at all, but rather as confusions arising from mistaken views concerning the functions of language. He does not consider himself to be taking sides with any of the traditional parties to these disputes, and hence would not want to opt for any of the positions in the realist/nominalist controversy over the status of universals. Indeed, at least one commentator, Alice Ambrose, has been so impressed by Wittgenstein's claim to have avoided taking sides in traditional disputes that she considers this feature of his philosophical method—viz., that which purports to show that ostensibly substantive disagreements are really grammatical confusions—as providing the key to Wittgenstein's 'solution' to the 'problem' of universals. Thus, she notes that philosophers other than Wittgenstein have also striven to 'command a clear view of the use of our words', but that, whereas they wanted to use this knowledge to gain an insight into the nature of reality,

> [t]he philosophical investigations of the later Wittgenstein were aimed neither at obtaining information about the world nor at refuting the positions of philosophers who claimed to have succeeded in this.[24]

It is a mistake, she says, to suppose that Wittgenstein holds that philosophers have been misled by confusions about language into pronouncing *false* views, or that he is *denying* what these philosophers assert to be true.[25] He

> ...is not concerned to question a matter of fact and is not to be construed as contesting the claimed truth value of any philosophical position, although he can be interpreted as concerned with removing the temptation to adopt one and defend it.[26]

Now, I do not doubt that Ambrose has accurately characterized what Wittgenstein conceives himself to be doing, and if this is in fact what he is doing, then my claim that he is a limited Aristotelian realist—or, for that matter, that he adheres to any ontological position—is incorrect. But I think that this claim of Wittgenstein's (and of Ambrose on his behalf) to have succeeded in maintaining ontological neutrality, as it were, is simply naive. This is not the place to attempt an extensive examination of Wittgenstein's philosophical method and of the discrepancy between the way he characterizes it and the way it actually works in practice, and I must therefore be content to make a few general observations.

Wittgenstein's conviction that philosophical positions cannot take a stand on any factual issue is, first of all, just a matter of the way he chooses to define 'philosophy'. Insofar as factual issues bear on any position, he regards this position as a 'scientific' one, to be verified or falsified by empirical methods.[27] Philosophy, on the other hand, is an activity of conceptual clarification brought about by a consideration, from a non-empirical perspective, of the workings of language, i.e., language is investigated, not *qua* anthropological phenomenon in which the causes of it being the way it is are to be ascertained, but rather *qua* rule-governed activity, where we look at the way words are used, in the sense of looking at the rules (to the extent and in the manner which rules operate at all) according to which the various language-games are played. On this view, there can be no distinctively philosophical propositions, and therefore no formulation of distinctively philosophical positions. (In this respect, Wittgenstein never departs from the views of the *Tractatus*.) All that philosophy can properly do is to draw attention to the actual uses of words and thereby remove the illusions of traditional philosophers, whose misconceptions about the functions of words results in the mistaken conception of philosophy as an area of substantive inquiry distinct from science.

Leaving aside the claims that the disputes of traditional philosophers concern no matters of fact and arise solely from a mistaken view of the functions of language, both of which are certainly open to question, Wittgenstein's own claim to be investigating language as it is actually used does not in any case absolve him from the charge of taking some sort of position on what there is. We can, of course, allow that insofar as his remarks about the functions of certain words commit him, for example, to the existence of particular things like bricks, apples, and people, he is speaking in his capacity as a scientist—or at least as a representative of ordinary common-sense, if we hesitate to call these sorts of mundane judgements 'scientific'. In the same way, if his remarks show him to be committed to the existence of color-qualities, we may then include universals within his ontology as well, and need only to be careful not to call his (implicit) affirmation of the existence of universals the affirmation of a *philosophical* position.

Needless to say, a Wittgensteinian account of the way our use of words commits us to an ontology is not a simple matter to express. It would clearly be excessive to hold that a sufficient condition for having ontological status is to be the subject-matter of a language-game. Even the more narrow criterion of 'being a named object within a particular language-game' will not do, as is shown by Wittgenstein's implicit uneasiness about allowing that the universe is populated by such entities as numbers and directions, even though they are in some sense named objects, as well as by the consideration of, e.g., fictitious objects such as elves and unicorns. While the users of language (2) seem committed to an ontology of bricks, slabs, etc., in that the existence of such objects is required if the language-game is to be played at all, our speaking of elves or the number three need not be taken to commit us to the existence of such entities. We might say that the existence of the named object may or may not be presupposed, depending on the language-game, but this is equivalent to admitting that there just is no handy formula which can be invoked to determine ontological commitment; rather, we must approach this issue on a case-by-case basis, so that it will depend upon the particular language-game whether or not the existence of an object, whose name is used in that language-game, is thereby presupposed, and what 'ontological weight' is given to any such presupposed object, i.e., whether it is an 'object' in more than a Pickwickian sense. It might be thought that ontological commitment could be characterized in a general way as being that which arises at the juncture at which language connects up with reality, i.e., at the place where non-linguistic things serve as paradigms for the use of their names; for reasons which will become apparent in Chapter Seven, however, even this way of putting the matter is misleading, and Wittgensteinian ontological commitment will turn out to be a less obscure business, though perhaps less interesting as well, than this admittedly odd-sounding talk about ontological commitment to bricks and colors may suggest.

Whatever is involved in the Wittgensteinian notion of 'ontological commitment', there is in any event another peculiar feature of Wittgenstein's own conception of his philosophical method which has ontological implications, viz., his assumption that as long as criticism is directed against a philosophical position on 'grammatical' rather than factual grounds, the criticism cannot be said to bear on an ontological dispute. The clearest example of this assumption at work is in Wittgenstein's attack on the notion of a private object, which he feels can be carried out without falling into the behaviorist's error of *denying* that private objects exist. In #304-308 Wittgenstein assures us that his criticism of the view that a mental process is a private experience does not mean that he wants to deny that we have mental processes. Behaviorists speak of mental processes as fictions, but this makes the diepute between behaviorists and introspectionists appear to be over a matter of fact, like the dispute about the existence of the Loch Ness monster, whereas Wittgenstein does not want to appear to be taking one side of a factual dispute, and therefore he speaks only of the introspectionist account as involving a *grammatical* fiction—a 'fictional' (i.e., untrue) account of the function of language as it is used to talk about inner experience. As he says in the "Notes on Privacy,"

> [t]he 'private experience' is a degenerate construction of our grammar (comparable in a sense to tautology and contradiction). And this grammatical monster now fools us; when we wish to do away with it, it seems as though we had denied the existence of an experience, say, toothache.[29]

Ambrose cites this strategy, in which Wittgenstein is claiming to correct only misconceptions about the grammar of expressions concerning inner experiences, as being a prime example of how he does not attempt to refute philosophers' claims about the nature of the world. It seems patently obvious to me, however, that a philosopher who believes that the word 'pain' is a generic name for a certain kind of private object, and who includes such objects in his ontology, has every right to feel that Wittgenstein is attempting to refute him in arguing that 'pain' is not the name of an object at all, and that we are only fooled by the superficial grammatical parallels between expressions like 'I have a pineapple' and 'I have a pain' into thinking that in both cases I am talking about an object that I have. Granted, Wittgenstein is not *denying* that there are objects answering to the name 'pain', in the sense that there are no objects answering to the name 'unicorn', because, as he contends, 'pain' is not used as the name of an object at all.[30] Nevertheless, this is small consolation to the philosopher who wants to include private objects in his ontology and who, if he accepts Wittgenstein's arguments, will have to consider his former position refuted, just as surely as if it had been denied on the basis of empirical fact.

So, whatever Wittgenstein thinks he is doing, his actual practice is

118

not one of preserving neutrality on ontological issues; and when I say that he is a realist, I am referring only to the ontological position implied by what he says in the course of doing philosophy, and not to the position—or lack of one—that he conceives himself as having when he self-consciously tries to characterize what he is doing. Ironically, Ambrose—who thinks she is defending Wittgenstein's claim of neutrality—in effect concedes my interpretation of Wittgenstein as a moderate realist when she says:

> Now it is quite true that many substantives do have a naming function, e.g. proper names, like "John", names of specific colors, like "cerise", general names, like "chair" (though amongst these are important differences). But not all words stand for things that can be pointed to....[31]

Aside from Ambrose's general conviction that nothing Wittgenstein says commits him to an ontological position, there is an additional reason for her failure to see how his admission that there are specific color-qualities bears on the question about universals, and this is that she poses the question exclusively in terms of a Platonist account of universals. Thus, the metaphysical position that there are universals is identified with the position that there are "...refined object[s] being apprehended by an inner vision..."[32] and existing in their own "shadow world".[33] We can only suppose that she is so concerned to exhibit the 'linguistic obsessions', as she calls them, manifest in Platonism, that the possibility of examining Wittgenstein's remarks from the perspective of another version of realism simply does not occur to her.

This leads us to the second reason for Wittgenstein's own lack of an overt proclamation of his realism: like Ambrose, Wittgenstein himself is preoccupied with Platonism, and that he does not totally reject realism as such in the course of his repudiation of Platonism is a matter which he considers to be of only incidental importance, if he considers it at all. To show that his interest in the problem of universals does indeed center almost exclusively around the issue of Platonism, and that his opting for Aristotelian realism occurs merely as a casual by-product of his repudiation of Platonism, will be the task of the next chapter, where I study Wittgenstein's views in the context of their historical development.

CHAPTER SIX

FROM PLATONISM TO ARISTOTELIANISM: THE TRANSITION TO THE LATER PHILOSOPHY

In the history of western philosophy, Plato and Aristotle are undoubtedly the two outstanding exponents of ontological realism. Now it is obvious, and will not be argued here, that Wittgenstein's ontology, in both his early and later philosophy, differs in fundamental ways from that of either Plato or Aristotle. Still, there is a certain issue with respect to which any version of realism would seem to be either Platonic or Aristotelian.[1] I have called 'Aristotelian realism' any view which holds that universals exist only because, and insofar as, they are instantiated in particulars; 'Platonic realism', on the other hand, is the view that the existence of universals is independent of any such instantiation.[2] Thus, if we suppose the color red to be a universal, an Aristotelian realist would have to regard the destruction of all red things as tantamount to the destruction of redness itself, or at least as amounting to its consignment to a kind of metaphysical limbo where it would remain without genuine ontological status unless and until particular red things were again to exist. For a Platonic realist, however, the destruction of red things would have no bearing on the existence of the universal redness; the latter would continue to exist in any case.

The question, then, is how to classify Wittgenstein's realism with respect to this distinction. I have been characterizing the transition from Wittgenstein's early philosophy to his later philosophy as a transition from Platonism to Aristotelianism, and it is now time to justify this characterization. Within the context of the *Tractatus*, the issue can be put as follows: could properties exist even if there were no facts in which such objects figured as constituents? Let us suppose, for example, that the color red is such an object.[3] Does the existence of this object depend on its being configured with some particular or other, or would redness exist even though there were no such configuration? Although the *Tractatus* does not specifically address itself to this question, there is little doubt that the early Wittgenstein must be considered a Platonist. An Aristotelian version of realism is precluded by the configuration of universals and particulars being a *contingent* matter, so that the existence of universals can never depend upon any such configuration. It must be possible sensibly to assert of some particular that it is red (i.e., configured with the universal redness) even if in fact it is not, or even if there are no red things in the world at all.

The issue is somewhat complicated, in that a good case could be made for saying that particulars, at any rate, must be part of some configuration even to be able to be picked out and named. Thus, as 2.0233 maintains, apart from having different external properties, different objects—and here 'object' must mean 'particular', since that is the only kind of object which could have external properties—are indistinguishable. And since our ability to use language shows that we do somehow have the capability of understanding its ultimate components, i.e., of being able to make (or, in some mysterious sense, of already having made) the correlation between name and simple object, it seems to follow that such objects cannot exist apart from some configuration or other, for it is only within a configuration that objects can be distinguished and, consequently, named.[4]

This is an interesting argument, but, if my reading of 2.0233 is correct, it concerns only particulars, and not universals. The notion of a particular is in any case problematic for the *Tractatus*. Objects are supposed to have both a form and a content, and though it is understandable that a property should be supposed to have a content—that, for example, there is a difference in the intrinsic natures of redness and blueness, not further characterizable, which distinguishes one from the other—what sort of analogously distinguishing feature could a particular, which in itself is 'bare', possibly have? That is, a particular's external properties are not part of its own nature, its internal properties concern only its form, and there seems to be nothing left to comprise its content.

These considerations should make us wary to assume that the difficulties involved in the notion of an isolated, unconfigured particular carry over to the notion of an isolated universal. Possibly, regarding this issue, universals and particulars ought to be treated quite differently. It is, I think, significant that Wittgenstein's description in the *Blue Book* of what we can presume is his own earlier position—in which he says that the elements themselves must exist, though their arrangements need not—gives only universals, viz., redness, roundness, and sweetness, as examples of unconfigured elements. Is this neglect of particulars perhaps evidence that Wittgenstein himself, in retrospect, saw that the assimilation of particulars with universals breaks down at this point, i.e., at the notion of an isolated particular? In any case, provided that the view of the *Tractatus* is what is being discussed in this passage in the *Blue Book*—and I see no reason to think otherwise—then the version of realism presented in this passage shows the early Wittgenstein to have been a Platonist. Of course, considering that the early Russell's brand of realism is itself overtly Platonic, Wittgenstein's own adoption of such a position should hardly come as a surprise. In the remainder of this chapter, I will show in detail how Wittgenstein's movement towards his mature position, including his Aristotelianism, is in large part shaped by a reaction to the Platonism of the *Tractatus*.

An examination of Wittgenstein's transition from his earlier to his later philosophy reveals his pre-occupation with a theme which can be expressed by the question: what is the connection between language and reality? A fundamental aim of the *Tractatus*, certainly, is to provide an answer to this question. The connection must be such as to allow the expression of propositions whose sense is independent of their truth or falsity. This separation of sense from truth-value is achieved by the picture theory, in which a proposition has sense by being a picture of a (possible) fact, the arrangement of elements in the proposition corresponding to the (possibly existing) arrangement of objects in reality. Whether the arrangement of objects pictured by the proposition actually occurs in reality is an empirical issue; in either case, the proposition succeeds in being a picture.

As opposed to facts, whose existence is contingent, objects must necessariy exist. If the existence of objects were a contingent matter, then we would again have failed to separate questions of sense from questions of truth, since, for example, the sense of a proposition containing the name 'A' would depend upon the truth of another proposition, viz., that proposition which said, in effect, that A exists. It is for this reason that we cannot sensibly assert of objects that they exist or do not exist; their existence is already guaranteed by the very meaningfulness of their names.

At the level of propositions, the connection between language and reality consists in propositions having the same form, or logical multiplicity, as (possible) facts. Since, however, there need be no actual fact corresponding to a proposition, the connection between language and reality is ultimately made at the level of names and their corresponding objects, for it is the connection at this juncture that is presupposed even for propositions to make sense.[5] As we have already seen, the manner in which this doctrine of the necessary existence, or 'indestructibility' of objects is, in the *Tractatus*, bound up with Platonism is simply that some of these objects are universals.

It is these key features of the picture theory—viz., that propositions have the same possibilities of arranging their elements as there are arrangements of elements in possible facts, thereby giving language and reality a common logical form, and also that the elements corresponding to names must exist—whose repudiation provides a dominant theme in Wittgenstein's later work, especially in the transitional period beginning with his paper of 1929, "Some Remarks on Logical Form," and ending with *Philosophical Grammar*, where the essentials of his mature position are established. I shall now trace the development of his views on this issue of the connection between language and reality, with the purpose of showing that, to the extent that Wittgenstein is concerned in his later philosophy with the question of universals at all, it is almost exclusively within the context of trying to elucidate the nature of the connection between language and reality while avoiding the Platonism of the *Tractatus*.

The process which eventually leads to the total collapse of the picture theory begins innocently enough, when Wittgenstein observes, in his paper of 1929, that the forms of elementary propositions cannot be foreseen. It might be thought that he already says the same thing in the *Tractatus*, 5.55 to 5.5571, but his point there is that although the general form of an elementary proposition is known *a priori,* the existence of propositions of any specific form—e.g., whether there are elementary propositions of a twenty-place relational form, or even of a two-place relational form or a subject-predicate form—remains to be somehow discovered by analysis.[6] Still, if he refrains in theory from making any dogmatic commitment, there is no doubt that he assumes in practice that there probably are, e.g., elementary propositions of the subject-predicate form and of the two-place relational form (as is shown by 4.24 of the *Tractatus*), and it is this comfortable assumption that is attacked in his paper of 1929. He there admits that the most we can say about the subject-predicate and relational forms is that "[t]hese forms are the norms of our particular language into which we project in *ever so many different* logical forms."[7]

To show how different the actual logical forms of propositions are from these norms of ordinary language, Wittgenstein cites as his prime example the fact that "...for their representation numbers (rational and irrational) must enter into the structure of the atomic propositions themselves."[8] Thus, a description of our visual field in which the shape and position of every patch of color is given with respect to a co-ordinate system "...by statements of numbers which have their significance relative to the system of co-ordinates..."[9] is the only kind of description which will have the right logical multiplicity. Also, numbers will have to enter those propositional forms

> ...when—as we should say in ordinary language—we are dealing with properties which admit of gradation, i.e. properties as the length of an interval, the pitch of a tone, the brightness or redness of a shade of colour, etc.[10]

Although Wittgenstein does not in this paper go on to spell out the consequences of these observations for the doctrines of the *Tractatus*, he makes clear, in remarks recorded a few months later by Waismann, that the very possibility of forms of description other than that of subject-predicate, etc., renders gratuitous the account of objects—implicit in the

Tractatus—which characterizes them with respect to their different grammatical functions. As he says:

> Now the question has no sense: "Are objects thing-like, standing as it were in the subject-place, or property-like, or are they relations and so on?"[11]

And he concludes: "We speak of objects simply where we have equal (*gleichberechtigte*) elements of representation."[12]

The example used by Wittgenstein to illustrate what sort of thing he means by an 'element of representation' is that if we were to describe the surface of a room analytically by an equation and describe the distribution of colors on these surfaces, and if we were to give an analysis of these colors themselves by saying how they were to be produced by the four primary colors,[13] then the primary colors themselves, viz., red, yellow, blue, and green, would be the elements of representation. Presumably, then, the primary colors would be the only simple objects involved in descriptions of visual space, and the phrase 'element of representation' is merely intended to remind us not to try to classify these objects according to a grammatical function. In *Philosophical Remarks* Wittgenstein speaks of 'elements of knowledge' rather than 'elements of representation', but the two expressions are probably intended to mark out the same province, since he gives as examples of elements of knowledge "...the four primary colors, space, time, and such else that is given."[14] These elements of knowledge are characterized as the "things themselves",[15] the "simple objects",[16] and are contrasted with the "things of physics",[17] and also with "inessential (*uneigentlichen*) objects" such as particular sense data.[18]

It might be thought that what we have here is still Platonism, though of an austere variety, having little else in its ontology than primary colors. But to claim even this much would be a mistake, for *Remarks* clearly indicates that colors ought not to be supposed to have an independent ontological status outside of their specific spatial and temporal manifestations. Thus:

> In what way is endless time a possibility and not a reality? For one could object against me that time must be a reality just as much as color. But is

not color by itself also just a possibility so long as it does not exist at a specific time and in a specific place?[19]

In this off-hand remark, made entirely without fan-fare, we find the clear implication that Wittgenstein has abandoned the Platonism of the *Tractatus*. The way in which the doctrine of 'elements of representation', or 'elements of knowledge', contributes to the erosion of Platonism is that, in arriving at this doctrine, Wittgenstein establishes the tactic of diminishing the role of reality and increasing that of language in explaining their connection. That is, whereas in the *Tractatus* various kinds of objects—particulars, properties, and relations—were thought to be needed to provide the requisite content for the sense of propositions, these objects are now rendered superfluous by co-ordinate systems, etc., which are themselves part of language. And it is this same strategy of transferring what seems to belong to the province of reality into the province of language that provides Wittgenstein with a way of escaping from the Platonist assumptions of the *Tractatus* altogether.

The *Remarks* is a transitional work which shows Wittgenstein's dissatisfaction with the *Tractatus'* version of the picture theory and his effort to provide a new account, but the strategy to be employed is still only hinted at here, and only in the *Philosophical Grammar* does it emerge with full force. I shall now trace the course of this development from the *Remarks* to the *Grammar*.

In the *Remarks* Wittgenstein wants, among other things, to defend the picture theory of language against a causal theory of the connection between language and reality.[20] According to the picture theory, the truth of a thought (or a proposition) involves only the thought and the fact that makes the thought true, while the causal theory involves an additional factor, viz., the feeling of satisfaction which results when the fact fulfills the thought. On the causal account, the way I intend a proposition to be taken depends upon my subsequent reaction; for example, if I say 'It is raining' and—after looking out the window and seeing the drops of water falling from the sky—do not experience the requisite feeling of satisfaction, or whatever, then I must conclude that I could not have meant what is normally meant by the words 'It is raining'. But, as

Wittgenstein contends, the sense of a proposition can never be decided by experience, and I must be able to know at the time I assert a proposition how I intend it to be taken. As he says: "The intention expresses even now how I *now* compare the picture with reality."[21] Likewise, to expect, wish for, or search for something presupposes that I know what it is that I am expecting, wishing for, or searching for (or at least this is so for one commonly used sense of 'expecting', etc.), which can be summed up by saying that

> ...the fact which satisfies the expectation of p is represented by the proposition p.... Therefore, not by the description of an *entirely* different event.[22]

From here, Wittgenstein is led into considering more precisely what it is that thoughts, expectations, wishes, searches, etc., presuppose, and this brings us back to the issue of Platonism:

> Searching presupposes that I know what I am searching for, without what I am searching for really having to exist. I expressed this earlier by saying that searching presupposes the elements of the complex but not *the* combination for which I search. And this is not a bad comparison. Linguistically, this is expressed by saying that the sense of a proposition presupposes only the grammatically correct application of certain words.[23]

This sounds like an endorsement of the *Tractatus*, but a few pages later, while re-iterating the point that the expectation, thought, wish, etc., that p must have the same multiplicity as that expressed in p itself, Wittgenstein makes an interesting qualification. After calling such processes of expectation, etc., *articulate*, in virtue of their possession of the same logical multiplicity as the propositions with which they are involved, he says that these articulate processes might also be called the interpretation of signs (meaning by this that the same interpretation of signs is involved in the expectation that p as is involved in p itself), and then adds:

> Perhaps one must say that the expression 'interpretation of signs' is misleading, and instead of this one should say 'the use of signs'. For 'interpretation' sounds as if one now correlates with the word 'red' the color red (even when it is not present) and so forth. And again the ques-

tion arises: What is the connection between sign and world? Could I search for something if the space were not there in which I could search for it? Where does the sign connect to the world?[24]

The problem arises here because Wittgenstein has rejected the solution of the *Tractatus* which tells us that the color red is always 'present' in the world as a Platonic universal. If, as he now holds, the color red is an actuality only in its specific spatial and temporal manifestations, what does the word 'red' mean when the color is not being manifested?

There is a further problem involved in the identification of the meaning of, e.g., the word 'red' with a Platonic universal (or with any one object, for that matter). In "Some Remarks on Logical Form" Wittgenstein had shown that, contrary to the views of the *Tractatus*, it is possible for elementary propositions to be mutually exclusive, a view which he now expresses in the *Remarks* by saying: "I do not apply the proposition as a measuring rule to reality, but rather the *system* of propositions."[25] Thus, in applying the proposition 'This is red' to reality, I am simultaneously applying the propositions 'This is not green', 'This is not blue', etc., since, if the first proposition is true, all these other propositions will be true as well. This admission is by itself a significant alteration of the picture theory, as it removes the one-to-one correspondence between propositions and possible situations (i.e., if the possible situation is determined to be an actual fact, this makes true a whole system of propositions, and not just one proposition). But the *Tractatus'* account of the connection between language and reality is thereby affected, not just at the level of proposition and fact, but also at the level of name and object, because, for example, the measuring rule for colors must be involved in the very meanings of the color-words themselves. I cannot understand the meaning of 'red' just by seeing something red; in addition, I must understand the operation of the whole measuring rule of which red is but one graduation mark, which amounts to knowing what colors there are besides red and how they are all grammatically related to one another.[26]

Obviously, the *Tractatus'* account of what it is for a name to have meaning is no longer tenable. Nor does Wittgenstein, in the *Remarks*, provide an entirely satisfactory alternative, though he moves in the direction of his ultimate solution by holding that the measuring rule for the representation of colors is itself an instrument *(Mittel)* of language,[27] and thus stressing that difficulties in understanding how propositions have sense—i.e., how language ultimately connects up with reality—are to be resolved by seeking an explanation in the operations of language itself rather than in the extra-linguistic reality to which language is applied. Still, merely to diminish the role of objects in determining the meanings of names does not solve the problem of the ontological status of such objects. Only in the *Grammar* does the strategy for eliminating Platonism receive its definitive formulation, and so it is to this work that we now turn.

As we would expect from the title, the underlying theme of *Philosophical Grammar* is to show how ostensibly 'philosophical' problems are really nothing but confusions about the grammar of the language. In principle, of course, Wittgenstein had even in the *Tractatus* rejected the view that philosophy had its own distinctive subject-matter, since the contingent status of all propositions, which placed them all in the province of 'science' (this term being used in a very extended sense), left no room for philosophy other than as an activity of making clear the actual logical structure of these propositions. In practice, however, his effort to explain the connection between language and reality, which led him to posit simple objects, i.e., indestructible substance, as an *a priori* requirement of the picture theory, placed him firmly in the ranks of traditional metaphysicians. Even when, in the *Remarks*, this doctrine of indestructible substance became a source of embarrassment, Wittgenstein had no ready solution for avoiding entanglement in this apparently substantive metaphysical issue. But by the time of the writing of the *Grammar*, the way out has become clear: the ostensibly metaphysical issue involved in explaining the connection between language and reality is not really a substantive issue, for, "[l]ike everything metaphysical, the harmony between thought and reality is found in the grammar of language."[28]

Simply put, Wittgenstein's contention is that insofar as an object is relevant to determining the meaning of the name corresponding to it, as in the case of ostensive definition, the object is in this capacity part of language and not part of the reality which language represents. Thus:

The interpretation of written and spoken signs through ostensive explanations is not the *application* of language, but part of the grammar (*Sprachlehre*).[29]

The connection between language and reality is made through the explanation of words—which belongs to the grammar, so that language remains in itself closed, autonomous.[30]

The correlation of name and object is produced in no other way than through a table, as ostensive gesture and a pronouncing of the word, etc. It is part of the symbolism.[31]

In short, there is no longer a problem of explaining the connection between language and reality in a way that avoids Platonism, because there is no such connection at all. This absence of any connection is not itself known through a metaphysical discovery whose articulation competes with the claims of Platonism, but is rather the result of a linguistic stipulation—though Wittgenstein does not himself describe the situation so bluntly—to include in the realm of 'grammar' "...all conditions (methods) of comparing a proposition with reality...,"[32] which by definition places objects themselves, insofar as they are relevant to the ostensive explanation of words, within the realm of language.

In the *Remarks*, Wittgenstein comes very close to this doctrine of linguistic autonomy[33] when, in trying to make the point that colors we imagine have the same 'grammatical behavior' as colors we see, he notes that our ordinary language does not have the means of describing precise shades of color, so that

...when I want to communicate to someone which color some thing should have, I send him a sample, and obviously this sample belongs to language; and the memory-image or other image of the color, which I produce by a word, belongs to language in just the same way...,[34]

the point being that the grammatical possibilities of color-samples we actually see are no different from those of colors we imagine (e.g., we can no more imagine reddish-green than we can see a sample of it).

The view that colors are at least sometimes instruments of, rather than the object of, communication—viz., in their status as samples—is but a short way from the view that colors *always* funtion in this paradigmatic capacity when they are being ostensively defined, and although

Wittgenstein extends this grammatical status to all objects that can enter into ostensive definitions—e.g., to people, activities, etc.[35]—colors are probably the most natural and obvious candidates for this dual- or shifting-status treatment, and there is little question that in making this distinction between the function of objects as part of grammar and as part of reality, Wittgenstein has in mind chiefly the example of colors. This preoccupation with colors, which issues in the development of a strategy particularly appropriate for them[36] is also explainable by the fact that colors are a prime example of that seemingly recalcitrant, extra-linguistic residue which had been collectively referred to in the *Remarks* as the 'elements of knowledge'. If colors can be disposed of, Wittgenstein no doubt feels that the rest will take care of itself. Accordingly, *Grammar* uses the example of colors in formulating the general problem:

> ...[T]he thought that p is the case does not presuppose that it is the case. ... [O]n the other hand something must be a presupposition for the thought itself (I cannot think that something is red, if the color red doesn't exist).[37]

And then it gives the solution:

> The proposition 'I could not think that something is red if red didn't exist' really means the image of something red, or the existence of a red sample, *as part of our language*. But, of course, one cannot say that our language *must* contain such a sample. If the language does not contain the sample, it is just another language. But one can say and emphasize that the language does contain the sample.[38]

It is this notion—that, in the name-object relation, the object is relevant only as a component of a grammatical rule—which removes the last excuse for equating the meaning of a word with the object for which it stands, and clears the way for the idea that the meaning of a word in every case just is its use in the language, no more and no less. For this reason, the doctrine of the autonomy of language has a good claim to be regarded as the decisive step in Wittgenstein's transition to his later philosophy.

The implications of this doctrine of linguistic autonomy will become clearer in the next chapter; for now I wish to note only that the absence of any explicit mention of the 'autonomy' of language in the *Investiga-*

tions marks, not any change in Wittgenstein's basic position, but only a realization that this position can be expressed in a way that is not needlessly provocative. Thus, once the point has been made that the meaning of a word is its use, and not the object, if any, that corresponds to the word, then whether or not we continue to insist that the object, *qua* component of an ostensive definition, is part of *language* is a matter of only secondary importance, since, in any case, there is no longer thought to be one fundamental semantic link which we can call the name-object relation; there are many such relations, constituted by various linguistic practices, and this is enough to repudiate the myopic outlook of the *Tractatus* without insisting that, for example, in the proposition 'That is called the Eiffel Tower' (said while one points to the Eiffel Tower), the Eiffel Tower is part of the grammar. I am not saying that in the *Investigations* Wittgenstein would have denied that it is part of the grammar, but only that he there uses more muted tones to make in effect the same point. Thus, it is enough to say that in making the connection between the Eiffel Tower and its name, we have not yet made a move in any language-game, but have only made the preparation for a move. And since the kind of preparation we make varies from one language-game to another, and does not consist in establishing some simple, invariable name-object relation,

> [w]e may say: *nothing* has so far been done, when a thing has been named. It has not even *got* a name except in the language-game (#49).

For our purposes, anyway, the important point is that in the *Investigations* Wittgenstein does explicitly retain expressions characteristic of the doctrine of linguistic autonomy in discussing the status of those ostensibly simple objects with reference to which the *Tractatus*' account of the connection between language and reality is conceived in the first place.[39] So, for example, in describing language-games in which color-samples are employed, he calls such samples 'instruments of language' (#46) and a means of representation rather than something that is represented (#50). And even in language-games which involve no direct appeal to color-samples as paradigms, so that the color signified by a word has simply to be borne in mind, the status of these imagined colors is essentially no different from that of external paradigms. One might suppose otherwise, in that, while external paradigms can be destroyed, we always retain the ability to bring forth images of these colors, which shows that the colors themselves, though not their external paradigms, are indestructible. But against the view that it must always be possible to remember, e.g., what color is called 'red', Wittgenstein argues that the criteria for judging memories to be correct cannot be provided exclusively by these acts of memory themselves. Sometimes, it is true, we judge on the basis of memory that a sample has changed color, but sometimes we appeal to the sample in judging that our memory-image itself has changed. As he had said earlier in the *Grammar*:

> When the color-sample appears darker to me than I remember it from yesterday as being, I need not, and sometimes do not, suppose my memory is correct. And I could very well speak of a darkening of my memory.[40]

But if memories cannot, by some intrinsic feature, ensure their own correctness, and are themselves sometimes judged by external paradigms, then, were all such paradigms, and red things generally, destroyed, the situation could come about that we no longer remembered which color our image was an image of. And

> [w]hen we forget which color it is that has this name, it loses its meaning for us; that is, we are no longer able to play a particular language-game with it. And the situation then is comparable with that in which we have lost a paradigm which was an instrument of our language (*Investigations* #57).

So, even though the meaning of the word 'red' is independent of the existence of red things *qua* objects in reality, if we assume the destruction of red things *qua* paradigms of language—which, Wittgenstein seems to imply, would result in the absence of an external check for the correctness of our memory-images, and would thus remove them from relevance to our language-games just as effectively as if they had been destroyed in the manner of external paradigms—then there is a sense in which we could very well say that the color 'red' had been destroyed. That is, with the destruction of the relevant paradigms, we could no longer play our accustomed language-game with the word 'red'.

What all this is intended to show is that the so-called 'indestructibility' of red is not a matter of the existence of a Platonic universal, but merely of the existence of a paradigm as part of the language. To assign the responsibility for providing the meanings of words to linguistic paradigms is not, however, to dispose of the ontological issue entirely, because we must now consider the ontological status of the paradigms themselves. Granted, things in their function as paradigms do not have an ontological status, since they are in that capacity part of language rather than part of reality. But a paradigm, after all, just *is* a thing like a piece of colored paper, and is exempt from ontological status only in respect of its special role in the language-game. Indeed, Wittgenstein admits that the same colored thing could function simultaneously as a paradigm and as an object in reality, depending on the perspective from which it is regarded. Thus, in discussing how the words *'That* is blue' can function either as a statement about the object pointed to, or as an explanation of the word 'blue', he adds: "It is also possible for someone to get an explanation of the words out of what was intended as a piece of information."[41] In this case, what functions for the speaker as a real object, functions for the hearer as a paradigm. So the question still remains as to the ontological status of paradigms apart from their function as paradigms. If colored things can serve as paradigms for color, we must still consider the ontological status of the colored things themselves.

Now, although Wittgentein's main ontological concern—as I have here tried to show—is to repudiate Platonism, and not to argue for any alternative position concerning universals, his remarks suggest that, regarding the ontological status of colors as they are instantiated in colored things, he does implicitly endorse Aristotelian realism. We have already seen in the *Remarks* how Wittgenstein is tending towards this version of realism (though his view in the *Remarks* is complicated by the subsequently abandoned doctrine of 'elements of knowledge', from the standpoint of which colors—and only primary colors at that—are the things themselves and are thus not amenable to an Aristotelian treatment in which they are regarded as properties of particulars), and the *Gram-*

mar makes his position even clearer. Thus, in contrast to any view which would deny that a color really exists in objects themselves as their common quality, Wittgenstein expresses his position as follows:

> This is a possible definition: "to point to a color" means to point to the object which has the color.[42]
> ..."The color brown exists" means nothing at all, other than that it is present here or there as the color of an object....[43]
> ...[W]e calculate with the word 'red' by describing the place where the color is found, which shape or size the patch (*Fleck*) or the body has which bears the color, whether it is pure or mixed, darker or lighter, changes or stays the same, etc.....[44]

That this remains his view throughout the *Investigations* as well is evident, not only from #72, which, as I have already argued, implies that it is possible for two or more objects to have precisely the same color as their common quality, but also by #58, in which, after explaining the sorts of consideraions which would lead us to deny that we could sensibly assert that red exists (or that red does not exist), he adds:

> In reality, however, we quite readily say that a particular colour exists; and that is as much as to say that something exists that has that colour. And the first expression is no less accurate than the second; particularly where 'what has the colour' is not a physical object.

This passage shows how willing Wittgenstein is to embrace Aristotelian realism as an account of the status of colors—i.e., that they exist only as properties actually instantiated in things—even when the 'things' in question are only mental images (it being evident from the context that these are the kind of non-physical objects Wittgenstein has in mind), which, if not for the generally adopted strategy of eliminating Platonism by insisting that universals exist only as qualifying actual particulars, might not otherwise be so readily assumed to be property-bearing things at all. (Of course, the question of the status of mental images, after-images, and the like, is further complicated by considerations advanced elsewhere in the *Investigations* against the possibility of naming or describing private objects; I return to this issue in Chapter Eight.) So, what was only an implicit suggestion in #1, viz., that 'red', like 'apple', is the name of an object, is finally given an explicit confirmation in #58: the color red is, indeed, an object, whose mode of existence is that of being the property of existing red things.

From the foregoing, it is evident that the 'grammatical' solution of the problem of the connection between language and reality does not go as far as Wittgenstein might have hoped towards removing him from the ranks of metaphysicians, since the strategy of invoking paradigms—while allowing him to dispose of Platonism—involves an ontological commitment of its own. Still, although Wittgenstein does not succeed in totally expunging ontological implications from his later views, the next chapter will show that, from the perspective of this later philosophy, the nature of ontological commitment as such is radically transformed, so that an important qualification must be made in calling him a moderate Aristotelian realist.

CHAPTER SEVEN

THE PRIMACY OF LANGUAGE

As opposed to the view that universals are fictions of language (nominalism) or mental creations (conceptualism), realism—whether of the Platonic or Aristotelian variety—holds that such items are actually to be found in that extra-linguistic, extra-mental, objective realm which, for short, we call 'reality'.[1] Now, although Wittgenstein obviously is a realist in the sense that he regards colors as items just as objectively real as the things they qualify, his ontological position must be distinguished from traditional realism—or from any traditional ontological position, for that matter—with regard to the nature of reality itself and its relation to language. In other words, the qualification I am about to make is not especially directed to Wittgenstein *qua* realist, but to Wittgenstein *qua* ontologist, so that the qualification which applies to his acknowledgement of the existence of universals equally applies to his acknowledgement of the existence of particular things.

Wittgenstein's departure from the more traditional approach to ontology—including that of Frege and Russell as well as that of the *Tractatus*—concerns the issue of the *justification* of language, i.e., the grounding of language in reality. Briefly, the usual view is that such a justification can, and indeed must, be had if there is to be such a thing as fact-stating language at all, whereas the view of the later Wittgenstein is that language is not, nor can it possibly be, grounded in reality. In his view, language is a free-floating structure, having no ontological basis as its anchor and foundation. Not only can we say that for Wittgenstein language is not answerable to reality, but we can even affirm the opposite: reality, and therefore ontology, is answerable to language. So we cannot say that the nature of extra-linguistic reality is such as to force us to include expressions in our language which designate this or that universal, or any universal at all, on pain of our language being somehow incomplete, i.e., incapable, because of the lack of these expressions, of saying all that it ought to be able to say if it purports to deal thoroughly with the reality with which it is ostensibly concerned. We can no more contend that a language lacking expressions for universals is incomplete than we can say that checkers is an incomplete game because it contains no bishops or knights. Checkers is simply a different game from chess, and in the same way, a language lacking names for universals is just different from a language containing such names, and is not an incomplete version of the latter.

This comparison between languages and games is not my own, but Wittgenstein's; so apt and illuminating does he consider this comparison, in fact, that he incorporates it into the concept of language itself. Language, for the later Wittgenstein, becomes the language-game. Granted, the notion of a language-game cannot be said to have as its rationale only one consideration. As Wittgenstein himself indicates in the *Investigations*, the expression 'language-game' serves partly to remind us that language is primarily an *activity*, whose function must be understood against a specific background of the customs and practices of a culture. The expression 'language-game' is also particularly appropriate for characterizing the more primitive and simple linguistic practices of savages and infants which serve as perspicuous objects of comparison with our own more complex linguistic practices (which are, nevertheless, also called 'language-games'). But the one fundamental consideration which gave rise to the notion of a language-game in the first place is undoubtedly the one I have suggested, viz., that language, like a game, is not answerable to reality. Thus, Wittgenstein holds that a game is defined by its rules, and not by some purpose lying outside of the rules which serves to justify the rules depending upon how well they facilitate the achievement of this purpose; if the rules are changed, we do not have a better or worse version of the same game (judged by the increased or decreased effectiveness of the game in satisfying some purpose outside the game), but merely a different game.[2]

In the same way, language is not to be characterized in terms of the achievement of some purpose outside of itself which it is supposed to facilitate, such as the purpose of describing reality; rather, language is defined by its grammatical rules, which are no less arbitrary than the rules of a game. Two languages having different grammatical rules are simply different language-games, and nothing more can be said—certainly not that one language is more adequately grounded in reality than the other. In order to show that it is indeed this concern—viz., to emphasize the absence of an ontological justification for grammatical rules—which is the fundamental consideration underlying Wittgenstein's notion of a language-game, I shall once again examine his views in the context of their historical development, from which we can readily see that the notion of a language-game is essentially a reformulation and recasting of the formalist strategy as it is described and criticized by Frege.

Part Two of the *Grundgesetze der Arithmetik* contains a lengthy discussion of the views of two mathematicians, E. Heine and J. Thomae, whom Frege groups together as advocates of what he calls formal arithmetic. In contrast to meaningful (*inhältlich*) arithmetic, whose subject-matter is actual numbers, i.e., those entities which the signs for numbers designate, formalism[3] is concerned only with the manipulation of number-signs themselves and regards the meaningful arithmetician's concern with the designata of number-signs as irrelevant for the purposes of arithmetic and liable to lead to 'metaphysical difficulties', e.g., when we wonder what sort of entity corresponds to a sign for an irrational number. Heine's is the cruder version of formalism—he apparently believes that numbers just *are* the tangible ink marks on pieces of paper, or chalk marks on blackboards, etc.—and Frege has no trouble disposing of this version.[4] The more interesting version is that of Thomae, who does not identify numbers with tangible signs, but instead characterizes numbers in terms of the rules according to which number-signs are manipulated. The following quotation, cited by Frege, gives the crux of Thomae's position:

> For the formalist, arithmetic is a game with signs, which are called empty. That means they have no other content (in the calculating game) than they are assigned by their behaviour with respect to certain rules of combination (rules of the game). The chess player makes similar use of his pieces; he assigns them certain properties determining their behaviour in the

game, and the pieces are only the external signs of this behaviour. To be sure, there is an important difference between arithmetic and chess. The rules of chess are arbitrary, the system of rules for arithmetic is such that by means of simple axioms the numbers can be referred to perceptual manifolds and can thus make important contribution to our knowledge of nature.[5]

The fact that the numbers in the calculating game can be 'referred to perceptual manifolds' is supposed to mitigate the charge of arbitrariness, but Frege correctly points out that, before we consider any possible *application* of the calculating game to our perceptual manifolds, the calculating rules—as they occur within the domain of formal arithmetic itself—are no less arbitrary than the rules of chess. As Frege says:

> In formal arithmetic we need no basis for the rules of the game—we simply stipulate them.... [W]e absolve ourselves from accounting for one choice of rules rather than another.[6]

From the standpoint of meaningful arithmetic, on the other hand, calculating rules are saved from the accusation of arbitrariness in that the number-signs designate entities which "...supply the grounds for the rules..."[7] by which these signs are manipulated. On Thomae's view, we can appeal to no such entities. Frege expresses Thomae's position thus:

> We do not derive these rules from the reference of the signs, but lay them down on our own authority, retaining full freedom and acknowledging no necessity to justify the rules; though we exercise this freedom with an eye to possible applications, since otherwise arithmetic would be a game and nothing more.[8]

Even this concession—that the rules of formal arithmetic, though applicable to reality, are in themselves arbitrary—would not satisfy Frege, since, he argues, a prerequisite for the applicability of a calculus just *is* that it is grounded in reality. Thus, considered merely as ink marks on a piece of paper, a formula can no more be applied to reality than can a configuration of chess pieces on a chess board; what makes the formula, but not the configuration of chess pieces, applicable to reality is that the ink marks of the formula express a sense, which they can only do if number-signs purport to stand for entities. And once it is admitted that arithmetical formulas express a sense, we have an additional reason, Frege thinks, for denying that the calculating rules can be arbitrary: the rules must be so chosen as to ensure that, from formulas expressing true propositions, there can only be derived other formulas which likewise express true propositions. So, in order for the gulf to be bridged between arithmetical formulas and their applications, "...it is necessary that formulas express a sense and that the rules be grounded in the reference of the signs...,"[9] and these two requirements are incapable of fulfillment in formal arithmetic.

Lest we suppose that Thomae is misrepresented in being said to hold that numerical signs designate nothing at all, since he does say that such signs do have a kind of content in virtue of their behavior with respect to the rules of the calculating game, Frege assures us that Thomae's apparent ascription of a kind of content to numerical signs or chess pieces

> ...is due to an inaccurate formulation, prompted perhaps by a certain repulsion from empty signs.... I am aware that the chess pieces are given, likewise that rules for their manipulation have been established, but I know nothing of any content. It can surely not be said that the black king, in consequence of these rules, designates something, as, say, the name 'Sirius' designates a certain fixed star. On the contrary, the appropriate way of speaking is to say that the rules of chess treat of the black king.[10]

Frege adds that it is misleading to speak of the behavior of signs with respect to rules, since it is the player or calculator who, by obeying or disobeying the rules, behaves with respect to them, and also that it is eccentric to speak of a numerical sign or a chess piece as an external sign of its behavior, since the more natural way of speaking would be to say that the rules of the calculus or of chess treat of the manipulation of the signs or pieces.[11] In short, Frege altogether dismisses the attempt to give numerical signs a kind of content constituted by rules rather than by designated entities, and he continues to see the contrast between meaningful arithmetic and formal arithmetic—in Thomae's as well as in Heine's version—as that between arithmetic whose formulas have a content, in virtue of their ontological ground, and arithmetic whose formulas are composed of empty signs.

In this dispute between Frege and Thomae, as presented in the *Grundgesetze*, we find a large part of the background against which Wittgenstein works out his own views concerning the necessity of grounding linguistic signs in reality. We can roughly characterize the evolution of his position by saying that the early Wittgenstein sides with Frege and that the later Wittgenstein sides with Thomae. Thus, in the *Tractatus*, Wittgenstein goes along with Frege's view that the use of all primitive signs must be justified by the existence of entities corresponding to these signs and providing their ontological ground, since the only primitive signs recognized by the *Tractatus* are names of simple objects, and it is of course these objects themselves, in virtue of their form, which provide the ground for the syntactically correct use of their names in propositions. Even in rejecting the Fregean approach to arithmetic, as is done in the *Tractatus*, Wittgenstein shows his respect for Frege's principles by holding that numerical signs are merely exponents of operations (6.021) and not primitive signs, implying that if they *were* primitive, then there would have to exist entities as their ontological ground, and mathematical equations would presumably then be expressions of thoughts, as Frege supposes but as the *Tractatus* denies (6.21).

Then, beginning with the *Remarks*, we see Wittgenstein breaking away from this Fregean position and adopting Thomae's position, not only for arithmetic, but for language as such. So, whereas Thomae implicitly contrasts the calculating game of arithmetic, where signs have only a rule-constituted meaning, with language proper, where words and their syntactical behavior presumably are ontologically grounded in entities designated by these words, we find Wittgenstein saying in *Remarks* that the syntax of language generally, and not just of the signs of the arithmetical calculus, cannot and need not be justified by reality.[12] We also find that Thomae's analogy between chess pieces and numerical signs has been replaced by the broader analogy between chess pieces and words generally,[13] though there still seems to be at least implicitly a contrast between those kinds of words which have merely a rule-constituted meaning and those which have an object-designating meaning.

These points are re-iterated and amplified in the notes recorded by Waismann, where Wittgenstein again takes up the formalist strategy by contending that mathematics deals with ink marks on paper in the same sense that chess has to do with figures of wood. That is, we are not concerned with chess pieces *qua* physical properties, but rather, so to speak, *qua* logical properties which these pieces have in virtue of the rules of chess. So, when I say that the knight *can* only move over three squares, the castle only in a straight line, etc., this 'can' means a grammatical, and not a physical, possibility; i.e., I am saying something about the syntax, or grammar, of chess, and not enunciating a law of physics.[14] That pawns, kings, etc., are not to be characterized merely as pieces of wood of certain shapes, nor are they to be regarded as functioning as representatives of other objects, shows that Frege is wrong in objecting to the formalists' notion of rule-constituted meaning (and at this place in Waismann's notes Wittgenstein explicitly refers to Frege).[15] The moral which Wittgenstein is anxious to draw from this is that "...not only the axioms of mathematics, but all syntax is arbitrary...,"[16] and that "...apart from its applications, considered for itself alone, it [i.e., syntax] is a game, exactly as chess is."[17] Here, we can plainly see that Wittgenstein's interest in games is from the perspective of the formalist: games are the most obvious example of rule-governed activities in which the rules require no ontological ground. Wittgenstein's advance beyond the formalist conception is to regard not only mathematics, but all of language, as a game in this respect.

With the advent in *Grammar* of the doctrine of complete linguistic autonomy, the formalist strategy is extended still further. Rule-constituted meaning is no longer contrasted with object-designating meaning, for even objects are now considered to be components of grammatical rules with respect to their role in ostensive explanations. Witt—genstein is now able to say quite generally that the meaning of a word is its use, which, from the context in which this slogan first appears, can be seen to be largely a response in the formalist vein to the view that the meaning of a word is an object which provides the ontological ground for the word's use, the latter being thought of as distinct from, and a consequence of, its meaning. Thus, Wittgenstein begins by saying that the rules governing the use of the negation-sign seem to follow from the nature of negation, which is an independently describable process,[18] and in general that a sign, in virtue of having a meaning by standing for something, seems to contain within it the whole grammar of its use, in the way that a box contains a string of beads which are waiting to be taken out.[19] But this way of thinking of the relation of meaning and use rests on a primitive conception of meaning, which sees everything as being accomplished in the simple act of naming an object.[20] Actually, words have many different kinds of uses,[21] and an apt comparison can be made between the different kinds of words and the different kinds of chess pieces.[22] The appropriateness of this analogy gives us a more helpful way of viewing the relation between meaning and use, viz., by identifying them. Thus, the meaning of a word is its place in the grammar,[23] or its use in the language.[24] Immediately after stating the meaning-is-use doctrine, Wittgenstein adds:

> Grammar describes the use of words in language. It is thus related to language similarly to the way that the description of a game, such as is given in the rules of the game, is related to the game.[25]

The influence of the formalist outlook on Wittgenstein's formulation of the meaning-is-use doctrine is therefore readily apparent.[26]

Lest we overlook the implication which this comparison of grammatical rules with rules of a game has for the relation of language to reality, Wittgenstein tells us a few pages later that

> ...a name has meaning, a proposition has sense, in the calculus to which it belongs. This [calculus] is, so to speak, autonomous.—Language must speak for itself.[27]

And to say that language is autonomous is to say that, while we justify moves within the calculus of language by appealing to the grammatical rules which sanction these moves, the rules themselves have and need no justification. In other words,

> [g]rammar is not accountable to reality. Meaning is first determined (constituted) by grammatical rules, and therefore they are not answerable to any meaning and are in this respect arbitrary.[28]

The rules of grammar are arbitrary in a way that the rules of cooking are not, because the concept 'cooking' is defined by the purpose of cooking, while the concept 'language' is not defined by some purpose outside of itself. Thus:

> Whoever cooks by other than the correct rules cooks badly; but whoever follows rules different from those of chess plays another game; and whoever follows other grammatical rules than the usual ones does not speak falsely, but just speaks of something else.[29]

All of this goes to show that the expression 'language-game' has been carefully chosen to emphasize that the formalist contention that the arithmetical calculus is like a game, in having and needing no ontological ground for its rules, should be extended to cover language in general; as such, the notion of a language-game marks as extremely important step in Wittgenstein's philosophical development. Clearly, standard accounts such as Quinton's of the rationale for the expression 'language-game'—which is that various linguistic practices are all called 'language', not because they possess some common element, but because they have certain family-resemblances with one another, and that since linguistic practices are in this respect like games, the two terms of the simile are run together to emphasize that both 'language' and 'game' have a multiplicity of uses—are superficial at best.[30]

Perhaps the widespread failure to recognize the influence of formalism in Wittgenstein's notion of a language-game is to some extent his own fault, since in the *Investigations* the formalist strategy is greatly de-emphasized, though why this should be so I cannot say. Still, I assume that in the *Investigations* Wittgenstein does continue to hold that language has no ontological ground, an assumption based chiefly on the evidence of #561-564. In #561, Wittgenstein asks why we want to say, as we do, that our use of the word 'is' both for the copula and for the sign of equality constitutes two different meanings for the word 'is' rather than one meaning whose use consists, as it were, in both of these component uses. We want to say that the use of the same word in both cases is inessential, and that two different words could serve just as well. He then poses, in #562, some important questions:

> But how can I decide what is an essential, and what an inessential, ac-

cidental, feature of the notation? Is there some reality lying behind the notation, which shapes its grammar?

If he were now inclined to answer this question in the affirmative, thereby rejecting his earlier assimilation of grammatical rules to rules of a game, we should expect as a follow-up to the question some kind of remark to this effect, considering the significance of such a shift from his earlier position. What he says instead is this:

> Let us think of a similar case in a game: in draughts a king is marked by putting one piece on top of another. Now won't one say it is inessential to the game for a king to consist of two pieces? (#562)

In #563 he then considers a similar example pertaining to the use of the king in chess to determine which player moves first, depending on the color of the king one player selects from the closed fist of the other; he asks whether we want to count this as part of the role of the king in chess, and, implying that he does not, concludes in #564:

> So I am inclined to distinguish between the essential and inessential in a game too. The game, one would like to say, has not only rules but also a *point*.

That is, even though a game is constituted by its rules—and not by the way and the extent to which these rules happen to be grounded in some external reality—we nevertheless are able to distinguish essential from inessential rules, and the point of making this observation where he does can only be to argue that grammatical rules, too, can be distinguished into those that are essential and those that are inessential for a particular language-game, without our having to suppose that this distinction requires that the language-game be grounded in reality.

There is still other evidence that Wittgenstein continues to characterize language from the formalist perspective. In #492 he says:

> To invent a language could mean to invent an instrument for a particular purpose on the basis of the laws of nature (or consistently with them); but it also has the other sense, analogous to that in which we speak of the invention of a game.

This other sense of 'invent' means simply the act of stipulating a system of rules so as to constitute a language-game; in this sense, we are looking at language, not as an instrument for bringing about some effect, but as a grammatical system. Thus:

> Grammar does not tell us how language must be constructed in order to fulfill its purpose, in order to have such-and-such an effect on human beings (#496).
>
> The rules of grammar may be called "arbitrary", if that is to mean that the aim of the grammar is nothing but that of the language (#497).

Of course, there is also a sense in which our grammatical rules are not arbitrary, viz., in the sense in which our grammar gets its character from our form of life, i.e., our cultural background, customs, education, instinctive behavior, etc. But these factors provide, not an ontological ground or justification for our grammatical rules, but rather a genetic, or causal, explanation of why we have them. Likewise, though our form of life depends in turn upon facts of nature being as they are, such facts themselves are relevant to our grammatical rules only as causes and not as grounds. To insist that grammatical rules must have not only causes, but grounds as well, is to display a misconception about the justificational process, which Wittgenstein opposes no less explicitly in the *Investigations* (e.g., in #217) than he does in the *Grammar* when he says that

> [a] reason (*Grund*) can be given only *inside* a game. The chain of reasons comes to an end, and indeed does so at the boundary of the game. (Reason and cause.)[31]

Even in one of his latest philosophical works, *On Certainty*, Wittgenstein continues to maintain this line of thought by saying that a language-game "...is not based on grounds. It is not reasonable (or unreasonable). It is there—like our life."[32]

Still other evidence that Wittgenstein never renounces the view that grammar has no ontological ground is to be found in a number of remarks preserved in *Zettel*, including two of the more explicit remarks to this effect, which closely resemble remarks previously made in *Grammar*. These include the passage comparing rules of grammar and rules of cooking—to which is added, in the version in *Zettel*: "That is why the use of language is in a certain sense autonomous, as cooking and washing are not…" (#320)—and also *Zettel* #331, which begins:

> One is tempted to justify rules of grammar by sentences like "But there really are four primary colors". And the saying that the rules of grammar are arbitrary is directed against the possibility of this justification, which is constructed on the model of justifying a sentence by pointing to what verifies it.

And the passage concludes by suggesting that, although we do in fact classify red, green, yellow, and blue as primary colors, it is not as though the nature of objective reality provides grounds for this classification as opposed to some other one. We could, if we so chose (or if our form of life so dictated), group red, green, and circular together; such a classification would be no less legitimate than any other, since the notion of an intrinsically legitimate classification, grounded in the true nature of reality, simply has no place. I conclude, therefore, that Wittgenstein's considered, mature view continues to be that language is not grounded in reality.

How this conclusion bears on Wittgenstein's status as a realist can be seen, e.g., by examining the language-game described in *Investigations* #48. The words of this language are 'R', 'G', 'W', and 'B', which name red, green, white, and black squares, respectively. Now, if Wittgenstein were a traditional realist with respect to shades of color, he would have to maintain that a colored square is, in a fundamental sense, undeniably *composite*, since it contains as a component a color which is a (universal) element in its own right. What he actually says, however, is that the *colored squares* are the primary elements. Then, to the question: "But are these simple?" he replies:

> I do not know what else you would have me call "the simples", what would be more natural in this language-game. But under other circumstances I should call a monochrome square "composite", consisting perhaps of two rectangles, or of the elements color and shape (#48).

He does not specify what these 'other circumstances' might be, but one such circumstance in which we would be inclined to treat color and shape as distinguishable components would be where the elements were different shapes as well as of different colors. As it is, with every element dealt with in language (48) being a square, the distinction between color and shape becomes irrelevant. If we insist that, relevant or not, the distinction is still *there* waiting to be made, this is to miss the point that the only distinctions which exist are provided for in the language-game itself. It should be noted that even in the situation in which things were of different shapes as well as of different colors, it does not follow that the distinction between color and shape must then become relevant. In *Remarks on Colour* Wittgenstein observes that there might be people in just such a situation who nevertheless have only color-shape concepts, so that "...they would have a special word for a red square and one for a red circle, and one for a green circle" (III, #155). Concerning such a situation, Wittgenstein comments:

> Should I say of them that they do not *see* that a green leaf and a green table—when I show them these things—have the same colour or have something in common? What if it had never 'occurred to them' to compare differently shaped objects of the same colour with one another? Due to their particular background, this comparison was of no importance to them, or had importance only in very exceptional cases, so that no linguistic tool was developed (III, #130).

Again, I take the point to be that distinctions which exist for us, because they matter for us and are accommodated in our language-games, simply do not exist for such people.

That ontological distinctions are relative to, and dependent on, the language-game being played receives further illustration from #64 of the *Investigations*:

> Let us imagine language game (48) altered so that names signify not monochrome squares but rectangles each consisting of two such squares. Let such a rectangle, which is half red half green, be called "U"; a half green half white one, "V"; and so on. Could we not imagine people who had names for such combinations of colour, but not for the individual colours?... In what sense do the symbols of this language-game stand in need of analysis? How far is it even *possible* to replace this language-game by (48)?—It is just *another* language-game; even though it is related to (48).

In other words, we cannot say that language (48) allows for a more accurate representation of reality by providing for distinctions which are slurred over by language (64), and this is because there is nothing that can be called 'reality' which functions as a standard external to all language-games and against which they can be compared. Insofar as we talk about reality at all, we can only be understood within the framework of a particular language-game.

In a manner reminiscent of Kant's categories and forms of intuition, the language-game has been placed as a necessary intermediary between us and noumenal reality, as it were ,even to the point, as could be contended is also the case for Kant, that the very intelligibility of the notion of a reality standing on the other side of this medium is in question. 'Reality' just is 'reality as defined by the particular language-game'. Therefore, when I say that Wittgenstein makes statements implying that he is a realist with respect to specific shades of color, or whatever, what I really mean is that he makes statements which show that he is playing a language-game appropriate to realism, or at least describing realist language-games and implying that in our form of life we do sometimes play them. So, for example, when he says that colors exist, i.e., that things exist which have colors as properties, we should on his behalf contend at most that he is committing himself to a realist ontology only in the sense that he happens to be playing or describing a language-game from which this ontology issues. To go further than this, saying some such thing as that reality compels us, upon pain of inaccuracy or incompleteness, to acknowledge the existence of universals such as colors, and to provide for the possibility of naming or describing them in language, would be inadmissible. If this appears to be a rather drastic qualification to be made about Wittgenstein's status as a realist, I should again point out that the qualification applies generally to any ontological position to which one might want to say that Wittgenstein is committed. He is, at any rate, no less committed to the existence of colors as properties of things than he is to the existence of such particular things themselves.

With this conclusion, I am now in a position to examine still one more argument—advanced this time by Pitcher—purporting to show that Wittgenstein provides the basis for disposing of the errors of realism (and which, of course, takes for granted that Wittgenstein himself is not a realist). Pitcher claims that part of Augustine's over-simplified picture of language-learning attacked by Wittgenstein is the view that we can see the universal in the particular, or—less crudely put—that we can come to possess a concept by abstracting the relevant common features from many particulars. Claiming that Wittgenstein's doctrine of family-resemblances provides a powerful argument against the Augustinian picture of concept formation as regards some concepts, Pitcher concedes that the Augustinian picture has at least a *prima facie* plausibility for relatively simple concepts such as colors. Surely we want to say that all red things have the color red in common—(to avoid irrelevant complications I am continuing to assume that 'red' is being used as the name of a specific shade of color)—and that to apply the concept 'red' to future things I may encounter, I need only note whether they, too, possess this common feature. My contention has been that this is, in fact, Wittgenstein's view, viz., that while some concepts, even the vast majority, treat only of family-resemblances, other concepts are indeed applied to various particulars in virtue of common features which the particulars share, the most obvious example and the one usually given by Wittgenstein himself being that of colors. But Pitcher contends that Wittgenstein has a line of argument which can be used to show that even the modest claim that there are any common-feature concepts at all is mistaken.

To say that many particulars have a common feature, which is to say that they have the *same* feature, assumes, according to Pitcher, that sameness "...is a wholly natural, as opposed to a conventional, relation."[33] Pitcher contends, to the contrary, that "...there is an element of convention—indeed, a profound element of convention—in all sameness."[34] To support this claim as regards color, he argues that we can imagine a society embodying a quite different form of life from our own which would see nothing in common between two colors, such as light blue and dark blue, which we classify as being two shades of the same color. His conclusion of this part of the argument is that

[t]hese examples show that there is no answer to the question whether or

not two colours are different shades of the same colour apart from the conventions embodied in the colour-concepts of this or that language— concepts determined by the 'form of life' of the language users and by certain general facts of nature.... There is no sense to the claim that colours 1 and 2 just *are*, in and of themselves, shades of the same colour: according to our colour-concepts, they are indeed shades of the same colour—namely, of blue; but according to the colour-concepts of our mythical tribesmen, they are not.[35]

This part of the argument, however, does not yet undercut the realist's claim that two or more things can have as their common element precisely the same shade of color, so Pitcher tries to show that even the judgement that two things have the same color contains an element of conventionality. We can imagine a tribe, he says, who live

...in a jungle illuminated by an eerie light called *jungle light*. Most things are unchanged in colour when they are brought from sunlight into jungle light, but certain kinds of materials *x* change slightly in colour when this happens to them. Hence it is quite possible that we should judge two pieces of cloth—one of kind *x* and another of kind not-*x*—to have exactly the same colour when the jungle tribesmen would judge them to be of different colour.[36]

This argument, though ingenious, will not do what Pitcher requires of it; it shows at most that the color an object is judged actually to have—as opposed to the color it merely appears to have—is based partly on the convention of what we accept as standard lighting conditions. But it does not show that we are mistaken in supposing that a specific shade of color can and does qualify many different particulars as their common element. The realist need not deny that what we call a thing's 'real' color is partly based on convention; the crucial point is that, even though two cultures may disagree as to which objects have, say, fire-engine red as their 'real' color, both cultures will presumably agree that this same shade of red qualifies more than one thing.

Nevertheless, leaving aside this objection to Pitcher's argument, the more important objection to his whole approach is not that he over-estimates, but rather that he under-estimates, the element of conventionality which Wittgenstein would say is involved in our concept formation. That is, in saying that the relation of sameness is at least in part conventional (where 'conventional' can be taken to mean 'arising from our form of life rather than based on the way reality is in itself'), he implies that the relation is in part *not* conventional, so that when I judge of two things that they are in some respect the same, my judgement is justified at least in part by the way reality is. For Wittgenstein, however, the process of justifying a move in a language-game finally terminates in appealing to the rules of the language-game, and these rules can *never* be based on the nature of an extra-linguistic reality.[37]

In a way, then, I am making Pitcher's case against Wittgenstein's purported realism stronger than Pitcher makes it himself. If Wittgenstein's realism amounts to no more than his playing or describing language-games in which, e.g., different things are properly said to have the same color, then little or nothing seems to remain as a point of substantive contention between realists and nominalists. If, to take the example discussed earlier in Chapter Five, I cut in two a uniformly dyed piece of cloth, a realist will say that both pieces of cloth have the *same* color, while a nominalist will at most concede that the color of one piece *resembles* the color of the other. This is clearly not a factual dispute, since for the nominalist nothing even in principle could count as a case of two different things having the same color. Rather, the nominalist simply wishes to replace the language-game in which different things are said to have the same color, and thus share this color as a common property, with a language-game in which each thing has its *own* color, i.e., colors themselves are individuated in virtue of the things that they color. To the realist, this way of individuating colors seems arbitrary and counter-intuitive, as the example of the cut cloth is meant to show. Whereas the original piece of cloth was of one color, the two cut pieces are—on nominalist principles—no longer of one color, but are rather of two resembling colors. Were these pieces of cloth divided in turn, there would result four resembling colors, and so on. Finally, were all these pieces sewn back together, we would again have one uniformly colored cloth. Since we are assuming that the color of the cloth has not actually been affected by this process of cutting and resewing, the realist would contend that the nominalist's way of individuating colors is at best *ad hoc* and misleading, since it suggests that some change in color has actually taken place. Since a uniformly dyed cloth remains the same color whether or not it is cut into smaller pieces, why not just say so?

I take it that the realist's way of talking about colors does reflect our ordinary linguistic practice; if so, Wittgenstein's realism with respect to colors amounts to no more than his willingness to play these language-games as well, a willingness which does not preclude his recognition of the possibility of other language-games. As he says in the *Blue Book*:

> We use the phrase "two books have the same colour", but we could perfectly well say: "They can't have the *same* colour, because, after all, this book has its colour, and the other book has its own colour too". This also would be stating a grammatical rule—a rule, incidentally, not in accordance with our ordinary usage.[38]

Wittgenstein is saying that we could adopt the nominalist way of speaking, but also that in fact we do not. No scruples about 'the way reality is' force us to speak of two pieces of cloth of the same color rather than two pieces of cloth, each with its own color, and no additional amount of experiential data about colors, however carefully collected, could settle or even bear on the issue.

It is misleading, however, to say that realists and nominalists are engaged in a *mere* verbal dispute, as opposed to a substantive disagreement, since this suggests that there could be such a thing as an issue to be decided solely by an appeal to the non-linguistic facts. For certain purposes, of course, a distinction between verbal and empirical disagreements can indeed be made, and it is Wittgenstein's sensitivity to the peculiarly intractable character of traditional metaphysical disputes which convinces him that all such traditional views are really recommendations of particular notations—ways of speaking—masquerading as empirical or quasi-empirical positions. From the standpoint of the doctrine of the primacy of language, however, there can be no such thing as a purely empirical stance, i.e., one dictated solely by the way the world is, since 'the way the world is'—including what empirical facts there are to be taken account of—is always relative to a particular language-game.

If Wittgenstein's attempt to maintain a position of ontological neutrality thus appears doomed, given that ontological commitment, i.e., the presupposition of the existence of certain named objects, is built into many of the language-games that we ordinarily play—including an acknowledgement of non-particular items such as colors—this commitment is itself rendered metaphysically innocuous, from a traditionalist perspective, by the doctrine of linguistic primacy. Wittgenstein's realism just *is* his going along with ordinary usage rather than with nominalist revisionism.[39] If realism amounts to no more than this, we may feel dissatisfied with the result; nevertheless, Wittgenstein's contention would be that our longing for metaphysical foundations is misplaced, and that

> [o]ur mistake is to look for an explanation where we ought to look at what happens as a 'proto-phenomenon'. That is, where we ought to have said: *this language game is played* (*Investigations* #654).

It is a matter of irony, then, that one of the central themes of Wittgenstein's later philosophy—his attack on privacy—implies that a particular language-game which we commonly suppose that we play quite regularly, viz., the language-game of referring to and describing our inner experiences, cannot, despite appearances to the contrary, be the sort of language-game we suppose it is, if indeed it can be regarded as a legitimate language-game at all. In the next, and concluding, chapter I will try to show why this view of Wittgenstein's is untenable.

CHAPTER EIGHT

NONJUSTIFICATIONALISM AND PRIVACY

In the previous chapter I contended that, whatever else is packed into Wittgenstein's notion of a language-game, his fundamental rationale for comparing language to a game is to extend the formalist strategy to language in general. Just as the rules of a game are not answerable to reality, likewise, the grammatical rules of language have no ontological ground. Justifying a move in a language-game is ultimately a matter of appealing to the rules of the game, and beyond this the justificational process cannot go. If we try to push the process back any further, we can only refer to the form of life we actually have. This allusion to our form of life, however, is not really part of the process of *justification*, but is at best a *causal* explanation of why we have the language-games we do and why we follow the rules of the language-games in one way rather than another. The moral to be drawn from this, which appears as a theme throughout Wittgenstein's later works, is that justification comes to an end, i.e., we must always reach a point where the request for a justification no longer makes any sense.

Of course, the notion that the process of justification is finite is hardly original with Wittgenstein. What is distinctive about his approach is his willingness to stop short of the place where others have tried to push the justificational process. To give but one example, in Chapter IV of *Problems of Philosophy* Russell postulates a law of induction which, in conjunction with our past experience, is supposed to justify our belief that, say, fire will burn us—this law of induction itself constituting a justificational terminus, since we cannot in turn justify it. Wittgenstein prefers to omit the inductive principle from the justificational process altogether; if the process has to stop anyway, why not let it stop at those primitive, fundamental beliefs such as that if we put our hands in the fire, we will be burned? No appeal to an inductive law could make these kinds of beliefs any more certain, psychologically *or* epistemologically, than they are already, and this further appeal can therefore be eliminated as superfluous.[1]

This desire of Wittgenstein's to avoid any gratuitous extension of the justificational process, which makes him critical of the places at which many philosophers have traditionally drawn the justificational boundaries (e.g., at intuitively 'self-evident' propositions, a view which is criticized in *On Certainty*, #144 and #204), forms that part of his outlook which I have called his *nonjustificationalism*. Although many commentators have noted the presence of this theme of nonjustificationalism in Wittgenstein's work, it has not been given the emphasis it deserves as a theme lying at the very heart of Wittgenstein's later philosophy. Even Specht, who, in emphasizing that for Wittgenstein "...the rules of a language-game cannot be read off from reality..."[2] and that reality itself "...is only linguistically accessible, i.e., only given and attainable in language-games...,"[3] has grasped more clearly the fruits of the formalist strategy than most, and perhaps all, other commentators, nevertheless does not realize how deeply Wittgenstein is committed to nonjustificationalism as an integral part of this strategy. Thus, Specht observes that language-games are supposed to be able to create "...a new organization of objects into groups, according to certain points of view or paradigms..."[4] but that, since any such organization presupposes that we can recognize these objects as being relevantly the same, we have here the basis for a critique of Wittgenstein's theory of language. This is because the question of how this knowledge of sameness is possible is "...one of the most difficult problems of philosophy..."[5] and one to which Specht apparently feels that Wittgenstein provides no satisfactory solution, even though Specht's citation of two examples from the *Remarks on the Foundations of Mathematics*—the first of which says that we do not need a criterion for judging different things to be relevantly the same, that the word 'same' is not used wrongfully just because it is used without justification, and the second of which says that we neither need nor can we have a justification for judging that a color agrees with the color sample—shows that he is well aware of Wittgenstein's nonjustificational approach.[6] Specht's evaluation of this approach is that

Wittgenstein wishes to make clear by means of these examples that there is no justification for the use of the word "same"; in other words, that the question about knowledge of identity cannot be answered.[7]

To attempt an answer—Specht reads Wittgenstein as saying—would be to indulge in metaphysical explanation, but of course Wittgenstein

> ...from the beginning denies his theory the possibility of giving metaphysical interpretations in those cases where the problems cannot be solved along analytical lines.[8]

Specht is saying, in other words, that there is a genuine problem here, which Wittgenstein cannot solve with the only means at his disposal, since he has rejected 'metaphysical explanation', so he is forced by an *ad hoc* measure to appeal to the notion of a justificational terminus as a way of showing that this is just one of those problems that cannot be solved, one of those questions which admit of no answer. But this is to under-estimate seriously the force of the nonjustificationalist approach. The finitude of the justificational process does not mean that at some point we are relieved of the onus of solving certain problems or answering certain questions; it is rather that the point at which the demand for solutions or answers goes beyond the provisions of the language-game is also the point at which legitimate problems or questions cease to exist.

The nonjustificationalist theme crops up repeatedly in Wittgenstein's writings from *Grammar* onwards, in connection with such topics as knowing how to carry out an order, continuing a series, following a rule, using words, etc., and in his late work *On Certainty* the basic problems of epistemology are thoroughly explored from a nonjustificationalist perspective.[9]

There can be no doubt, then, that the nonjustificationalist theme assumes a central place in Wittgenstein's later philosophy. Ironically, however, the most famous and controversial doctrine of the later Wittgenstein—viz., his denial of the possibility of a private language, which involves the concomitant and, in my view, much more important doctrine of the unintelligibility of the notion of a private something (where the same argument applies whether we regard this 'something' as an object, an experience, a process, or an event)—is a product of his failure to take his own nonjustificationalism seriously enough.

Wittgenstein's argument against the possibility of a language being used to name or describe private objects is that the lack of public access to private objects prevents any intersubjective check to see if these private objects are being correctly named (i.e., re-identified) and described; furthermore, that the notion of a private check, in which one is applying language correctly, is also vacuous, since there is in such a case no external check by which one can distinguish correct from faulty memory; and therefore that we cannot make sense of the notion of a correct application of language to private objects. As he says in #258 of the *Investigations:* "Whatever is going to seem correct to me is correct. And that only means that here we can't talk about correctness." In his argument, Wittgenstein is not careful to distinguish between an object or experience as a *particular*—which would involve the problem of re-identifying something as, for example, this particular headache—and a *kind* of object or experience—which would involve the problem of recognizing an experience as, for example, an ache rather than a tingle. The lack of a clearly drawn distinction between these two sorts of identification-problems is probably due to the fact that Wittgenstein's argument, if correct, would apply to either sort of problem, though the context of his discussion of privacy in the *Investigations* indicates that it is the problem of qualitative sameness rather than that of numerical identity which Wittgenstein has chiefly in mind.

Be that as it may, what his argument boils down to is that the application of language to private objects cannot be *justified*. Now, it seems to me that the proper response to this argument—a response in the best Wittgensteinian tradition—would be: so what? I regard it as perfectly natural and untroublesome to suppose that when, for example, I say that I have a mental image of a farmer standing to the left of a cow, I am describing a scene to which only I have direct access and to which anyone else, through an examination of the state of my central nervous system or whatever, can have at best only an indirect, inferential access; furthermore, that no matter what happens to be the state of my brain, I alone, through introspection,[10] am the ultimate judge of whether, say, the farmer is standing to the left of the cow rather than to the right of it.

On Wittgenstein's argument, if I am not subject to some kind of external check, I cannot be sure that in my mental image the farmer really is to the left of the cow, nor can I even be sure that what I mentally picture is a farmer or a cow at all, and this consequence presumably helps dispose of the existence of mental images entirely, at least on the supposition that such images, were they to exist, *would* be essentially private rather than public.[11] It seems to me, on the other hand, that we can readily admit both (a) that mental images are private (which is not to deny that they may have public physiological correlates, though these correlates are themselves established only on the basis of first-person introspective testimony and may also be over-ridden by such testimony), and (b) that mental images *are* describable by public language. (a) and (b) are rendered compatible by my contention (c) that such descriptions are not amenable to justification, and that none is in their case required.

If I am able to play those language-games in which my use of language is subject to an intersubjective check, then the fact that I am able to transfer these linguistic techniques to a description of my own private experience is simply another related language-game, in which the function of the justificational demands is correspondingly restricted, or in which such demands are even eliminated altogether. Similarly, I use names of sensations to refer primarily to my own private experience, and then assume, not by a conscious, reasoned process of analogy, but by a spontaneous, instinctive attitude, that other people have the same kind of experience that I do when they make sensory contact with the same physical object as I do (or, generally, with the same kind of environment)—e.g., we both bite into the apple and I therefore assume that you, too, have the private experience of apple-taste—or when, in relevantly similar circumstances, other people manifest behavior similar to mine as, e.g., when I have a toothache. It is part of our form of life that we regard each other as private centers of experience, and a *justification* of this attitude, as is attempted in standard solutions to the other-minds problem, is neither possible nor is it needed. This attitude towards others is simply part of the background against which our language-games are played.

On at least one occasion Wittgenstein seems to be steering towards just such a nonjustificationalist strategy for dealing with private experiences, when, in a passage in Zettel, he remarks:

> ...[W]hen I say "It tastes exactly like sugar", in an important sense no remembering takes place. So I do not have grounds for my judgment or my exclamation. If someone asks me "What do you mean by 'sugar'?"— I shall indeed try to shew him a lump of sugar. And if someone asks "How do you know that sugar tastes like that?" I shall indeed answer him "I've eaten sugar thousands of times"—but that is not a justification that I give myself (#659).

This suggests that Wittgenstein is treating a taste as an experience identifiable apart from the physical stuff with which this taste-experience is associated, and that the identification of this experience as sugar-taste, along with its description in public language, can legitimately take place without an appeal to memory—indeed, without the need of any justification at all.

His more usual approach, however, is to suppose that language, in its fact-stating capacity, always requires justification for its employment, and if there are cases where no such justification is required, in these cases language must be functioning in some other capacity. Thus, in *Investigations* #290 he admits that one does not identify one's sensations by criteria, but he goes on to explain that this is only because there is no question here of identifying anything at all. The utterance of a sensation-word is the *beginning* of the language-game, and not the outcome of the process of identifying an object. Granted, one talks about describing one's sensations, but Wittgenstein warns us that this cannot be a description in the sense in which one describes one's room, or, generally, in the sense of using language to state facts (#292). So, although he does concede that there are nonjustificational uses of language—"[t]o use a word without justification does not mean to use it without right" (#289)—this nonjustificationalism is made to complement the attack on private experience rather than to render this attack unnecessary in the way I maintain he ought to have done to avoid being in the untenable position of having to explain away altogether the existence of such experience.

As a way of tying in my own remarks with the vast corpus of secondary literature on the subject, I have decided to focus on two articles—

the reviews of the *Investigations* by Malcolm and Strawson—whose discussion of the key issues has remained unsurpassed, and usually even unapproached, by the flood of literature which has arisen since these reviews made their appearance in the early 1950's. Strawson's position in his review is essentially the one I have been advocating, the main difference between us being his contention that this is essentially Wittgenstein's position as well. That is, Strawson believes that Wittgenstein wavers between a stronger and a weaker thesis, the stronger thesis being that no words name private experiences, and the weaker thesis being that "...certain conditions must be satisfied for the existence of a common language in which sensations are ascribed to those who have them...,"[12] where the sensations themselves are still regarded as private experiences. These conditions are that the names of sensations

> ...must always contain in a more or less complex way, within their logic, some allusion to what is not sensation, to what can be seen and touched and heard.[13]

This is because

> ...a common language for describing or reporting requires general agreement in judgements. So for a (descriptive) word or phrase to belong to a common language, it is essential that *the occasions on which it is right to apply it should provide shared experiences of a certain kind*, the existence of which is connected with the rightness of applying the word.[14]

And since sensations are private, i.e., non-shareable, experiences, we must look to people's observable behavior to provide the shareable experiences which constitute our criteria for ascribing sensations to them. Because of this need for behavioral criteria for a common sensation-language, Strawson concludes that

> ...it is necessarily empty and pointless (I will *not* say meaningless) either (a) to speculate about the ascription of pain to anything which does not exhibit behaviour compatible in the relevant respects with human behavior (i.e. the behaviour of those who use the concept), or (b) to raise generalized doubts about other people's experience of pain, or about one's own knowledge of this.[15]

He then adds: "It is the above points which I take Wittgenstein essentially to be making."[16] Now, while I disagree with Strawson's assumption that in the *Investigations* Wittgenstein is for the most part advocating the weaker thesis—he is too deeply committed to the stronger thesis for this—I agree with Strawson that the weaker thesis is the only defensible one, and the one Wittgenstein ought to have advocated.

Although Strawson emphasizes the need for a justification for our use of words in a common language, he is ultimately taking the same nonjustificational approach that I have set forth, since he clearly does not regard behavioral criteria as logically guaranteeing, by definition, the existence of the relevant sensations. If he were asked on what basis we suppose that another's pain-behavior shows the existence of a certain kind of private experience, he would presumably reply—based on his previous remarks—that we have no justification, but that such a skeptical doubt, though not strictly meaningless, would be empty and pointless (this distinction being one which Wittgenstein's own version of nonjustificationalism would not be concerned to draw). That is, for Strawson it is not the assumption of the existence of another's private experience that is empty, but rather the *doubt* of its existence.

Furthermore, to the extent to which the ascription of sensations does require justification, the shareable experiences which are supposed to provide this justification cannot themselves be justified in their claim to be shareable. Thus, Strawson says that we have a common impersonal language for describing colors because we can reach general agreement in our color-judgements; but if he were asked what justification he has for supposing that we ever do reach such an agreement—e.g., that when we all say that something is red we do not all have different color-experiences which we simply call by the same name—he could only dismiss this as an empty metaphysical speculation, the possibility of justification here being out of the question, and say that our forms of life makes any such justificational attempt irrelevant. Strawson must admit, then, that the ascription to others of shareable and non-shareable experiences alike must ultimately be carried on without a justification, and since he also explicitly says that one can recognize and identify one's own experiences, both shareable and unshareable, without the use of any criteria,[17] we can readily see that the nonjustificational approach is central to Strawson's strategy.[18]

I turn now to Malcolm's review, which is mainly concerned to elucidate Wittgenstein's account of how language is related to inner experience, and to rebut Strawson's criticism of Wittgenstein. Malcolm takes Wittgenstein's chief insight to be that the connection between a sensation and its outward expression is essential rather than contingent. The presence of behavioral criteria for pain guarantees, by definition, the presence of pain; these criteria *constitute* the pain (though Malcolm is put in the uncomfortable position of having to admit that even for Wittgenstein these criteria can only be a logical guarantee in certain circumstances). If behavioral criteria are regarded as anything short of logically guaranteeing that for which they are criteria, then their status as criteria, even in Strawson's weaker sense of being indications or signs of the inner experience, comes into question. If inner experiences are only contingently connected to their outward expression, then one is immediately faced with the problem of showing how anything can be known about these inner experiences other than in one's own case. Malcolm argues that the defender of the contingent-connection thesis is forced to admit that the public inaccessibility of inner experiences means that such experiences can be the subject-matter only of one's private language, and then raises the standard difficulties about criteria of correctness, etc., to show that even a private language for talking to oneself about one's inner experience is impossible. We are thus left with only the essential-connection thesis—which denies that so-called 'inner experiences' are really private experiences or objects at all, separable from their behavioral manifestation—as a viable position.

Without examining Malcolm's arguments in detail, I want to show only how the seeming impregnability of his position depends upon justificationalist assumptions which the nonjustificational approach, implicitly advocated by Strawson, sets out to challenge. Strawson's view, we will recall, is that the possibility of naming and describing non-shareable experiences in our common language requires that there be shareable experiences which are associated with, and thereby indicate the presence of, these non-shareable experiences. Were there no such association with shareable experiences, our non-shareable experiences could be the subject-matter only of each individual's private language, but as it is, they are the subject-matter, not of private language, but of our common language. Malcolm, on the other hand, characterizes Strawson's view as being "...that each of us not only can have but does have a private language of sensations...,"[19] and that this private language serves as the "...understructure of the language we all understand."[20] This must be Strawson's view, Malcolm supposes, because the claim that sensations are non-shareable experiences implies that there is a feature of the use of sensation-words that cannot be taught, viz., their reference. Only the possessor of the inner experience could be acquainted with it; everyone else would have to be content to be acquainted with the shareable experiences with which this non-shareable experience is associated. So, on this view (which Malcolm imputes to Strawson), "...sensation-words will have both a public and private meaning."[21] Malcolm then adds:

> But if my words, *without* these allusions, can refer to my sensations, then what is alluded to is only *contingently* related to the sensations. Adding the "allusions to what can be seen and touched" will not help one little bit in making us understand one another. For the behavior that is, for me, contingently associated with 'the sensation of pain' may be, for you, contingently associated with 'the sensation of tickling'; the piece of matter that produces in you what you call 'a metallic taste' may produce in me what, if you could experience it, you would call 'the taste of onions'; my 'sensation of red' may be your 'sensation of blue'; we do not know and cannot know whether we are talking about the same things; we cannot *learn* the essential thing about one another's use of sensation-words— namely, their reference.[22]

The phrase which Malcolm considers to be his knock-out punch— "we do not know and cannot know whether we are talking about the same things"—is a prime example of what Strawson calls 'empty and pointless metaphysical speculation'. Malcolm's claim that there is an epistemological gap here that demands to be filled by definitional criteria which guarantee that the reference of a sensation-word is a matter of public knowledge, can be rejected with the observation that our form of life makes no such demand. Granted that pains are non-shareable experiences, still, we all know what pains are, and the reference of the word 'pain' is therefore public, even though what is being referred to are private experiences. Malcolm's insistence that Strawson must believe that 'pain' has both a public and a private meaning stems from Malcolm's own assumption that the privacy of my inner experience implies that no one else can *know* what I have. But what kind of knowledge does Malcolm suppose other people are deprived of here? He seems to want something concerning other people's experiences which would be as good in every respect as anything they could have themselves, but it is precisely because our status as individual centers of private experience makes such a wish unfulfillable that our form of life takes no notice of such a wish and therefore does not give rise to language-games in which I can be said to 'know' something about my own sensations that no one else can possibly know, even if I tell him whatever I possibly can about my experience. Once we abandon this use of 'know'—which from the perspective of the language-games we actually play (in our non-philosophical moments) is illegitimate and irrelevant—the distinction between a sensation-word's public and private meaning also loses its point.

Malcolm's justificationalist assumptions again come to the fore in his discussion of how Strawson has failed to understand Wittgenstein on the topic of recognizing and identifying sensations. According to Strawson, Wittgenstein correctly notes, first, that the expression of doubt has no place in the language-game in which one says 'I am in pain', and secondly, that one does not, when one says 'I am in pain', identify one's sensation by criteria, but that Wittgenstein goes wrong in supposing

> ...that these facts can only be accommodated if we regard 'I am in pain' as an *expression* or manifestation of pain.... So regarded, 'pain' ceases to appear as the name or the description of a sensation. If we do *not* so regard it, then we shall require criteria of identity for the sensation; and with these there would enter the possibililty of error.... What he has committed himself to is the view that one cannot sensibly be said to recognise or identify anything, unless one uses *criteria*; and, as a consequence of this, that one cannot recognise or identify sensations.[23]

Strawson points out that we use no criteria to identify tastes or colors, and that we also discriminate and recognize aches and throbs, searing and jabbing pains, to which there do not obviously correspond different characteristic natural expressions of pain.[24]

Malcolm's way of getting around these difficulties raised by Strawson, without really facing them head-on, is to argue that we cannot in any straightforward sense be said to recognize or identify pains, in the way we can identify, say, rabbits, because only in the latter case is there the possibility of making a mistake; and only where such a possibility exists can we speak of a *correct* identification at all. So we can, if we like, still speak of *identifying* sensations, as long as we recognize that such 'identifications' are incorrigible. The fact that it is out of the question that one should make a mistake in identifying one's sensations shows that sensations and other inner experiences are not private objects, because if they were such objects, which I identify and from which I derive their description, "...why cannot my identification and description go wrong, and not just sometimes but always?"[25] For all we know, our memory is constantly deceiving us. Expressing Malcolm's conclusion in terms of my own earlier example, the fact that it does not make sense to ask me what my *grounds* are for supposing that, in my mental image, the farmer is standing to the left of the cow is supposed to show that my mental image cannot be a private object. What is it, then, a *public* object, accessible in principle to anyone? Or is it just nothing at all, the words 'I now have a mental image in which a farmer is standing to the left of a cow' being a non-indicative use of language on a par, in this respect, with a groan or a cry? Clearly, an alternative preferable to either of these is that mental images are indeed private objects or experiences, and that the incorrigibility of reports and descriptions of sensations, images, etc., rather than showing that these things are not private objects, simply shows that the request for grounds concerning reports and descriptions of objects of this status is irrelevant, and that Malcolm's challenge—'why cannot my identification and description go wrong'— is nothing less than a challenge to our form of life. This particular 'why' simply cannot, and need not, be answered.

It would be giving the wrong impression of Malcolm to say that he is totally oblivious to the notion of an ungrounded form of life. To the contrary, he is well aware of this notion, but he introduces it into the discussion so as to *lend support* to the attack on private objects. Thus:

> As philosophers we must not attempt to justify the forms of life, to give reasons for *them*—to argue, for example, that we pity the injured man because we believe, assume, presuppose, or know that in addition to the groans and writhing, there is pain. The fact is, we pity him![26]

Unfortunately, Wittgenstein would probably have approved of the way Malcolm takes advantage of the nonjustificationalist theme; Malcolm's discussion as a whole, in fact, appears to be an extremely accurate representation of Wittgenstein's own position. My contention has been that Wittgenstein and Malcolm would have employed the nonjustificationalist strategy more plausibly had they conceded that our pity for another on the basis of his pain-behavior is indeed occasioned by the unpleasant private experience which he is undergoing, and that the place where justification ceases is in the transition from our observation of his criterial pain-behavior to our instinctive assumption that he is in pain.

Criterial pain-behavior, in this sense, would provide something less than a definitional guarantee of the presence of pain, but it would provide something more than material for a hypothesis. The difference between merely symptomatic signs of pain and criterial signs of pain, on this account, would be the difference between those signs whose status as signs requires justification and those which are simply accepted as signs without further justification. Wittgenstein in effect makes just the distinction I want, in his discussion of criteria and symptoms in the *Blue Book*, where he says:

> When we learnt the use of the phrase "so-and-so has toothache" we were pointed out certain kinds of behaviour of those who were said to have toothache. As an instance of these kinds of behaviour let us take holding your cheek. Suppose that by observation I found that in certain cases whenever these first criteria told me a person had toothache, a red patch appeared on the person's cheek. Supposing I now said to someone "I see A has toothache, he's got a red patch on his cheek". He may ask me "How do you know A has toothache when you see a red patch?" I should then point out that certain phenomena had always coincided with the ap-

pearance of the red patch.

Now one may go on and ask: "How do you know that he has got toothache when he holds his cheek?" The answer to this might be, "I say, *he* has toothache when he holds his cheek because I hold my cheek when I have toothache". But what if we went on asking:—"And why do you suppose that toothache corresponds to his holding his cheek just because your toothache corresponds to your holding your cheek?" You will be at a loss to answer this question, and find that here we strike rock bottom, that is we have come down to convention.[27]

Regrettably, he immediately goes on to speak of criteria as if they were all *defining* criteria, implying that the convention we come down to, in asking how we know that cheek-holding corresponds to toothache, is simply the convention of a definition: cheek-holding in such-and-such circumstances just is what we *mean* by toothache. My view, on the other hand, is that the convention we come down to is not one of definition; it is just the convention that regards this sort of cheek-holding behavior as a primary, criterial sign of toothache. It is part of our form of life to respond with immediacy to these sorts of manifestations, whereas in this same form of life the appearance of red patches on cheeks would do no more than serve as the basis for a hypothesis, even though cheek-holding has no more intrinsic connection with toothache than red patches do. In fact, we could easily imagine a form of life where the red patch was the criterion, and cheek-holding the symptom, of toothache.

The foregoing discussion of privacy, though more directly concerned with issues in the philosophy of mind, is nevertheless relevant to the topic of universals on several counts. First, as I previously indicated in discussing Specht's concerns about judgements of sameness, the strategy of nonjustificationalism can be invoked at some point in response to the challenge to give one's grounds for asserting that a number of things share a common quality. Rather than having to insist that one just 'sees' that, e.g., two pencils are the same color, where 'seeing' here is meant to carry a peculiar force of epistemological finality, or appealing instead to self-evidence or intuition as a way of grounding one's judgement of sameness, the more appropriate response might simply be to deny that in such circumstances any request for justification is in order.

Secondly, if we are able once again to treat with epistemological respectability the view that memory-claims do not necessarily require the possibility of an external check, one of Wittgenstein's arguments in the *Investigations* against the 'indestructibility of red' etc. is weakened: if it cannot be ruled out that one's memory of what the color red is could continue to be trusted in the absence of external paradigms, and if we also reject the view which treats memory-images as simply another medium—only mental rather than physical—for instantiating redness, then we have opened the door once again to the possibility of a non-Aristotelian version of realism. I say 'non-Aristotelian', rather than 'Platonic', since, although I have been treating these two alternatives as exhaustive, I will later briefly discuss the possibility of a third, non-Platonic and non-Aristotelian sort of realism towards which Wittgenstein himself seems occasionally to be leaning.

Thirdly, my own discussion of universals has been guided by the assumption that the most obvious candidates for such items are sense-qualities such as colors, although tastes, odors, etc., could be included as well. The connection between private experience and sense-qualities is that we become acquainted with sense-qualities by having experiences of them: a blind man would not really know what red is, a person lacking operative taste buds would not know what sugar-taste is, and so on. Since experience is ultimately not an impersonal public commodity, but rather that which is had by individual conscious beings, there is an important sense in which access to universals such as sense-qualities is essentially private. Although I learn what the color red is by being shown public objects such as crayons or fire engines, or what sugar-taste is by being given some sugar to eat, these objects provide only the occasion for me to have the appropriate private experience.

A problem traditionally posed for this sort of account is to explain how knowledge of a public, intersubjective world can be built up from a foundation of the private experience of individuals. My own proposed solution along Wittgensteinian lines as to how, e.g., the public sense-quality of redness can be derived from private sense-impressions of redness is that, if we take Wittgenstein's nonjustificationalism seriously, the problem is seen to be really only a pseudo-problem, because our form of life presents no such gap to be bridged. The color red is just what normal observers under standard conditions see when they look at red things, and the fact that what each of us sees is a matter of our individually having (private) experiences—so that there is a theoretical possibility of each of us having a different sort of experience, a different phenomenological understanding, of redness—is simply irrelevant; the 'theoretical possibility' is something of which our non-philosophical form of life takes no account.

Although I have been defending this approach, I am not entirely confident that this way of dealing with the issue is satisfactory; perhaps the philosopher *ought* to be able to transcend our ordinary, non-philosophical language-games by formulating revised, philosophical language-games in which these sorts of theoretical possibilities receive expression. Such an approach, of course, would involve a fundamental repudiation of the views of Wittgenstein—much more fundamental, I believe, than an opposition to his views on privacy—but it might be none the worse for all that. In any event, the solution which Wittgenstein would himself propose to the problem of deriving knowledge of the public world from private experience—viz., to eliminate private experience altogether as being nothing more than a grammatical fiction—is to make knowledge of the public world incomprehensible. How can I see that a particular apple is red in the absence of a visual experience—which is necessarily *my* experience—of redness?

The account I have given here of Wittgenstein's criticism of the notion of a private object, or of private experience generally, might be resisted on the ground that if such experience is the obvious, pervasive stuff of consciousness that I take it to be, how could Wittgenstein have failed to notice it in his own case? I believe that there is an explanation for this puzzling situation, one indeed along Wittgensteinian lines. The explanation is that, with respect to this issue, Wittgenstein himself was under the grip of a particular philosophical theory; in attempting to free himself from certain aspects of the theory, he nevertheless did not recognize, or attempt to free himself from, its underlying presuppositions and was thereby ultimately led into an untenable position.

The philosophical theory in question is Frege's account of the relation between the public world and the realm of private experience, as set out in his article "Thoughts." According to Geach's account of conversations he had with Wittgenstein, the latter was well acquainted with this article, but considered it

> ...an inferior work—it attacked idealism on its weak side, whereas a worthwhile criticism of idealism would attack it just where it was strongest.[28]

Geach cautiously suggests that "...in spite of Wittgenstein's unfavourable view of 'Der Gedanke', his own later thought may have been influenced by it."[29] I would state the case more strongly: a careful comparison of "Thoughts" with Wittgenstein's discussion in the *Investigations* of privacy will show beyond reasonable doubt that Frege is one of the chief targets—though not, of course, the only target—of Wittgenstein's attack. So clearly, in fact, are Frege's and Wittgenstein's views intertwined here that the discussion of privacy from #243 to #315 of the *Investigations* can be fully appreciated only if it is read as a point-by-point rebuttal of Frege. Furthermore, Wittgenstein may very well have deliberately drawn on a Fregean strategy as the basis of his attack; if so, Wittgenstein's critique of the notion of private experience can be read as an attempt, in effect, to hoist Frege by his own petard. Finally, even the inadequacy of Wittgenstein's position can be traced back to Frege, inasmuch as Wittgenstein's attack goes awry in not taking his criticism of Frege far enough. While I shall not here enter into a detailed comparison of Frege's and Wittgenstein's texts, I wish at least to address these issues briefly.

In "Thoughts" Frege assumes without argument that there is a realm of private experience—we could even say a plurality of such realms, one for each conscious being. This inner world (or worlds) of ideas, moods, and feelings must be sharply distinguished from the outer, public world, since it is only the existence of the latter that renders intersubjective communication possible; the inner world of ideas, on the other hand, can be the subject-matter only of each individual's private language. When, for example, I use the word 'red' to refer to the property of an object in the public world, I mean one thing, but when I use 'red' to refer to my own private sense-impression, I mean something else,

> [f]or when the word 'red' is meant not to state a property of things but to characterize sense-impressions belonging to my consciousness, it is only applicable within the realm of my consciousness.[30]

It is surely to this passage that Wittgenstein is responding when he says:

> What am I to say about the word 'red'?—that it means something 'confronting us all' and that everyone should really have another word, besides this one, to mean his *own* sensation of red? Or is it like this: the word "red" means something known to everyone; and in addition, for each person, it means something known only to him? (#274)

Although Frege makes a brief attempt, along Cartesian lines, to explain the relation between the outer and inner worlds as an interaction between one's private sense-impressions and one's nervous system, his preferred strategy is to argue that we just do successfully communicate with one another about various subject-matters—e.g., social and natural sciences, logic, mathematics—so that knowledge of the public realm is a *fait accompli* and is therefore not imperilled even in the absence of a satisfactory account of how it is possible. Since "...the assumption that there are other men besides myself, who can make the same thing the object of their considerations..."[31] underlies Frege's entire account, we can see how Wittgenstein's making this same assumption the starting-point of his own inquiry allows him in clear conscience to treat the 'inner world of ideas' as an idle philosophical hypothesis. If the fact of intersubjective communication assumes the existence of the public world in any case, we lose nothing—or at least nothing we can talk about in a public language, including what is supposedly talk about the 'inner world' itself, since talk about sensations, moods, etc., is still part of public language—by eliminating the private realm entirely. If one objects that the private realm is still *something*, since it remains at least the subject-matter for each individual's private language, Wittgenstein can counter with the principle, developed by Frege himself in *Foundations of Arithmetic*, that giving a name to an object involves being able to re-identify that object on other occasions.[32] Since, according to

Wittgenstein's argument, in the case of private objects nothing could count as a successful re-identification, private objects cannot be named, etc., and so there can be no language having private referents. The postulation of a private realm is thus not only gratuitous but unintelligible.

The problem with this attack on the private realm is that it uncritically adopts Frege's way of framing the distinction between public and private. Frege just *assumes* that we cannot know anything about each other's private referents, which is why he supposes that each of us has his own private meaning for the word 'red' in addition to the public meaning that we all understand. Wittgenstein begins his discussion with the same assumption about the public unknowability of private referents. Thus, he asks whether we could

> ...imagine a language in which a person could write down or give vocal expression to his inner experiences—his feelings, moods, and the rest— for his private use?—Well, can't we do so in our ordinary language?— But that is not what I mean. The individual words of this language are to refer to what can only be known to the person speaking; to his immediate private sensations. So another person cannot understand the language (#243).

Now this is completely fair as a statement of Frege's own position, since Frege's considered view is that private experiences cannot be talked about in public language, on the grounds that none of us can know anything about anyone else's private experience. If, however, we read #243 without Frege's position in mind, the suggestion that private experiences can at best be the subject-matter of a *private* language should strike us as exceedingly peculiar. If we allow this assumption to be insinuated into the argument unchallenged, then Wittgenstein has thereby been conceded virtually everything he needs. We would do better to reject this Fregean assumption, taken over by Wittgenstein, and return to the common-sense view that there are private experiences, but that we talk about them in public language. Your experiences of pain, sugar-taste, the color red, etc., are of course private to you, just as my experiences of these things are private to me. Nevertheless, they *are* publicly knowable; I understand you when you say you have a toothache, are seeing (or imagining) something red, or tasting something sweet, because I have had these same sorts of experiences. To deny that such objects or experiences are publicly knowable on the grounds that the claim that different people have comparable private experiences cannot be *justified* is just to buy into the Fregean view, a view that Wittgenstein would have been much better off criticizing in the manner I have suggested. Had he done so, he would have brought his treatment of private experience into line with the most original and intriguing tendency of his later thought—his nonjustificationalism—rather than regressing as he did in this instance, to an outmoded verificationism.

It is fascinating to speculate about the direction Wittgenstein's thought might have taken generally, and specifically concerning the status of universals, had he felt free to acknowledge the realm of private experience. From a number of passages in *Remarks on Colour*, the indications are—surprisingly, perhaps—that he might have turned towards phenomenology.[33] As he says: "There is indeed no such thing as phenomenology, but there *are* phenomenological problems..." (III, #248), which suggests that while Wittgenstein would reject phenomenology in the Husserlian sense of a rigorous, comprehensive, philosophical science, he might nevertheless have appropriate recourse to a kind of phenomenological method—a concentration on the pure, uninterpreted data of experience. One area where the phenomenological method would seem to be particularly appropriate is in the investigation of color; in this connection, Wittgenstein makes the following revealing remark:

> One might be inclined to believe that an analysis of our colour concepts would lead ultimately to the colours of places in our visual field, which would be independent of any spatial or physical interpretation, for here there would be neither illumination nor shadow nor high-light, nor transparency nor opaqueness, etc. (III, #268).

As the guarded phrasing at the beginning of the passage shows, this is hardly a ringing endorsement of the view that an analysis of colors does ultimately lead in the phenomenological direction, in part because Wittgenstein is wary of any claim as to where analysis ultimately leads—this sounds too much like the *Tractatus*—but also because of the unease he must feel in dwelling on the data of visual fields, since a visual field is pre-eminently an example of the sort of thing revealed only within the private experiences of an individual consciousness. He even hedges the issue by using the peculiar expression "*our* visual field", as though to obscure the point that a visual field is not something different people can share. His desire to do phenomenology, but to do it in such a way as not to suggest that the data under consideration are objects of one's own private experience, is best shown by the following:

> I would like to say "*this* colour is at *this* spot in my visual field" (completely apart from any interpretation). But what would I use this sentence for? "This" colour must (of course) be one that I can reproduce. And it must be determined under what circumstances I say something is this colour (III, #262).

But on the nonjustificationalist approach, these are unnecessary scruples. It is not necessary for me to be able physically to reproduce a particular color in order to know that color as a phenomenological essence. And, from a phenomenological point of view, the circumstances under which I say that a particular area of my visual field is this color will be nothing more than that the area in question just *is* this color. Had Wittgenstein abandoned his attack on private objects and proceeded in the direction of analyzing colors and other sense-qualities as phenomenological essences, my neat dichotomy between Platonic and Aristotelian realism would also no longer seem to apply: phenomenological essences are not immanent in particulars (unless we want to regard as a particular that part of the phenomenological field in which the essence presents itself) since the conditions normally requisite for particularity (physical space, time, etc.) have been bracketed away; on the other hand, that such conditions can be bracketed off is not to imply that phenomenological essences are ontologically independent of particulars either, and Husserl himself disavowed Platonism in this sense. The important point, in any event, is that such a view would be no more compatible with nominalism than are the more straightforwardly classifiable versions of realism we have previously considered.

The question remains, however, whether any such attempt to return to the pure data of phenomenology can be reconciled with the view that reality itself is constituted only within language. Would the solution be to regard phenomenology as just one more language-game? Were this solution adopted, then such an activity, having no claim to fundamental status, would hardly merit the title 'phenomenology' after all; but if we decline to call phenomenology just another language-game, on the grounds that phenomenological analysis goes beneath all interpretative strata, including language, to reveal the 'things themselves', then phenomenology would seem to be incompatible with Wittgenstein's doctrine of the primacy of language. Whether consciousness reveals any such level of pure data is, of course, a matter open to dispute; it is at any rate an important issue which merits attention, and not a pseudo-problem, as it would be if Wittgenstein's attack on privacy were warranted.

APPENDIX

SOME SOURCES OF INFLUENCE ON WITTGENSTEIN

It goes without saying that Wittgenstein was a philosopher of exceptional creativity and originality; nevertheless, he was not an isolated genius, working in an intellectual vacuum, though the distinctiveness of the style of his prose and the frequent obscurity in the presentation of its content no doubt encourage this impression. My own view is that, quite to the contrary, Wittgenstein's philosophy owes a great deal to the works of others—much more than is commonly supposed—and in my book I have attempted to go at least part way towards making this case by concentrating on some of the writings of Russell and Frege. Much more could be said about the influence of these two, as well as other figures of a more peripheral influence such as Schopenhauer, Hertz, James, Weininger, etc., but a project of this magnitude deserves a book in itself and I will not attempt it here. In this appendix, I will confine myself, first, to a brief supplementation of my attempt in the text to show the influence of Russell's *Problems of Philosophy* and *Our Knowledge of the External World* on the early Wittgenstein, and secondly, to a more detailed examination of the influence of Ogden and Richards' *The Meaning of Meaning* on Wittgenstein's later philosophy, especially with regard to his views on universals. While we have Eames' authority that Wittgenstein knew (and apparently detested) *Problems of Philosophy*, the evidence I adduce for his familiarity with *Our Knowledge of the External World* and *The Meaning of Meaning* is circumstantial, consisting in the exhibition of parallels in passages of these works with passages of Wittgenstein's own works. Though evidence of this kind is not absolutely conclusive, I believe that the parallels are sufficiently striking and numerous to convince all except those whose skepticism about historical

influences would be assuaged by nothing less than an explicit acknowledgement in footnotes by Wittgenstein himself.

Of the two works by Russell, the internal textual evidence for the influence of *Our Knowledge* is the more striking, and I shall consider this
work first. When *Our Knowledge* was first published in the latter part of
1914, Wittgenstein was already scrving in the Austrian army, and one
might suppose it unlikely that he would have had access to this work.
Yet, a remark made in the *Notebooks* on May 1, 1915 criticizes Russell's
article "On Scientific Method in Philosophy," and since this article was
not published until a month or so after the publication of *Our
Knowledge*, we have no reason to doubt that Wittgenstein would be able
to procure a copy of one as well as of the other.

The first indication of the influence of *Our Knowledge* showing itself in the *Notebooks* consists in remarks made in March through May of
1915, where Wittgenstein's discussion at many points, e.g., concerning
the status of the so-called 'law of causality' (29.3.15), Occam's razor
(23.4.15), and the bearing of the nature of causality on the question of
free will (27.4.15), corresponds to comparable discussions in *Our
Knowledge*. This in itself is hardly conclusive evidence for the influence
of *Our Knowledge*, especially since the first two topics are also discussed in "On Scientific Method in Philosophy," but then we also have
Wittgenstein's remarks of 1.5.15, where he says that "[s]kepticism is not
irrefutable, but obvious nonsense...," which is very likely a response to
Our Knowledge, p. 57, where Russell says: "Universal skepticism,
though logically irrefutable, is practically barren...." Even here it is possible that Wittgenstein was responding to a comparable passage about
skepticism in *Problems of Philosophy* (p. 150) rather than to the passage
in *Our Knowledge*, but that the allusion is to the latter becomes plain a
few sentences later, when Wittgenstein says: "My method is not to
sunder the hard from the soft, but to see the hardness of the soft"
(1.5.15). This surely refers to the distinction between hard and soft data,
on p. 61 of *Our Knowledge*, which Russell introduces to foil universal
skepticism—i.e., we can be doubtful about the soft data, but not about
the hard—the expressions 'hard' and 'soft' data occurring to my
knowledge nowhere else in Russell's work through 1915. The com-

parable discussion in the *Notebooks* and *Our Knowledge* of still other topics, such as the bearing of logical complexity on spatial complexity (cf. 7.5.15 of the *Notebooks* with p. 116 of *Our Knowledge*), or the peculiar notion of an 'alien will' (cf. 8.7.16 of the *Notebooks* with p. 181 of *Our Knowledge*) is further evidence of the influence of *Our Knowledge* on Wittgenstein.

Turning to *Problems of Philosophy*, concerning which we have good authority as to Wittgenstein's familiarity with the text, we find many passages which might have served as stimuli for remarks in the *Notebooks* and the *Tractatus*, the most obvious being the material already cited in the main text concerning the world of universals. Apart from this, there is also Russell's discussion and criticism of Hegel in Chapter XIV where, in characterizing Hegel's doctrine of the absolute, Russell says:

> ...everything short of the Whole is obviously fragmentary, and obviously incapable of existing without the complement supplied by the rest of the world.... Every apparently separate piece of reality has, as it were, hooks which grapple it to the next piece; the next piece, in turn, has fresh hooks, and so on until the whole universe is reconstructed.... The fundamental tenet upon which the system is built up is that what is incomplete must be not self-subsistent, but must need the support of other things before it can exist. It is held that whatever has relations to things outside itself must contain some reference to those outside things in its own *nature*, and could not, therefore, be what it is if those outside things did not exist (pp. 142-143).

The 'nature' of a thing, in this sense, seems to mean 'all the truths about a thing', and Russell objects that we can surely know a thing, in the sense of being acquainted with it, without knowing any propositions concerning it. Russell concludes:

> Hence, (1) acquaintance with a thing does not logically involve a knowledge of its relations, and (2) a knowledge of some of its relations does not involve a knowledge of all of its relations nor a knowledge of its 'nature' in the above sense.... [T]he fact that a thing has relations does not prove that its relations are logically necessary. That is to say, from the mere fact that it is the thing it is we cannot deduce that it must have the

various relations which in fact it has (pp. 144-145).

It is at least very likely that this discussion of Hegel provides material for Wittgenstein's own distinction between internal and external relations, in which Russell's and Hegel's views are effectively mediated by the view that objects are externally related—or independent of one another—with respect to their content, while at the same time internally related—or dependent on one another—with respect to their form, i.e., their possibility of configuration with one another. So, by including within a thing's 'nature' both form and content, Wittgenstein is able to incorporate an Hegelian insight into a system of logical atomism by showing that there is indeed a sense in which acquaintance with a thing (viz., with respect to its form) involves a knowledge of its relations (viz., those of its relations which are internal) to other things. Russell's vivid metaphorical talk of 'hooks' and 'grappling' is probably also a further source of inspiration, along with the passage from Bradley found in *Our Knowledge*, for Wittgenstein's employment of a concrete model of his own, viz., the chain-simile.

The influence of *Problems of Philosophy* on Wittgenstein is also apparent with regard to the notion of self-evidence. On pp. 117-118, and again on pp. 136-139, Russell maintains that there are degrees of self-evidence, only the highest degree of which is an infallible guarantee of truth, all the lesser degrees giving only a greater or lesser presumption of truth. In what is almost certainly a response to this Russellian doctrine—articulated, so far as I am aware, only in *Problems of Philosophy*—we find the following passage from the *Tractatus*:

> If the truth of a proposition does not *follow* from the fact that it is self-evident to us, then its self-evidence in no way justifies our belief in its truth…(5.1363).

Finally, the general tenor of Chapter XV of *Problems of Philosophy*, which deals with the value of philosophic contemplation, is echoed in both the *Notebooks* and the *Tractatus*, but especially the former. For example, Russell says:

> The free intellect will see as God might see, without a *here* and *now*,

without hopes and fears, without the trammels of customary beliefs and
traditional prejudices, calmly, dispassionately, in the sole and exclusive
desire of knowledge—knowledge as impersonal, as purely contemplative,
as it is possible for man to attain (p. 160).

These same sentiments are expressed in the *Notebooks* as follows:
"Only a man who lives not in time but in the present is happy" (8.7.16),
and "[t]he life of knowledge is the life that is happy in spite of the misery
of the world" (13.8.16). It would thus seem that despite Wittgenstein's
professed disdain for *Problems of Philosophy*, he assimilated a number
of its teachings and incorporated them into his own thought.

I turn next to the question of the influence of *The Meaning of Meaning* upon the later Wittgenstein. The evidence for this influence—besides Wittgenstein's one specific reference on p. 63 of *Philosophical
Remarks* to Ogden and Richards, which indicates that he was acquainted
with their work (which interest on Wittgenstein's part should not be too
surprising, given that Ogden was the editor of the English version of the
Tractatus)—consists in numerous textual parallels between *The Meaning
of Meaning* (and its two supplementary essays by Malinowski and
Crookshank) and Wittgenstein's own writings from *Philosophical Grammar* onwards, of which I now proceed to list some of the more striking
instances. All quotations and page citations are from the eighth edition
of *The Meaning of Meaning*, though the wording of these quotations
remains unchanged from any of the earlier editions. Also, these passages
are not grouped according to topic, but are merely listed in their order of
appearance in the text, and are followed in each case by the appropriate
remark of Wittgenstein's.

1. If we stand in the neighborhood of a cross road and observe a
pedestrian confronted by a notice *To Grantchester* displayed on a post, we
commonly distinguish...(1) a Sign which (2) refers to a Place and (3) is
being interpreted by a person (p. 21).
   A rule stands there like a sign-post.—Does the sign-post leave no
doubt open about the way I have to go? (*Investigations* #85. See also #87
and #198).

2. Whenever we 'perceive' what we name 'a chair,' we are interpreting a certain group of data…and treating them as signs of a referent (p. 22).

Does it *follow* from the sense-impressions which I get that there is a chair over there? (*Investigations* #468. See also #356)

3. [There is] the primitive idea that Words and Things are related by some magic bond… (p. 47).

One could almost imagine that naming was done by a peculiar sacramental act, and that this produced some magic relation between the name and the thing (*Brown Book*, p. 172).

4. …[I]t is actually through their occurrence together with things, their linkage with them in a 'context' that Symbols come to play an important part in our Life… (p. 47).

…[I]f you are asked what is the relation between a name and the thing it names, you will be inclined to answer that the relation is a psychological one, and perhaps when you say this you think in particular of the mechanism of association (*Blue Book*, p. 3).

5. [Traditionally] thinking is regarded as an unparalleled happening (p. 48).

"Thought must be something unique" (*Investigations* #95. See also the *Blue Book*, pp. 3-4).

6. "What happens when we think?" is a question which should be of interest to every thinker.… [A]n attempt is made to outline an account of thinking in purely causal terms… (p. 50).

…[W]e are tempted to say "the mechanism of the mind must be of a most peculiar kind to be able to do what the mind does". But here we are making two mistakes. For what struck *us* as being queer about thought and thinking was not at all that it had curious effects which we were not yet able to explain (causally).… [T]his aspect of the mind does not interest us. The problems which it may set are psychological problems, and the method of their solution is that of natural science (*Blue Book*, pp. 5-6).

7. An account of the process of Interpretation is thus the key to the understanding of the Sign-situation… (p. 50).

…[A]ny interpretation still hangs in the air along with what it interprets, and cannot give it any support. Interpretations by themselves do not determine meaning (*Investigations* #198. See also #637-638).

8. There is no good reason for supposing that mathematics is fundamentally homogeneous... (p. 90)
....[T]he kinds of number form a family... (*Investigations* #67).

9. [S]o-called fictions are often indistinguishable from hypotheses.... But all fictions of this kind must be clearly distinguished from those due to manipulations of language itself (p. 99).
Aren't you at bottom really saying that everything except human behavior is a fiction?—If I do speak of a fiction, then it is of a *grammatical* fiction (*Investigations* #307).

10. ...[T]o go up the ladder and overlook the maze is by far the best method of mastering a subject (p. 116).
A main source of our failure to understand is that we do not *command a clear view* of the use of our words (*Investigations* #122).

11. At what point our definitions are thorough enough must be left for the occasion to decide (p. 128).
...[A]n explanation may indeed rest on another one that has been given, but none stands in need of another—unless *we* require it to prevent a misunderstanding (*Investigations* #87).

12. ...[W]e should provide ourselves with as complete a list as possible of different uses of the principal words.... It is extraordinarily difficult in such fields to retain consistently what may be called a 'sense of position.' The process of investigation consists very largely of what, to the investigator, appear to be flashes of insight, sudden glimpses of connections between things... (p. 131).
...[W]e do not *command a clear view* of the use of our words.—Our grammar is lacking in this sort of perspicuity. A perspicuous representation produces just that understanding which consists in 'seeing connexions' (*Investigations* #122).

13. ...[T]he ability to frame definitions comes...only with practice, like surgery, diagnosis or cookery, but, as in these arts, a knowledge of principles is of great assistance (p. 138).
Why don't I call cookery rules arbitrary, and why am I tempted to call the rules of grammar arbitrary? Because 'cookery' is defined by its end, whereas 'speaking' is not (*Zettel* #320. See also *Grammar*, pp. 184-185).

14. The symbolic use of words is *statement*.... The emotive use of words is a more simple matter, it is the use of words to express or excite feelings and attitudes. It is probably more primitive (p. 149).

...[W]ords are connected with the primitive, the natural, expressions of the sensation and used in their place (*Investigations* #244).

15. ...[I]t has been easy and natural for philosophers to hypostatize their definiendum...by inventing a peculiar stuff, an intrinsic property, and then saying let everything which possesses this be said to possess meaning... (p. 185).

The question "What is length?", "What is meaning?"...produce in us a mental cramp. We feel that we can't point to anything in reply to them and yet ought to point to something. (We are up against one of the great sources of philosophical bewilderment: a substantive makes us look for a thing that corresponds to it.) (*Blue Book*, p. 1)

16. ...[F]ew important psychological laws have as yet been ascertained.... To take an analogous case, before Newton's time scientists were in much doubt as to the 'meaning' of tidal phenomena, and peculiar 'sympathy' and 'affinity' relations used to be postulated.... Further knowledge of more general uniformities made it possible to dispense with such phantom relations. Similarly more accurate knowledge of psychological laws will enable relations such as 'meaning,' 'knowing,'...to be treated as linguistic phantoms... (pp. 200-201).

The confusion and barrenness of psychology is not to be explained by calling it a "young science"; its state is not comparable with that of physics, for instance, in its beginnings (*Investigations*, p. 232).

17. Some of these rules are of no great importance, those recorded in the parts of grammar which deal with literary usage and the conventions of sentence formation. Others however are of quite a different standing and are due to nothing less than the nature of things in general.... [T]hese rules are logical laws... (p. 204).

One would like to distinguish between rules of grammar which "establish a connection between language and reality" and those which do not. A rule of the first kind is: "this color is called 'red'",—a rule of the second kind: "$\sim\sim p = p$". But this distinction embodies a mistake.... (*Grammar*, p. 89).

18. ...[G]rammar...may be regarded as the Natural History of symbol systems (p. 221).

...[O]ur interest does not fall back upon these possible causes of the formation of concepts; we are not doing natural science, nor yet natural history—since we can also invent fictitious natural history for our purposes (*Investigations*, p. 230).

19. ...[T]he set of confusions known as metaphysics has arisen through lack of this true grammatical approach, *the critical scrutiny of symbolic procedure* (p. 222).

Our investigation is therefore a grammatical one. Such an investigation sheds light on our problem by clearing misunderstandings away. Misunderstandings concerning the use of words... (*Investigations* #90).

20. ...[L]anguage is essentially rooted in the reality of the culture, the tribal life and customs of a people, and...it cannot be explained without constant reference to these broader contexts of verbal utterance (p. 305).

...[T]o imagine a language means to imagine a form of life (*Investigations* #19).

21. The structure of all this linguistic material is inextricably mixed up with, and dependent upon, the course of the activity in which the utterances are embedded (p. 311).

...[T]he *speaking* of language is part of an activity, or of a form of life (*Investigations* #23).

22. How shall we conceive the formation of meaning at these earliest stages?... The child *acts* by sound at this stage.... [T]he meaning of an utterance is here identical with the active response to surroundings and with the natural expression of emotions (p. 319).

...[W]ords are connected with the primitive, the natural, expressions.... A child has hurt himself and he cries; and then adults talk to him and teach him exclamations and, later, sentences. They teach the child new pain-behaviour.... [T]he verbal expression of pain replaces crying and does not describe it (*Investigations* #244).

There are many other points of comparison, but these examples—chosen mainly because they admit of concise quotation and because they have easily recognized counterparts in Wittgenstein's own work—are sufficient to show the profound influence which *The Meaning of Meaning* has had on Wittgenstein's later philosophy. Two of the themes

188

sounded in these passages—viz., (a) that traditional philosophical problems arise from a misunderstanding of the workings of language and are resolved by a correct understanding of these workings; and (b) that the task of the grammarian is to promote this understanding by giving a *causal* account of the workings of language—are especially prominent in Wittgenstein's own work, where his whole-hearted agreement with (a) is matched by his constant fight against (b).

Concerning the topic of universals, the influence of Ogden and Richards upon Wittgenstein is again evident, though here, too, his aversion to a causal theory of meaning prevents him from embracing their viewpoint completely; he goes along with their attack on uncritical essentialiam and on Platonism, but he stops short of their thorough-going nominalism in which words which ostensibly designate universals are regarded as nothing more than handy symbolic devices which are eliminable in favor of talk about the resemblances of particular things (where 'resemblance' and 'similarity' are themselves just such symbolic devices and no more).

First of all, the debt Wittgenstein owes to Ogden and Richards in his criticism of essentialism is easily shown. In *The Meaning of Meaning*, a few pages after dismissing as 'primitive' Herbert Spencer's contention that

> [b]y comparing its meanings in different connections, and observing what they have in common, we learn the *essential meaning* of a word... (quoted on p. 109, ft. 1),

Ogden and Richards continue:

> The natural tendency of those accustomed to traditional procedure is to expect that since what appears to be one word is being defined, the alternative substitute symbols will stand for referents with some common character of a more or less recondite nature. This may sometimes occur, but the inquiry as to whether there is such a common character should be postponed to a much later stage. The slightest study of the way in which words in ordinary speech gain occasional derivative and supernumerary uses through metaphorical shifts of all degrees of subtlety, and through what can be called linguistic accidents, is enough to show that for a common element of any interest or importance to run through all the respect-

able uses of a word is most unlikely. Each single metaphorical shift does, of course, depend upon some common element which is shared by the original reference and by the reference which borrows the symbol. Some part of the two contexts of the references must be the same. But the possible overlaps between contexts are innumerable, and there is no reason to expect that any word at all rich in context will always be borrowed on the strength of the same similarity or overlap. Thus, Beautiful (A) and Beautiful (B) may symbolize references with something in common; so may Beautiful (B) and Beautiful (C), but it by no means follows that these common elements will be the same or that the three symbols will stand for referents which share anything whatever of interest. Yet few writers who concern themselves with such wandering words resist the temptation to begin their inquiry with a search for essential or irreducible meanings (pp. 128-129).

There can be little doubt that Wittgenstein owes his famous family-resemblance strategy to this passage; even Wittgenstein's discussion of the open-textured character of concepts, which is in close textual proximity with his discussion of their family-resemblance character (in a way which Jonathan Bennett, in an unpublished paper, suggests is a conflation of two quite separate features, Bennett's contention being that a concept may have either feature without the other) follows the comparable treatment of Ogden and Richards. Thus, after telling us that we should not expect to find a common property which distinguishes things as beautiful, they say that

...we must in fact always bear in mind that there is an indefinitely large number of ways in which any symbol may acquire derivative uses; any similarity, any analogy may provide a sufficient reason for an extension of 'meaning' or semantic shift. It no more follows that the two or more symbols which it then becomes...will stand for referents with some relevant common property, than it would follow from the common name of a man's step-mother and his daughter-in-law that they share his gout or his passion for the turf (pp. 146-147).

Whether or not a concept which is subject to 'semantic shift'—or, as Wittgenstein would say, a concept without fixed boundaries—is necessarily a concept without an essential definition, these two features are at any rate lumped together by Ogden and Richards, and Witgenstein—

rightly or wrongly—follows them in doing so as well.

I might also add—in connection with my argument of Chapter Five that Wittgenstein is not attacking essentialism as such, but only an *uncritical* essentialism—that Ogden and Richards, too, say only that it is unlikely, and not that it is in principle impossible, for a common element to run through all the respectable uses of a word (See p. 129). To be sure, where a non-essentialist account of the use of a word is correct, this word is precluded from being regarded as the name of a universal—as Ogden and Richards observe in their discussion of the expressions 'beauty' and 'beautiful' (See pp. 129, 144, and 146. as well as Wittgenstein's comparable remark concerning beauty on p. 17 of the *Blue Book*)—but as long as the possibility of an essentialist account of some words is admitted, the attack on realism *as such* must be made on another basis.

For Ogden and Richards, this attack consists chiefly in ridiculing the Platonic notion of "...another world of pure being..." (p. 97), where universals subsist, as well as in providing a causal account which explains our use of general words in a way that assumes no more than the existence of propertied things not further divisible into properties and things as distinct entities (p. 188). For example, the occurrence of the word 'green'

> ...causes in [us] a certain process which we may call the idea of green. But this process is not the idea of any one green thing... (p. 70);

rather, it is the idea of any of those entities which are similar to one another with respect to color (p. 117). This account, if it avoids Platonism, does not obviously avoid Aristotelianism, since it seems to be saying that the similarity of these things is with respect to their having the common quality of greenness. Presumably, Ogden and Richards are confident that a thorough-going causal account will somehow eliminate the need for specifying the respect in which various green things are similar, in which case theirs would be a pure resemblance-theory; for Wittgenstein, however, such an account is out of the question, and he is thus led to an account of the meaning of color-words which involves *paradigms*, whose relevance as paradigms does not concern the causal relation in which they happen to stand to us, but rather concerns (in the case of colors) the Aristotelian universals of which these samples serve as paradigmatic instantiations. So, while Wittgenstein's sudden distaste for Platonism, first manifest in *Philosophical Remarks*, can probably be attributed to his reading of *The Meaning of Meaning*, his equally great distate for causal theories of meaning prevents him, assuming he were otherwise inclined to do so, from following Ogden and Richards in their contention that general words are in every instance merely pieces of 'symbolic machinery' (p. 94) and that properties are merely 'linguistic fictions' (p. 99).

NOTES

INTRODUCTION

[1]Erik Stenius, *Wittgenstein's 'Tractatus'*; P.M.S. Hacker, *Insight and Illusion*; Frank Ramsey, "Review of 'Tractatus'"; Edwin Allaire, "The 'Tractatus': Nominalistic or Realistic?"; and John V. Canfield, "Tractatus Objects." Full bibliographical information for these and subsequently cited works is found in References
[2]Desmond Lee (ed.), *Wittgenstein's Lectures, Cambridge, 1930-32*.
[3]G.E.M. Anscombe, *An Introduction to Wittgenstein's Tractatus*; I.M. Copi, "Objects, Properties, and Relations in the 'Tractatus'"; George Pitcher, *The Philosophy of Wittgenstein*; James Griffin, *Wittgenstein's Logical Atomism*.
[4]Stenius, *Wittgenstein's 'Tractatus'*, p. 21, n. 1.
[5]In Frank Ramsey, *The Foundations of Mathematics*.

CHAPTER ONE

[1]See, for example, Anselm Müller, *Ontologie in Wittgensteins 'Tractatus'*, p. 81.
[2]G.E. Moore, "Wittgenstein's Lectures in 1930-33."
[3]*Blue Book*, p. 31.
[4]Müller, *Ontologie in Wittgenstein 'Tractatus'*, p. 81, quoting Russell, *Introduction to Mathematical Philosophy*, p. 142.
[5]Whitehead and Russell, *Principia Mathematica to *56*, p. 51.
[6]*Ibid.*, p. 8.
[7]*Ibid.*, pp. 54-55.
[8]*Ibid.*, p. 161.
[9]Russell, "Mathematical Logic as based on the Theory of Types," p. 76.
[10]In #49 of *Principles of Mathematics* Russell makes clear that the expressions 'human' and 'humanity' are meant to designate the same entity, and that their grammatical difference indicates only a difference in external relations between this entity and the other constituents of the respective propositions.
[11]Whitehead and Russell, *Principia Mathematica*, p. 51.
[12]Russell, *The Problems of Philosophy*, p. 128.
[13]*Ibid.*, pp. 105-106.
[14]See, for example, *Theory of Knowledge*, p. 80.
[15]Russell, "The Philosophy of Logical Atomism," pp. 205-206.
[16]Russell, *Our Knowledge of the External World*, p. 47.
[17]*Ibid.*

[18]Russell's determination here to avoid at all costs the employment of universals as logical subjects is also shown by the skepticism he is now willing to entertain concerning the possibility of general knowledge. That is, he is no longer able, as he was in *Problems of Philosophy*, to regard a general proposition such as 'All men are mortal' as involving merely a relation between two universals; instead, he must now analyze such a proposition as the logical product of elementary propositions such as 'Jones is mortal', 'Smith is mortal', etc., in which universals no longer occur as logical subject. Since, however, the knowledge of these atomic facts cannot by itself show us that these are *all* the relevant facts, Russell concludes his account of general knowledge on the skeptical note that he does not know whether, outside of logic, there is any general knowledge at all. See *Our Knowledge of the External World*, p. 51.

[19]Russell, *Principles of Mathematics*, #47. This passage, by providing a Russellian precedent for using 'individual' in a wide sense encompassing not only particulars but universals as well, shows only that Wittgenstein *may* have been thinking of Russell's individuals in this same wide sense when he compared them to the simple objects of the *Tractatus* in *Investigations* #44 (which, though not sufficient to count as evidence for a realistic interpretation of the *Tractatus*, is sufficient to defeat the argument against the realistic interpretation). Further—though hardly conclusive—evidence that *Investigations* #44 is using 'individual' in this wide sense is Wittgenstein's remark in *Investigations* #26 that "[o]ne thinks that learning language consists in giving names to objects. Viz, to human beings, to shapes, to colours, to pains, to moods, to numbers, etc." This bears a striking resemblance to Russell's statement in *Principles of Mathematics* #47 that "[a] man, a moment, a number, a class, a relation, a chimaera, or anything else that can be mentioned is sure to be a term." If, in *Investigations* #26, Wittgenstein has this passage of Russell's specifically in mind (as well as his own earlier view in the *Tractatus*) as a prime example of the name-object account of meaning he now wishes to attack, it is likely this same Russellian position that Wittgenstein has in mind in his closely proximate remark in *Investigations* #44 concerning the rationale for the name-object account of meaning. At the very least, the independent evidence which I will subsequently put forward to show that the objects of the *Tractatus* include universals will by implication show that, even though Wittgensteinian objects and Russellian individuals (in the wide sense) cannot be precisely equated, a comparison between them is particularly apt, whether or not Wittgenstein is actually making this comparison in *Investigations* #44.

[20]Russell, *Theory of Knowledge*, p. 92.

[21]*Ibid.*, p. 100.

[22]*Ibid.*, pp. 92-93.

[23]Russell, *Problems of Philosophy*, p. 92.

[24]The former notion appears to be much broader than the latter. A "...classification...according to the logical character of the object, namely according as it is (a) particular, (b) universal, or (c) formal, i.e. purely logical..." (*Theory of Knowledge*, p. 100), seems to be a classification more ontologically basic than that of a hierarchy of types. All universals, for example, are of the same logical character, whereas there are functions of indefinitely many logical types. The relevant issue for us, of course, is not whether objects of the same logical character can be of different logical types, but rather whether objects of different logical character can be of the same logical type.

CHAPTER TWO

[1]I shall subsequently argue that Wittgenstein's characterization of (2) as the view which denies that any content is symbolized by signs for properties and relations is belied by implications of position (2) itself.

[2]Russell, *Principles of Mathematics*, #54 and #135-136.

[3]Russell, *Problems of Philosophy*, p. 127.

[4]Russell, *Principles of Mathematics*, #138.

[5]Wittgenstein undoubtedly has his earlier view in mind when he says, in the "Notes on Logic" (in *Notebooks*, p. 104): "It is easy to suppose only such symbols are complex as contain names of objects, and that accordingly '$(x, \phi)\phi x$' or '$(\exists x, y)xRy$' must be simple. It is then natural to call the first of these the name of a form, the second the name of a relation. But in that case what is the meaning, e.g., of '$\sim(\exists x, y)xRy$'? Can we put 'not' before a name?" And again: "There is no *thing* which is the *form* of a proposition, and no name which is the name of a form" (p. 99).

[6]This might be the appropriate place to note that, while in the *Tractatus*, Wittgenstein himself distinguishes symbols from signs, the latter being the physical medium of the former, I do not need this distinction for my purposes and shall consider symbols and signs, indifferently, as characterizing that which *represents* in contrast to that which is *represented*. So, while Wittgenstein would call the letter 'R' itself a sign rather than a symbol (the latter involving not only a physical sign but a mental correlation of sign and object), I will speak indifferently of 'R' as a sign or a symbol, as a matter of stylistic convenience.

[7]The remark in the "Notes on Logic" is instructive here: "[Philosophy] consists of logic and metaphysics, the former its basis" (*Notebooks*, p. 93).

[8]*Notebooks*, p. 109.

[9]It is possible that someone who holds what I have called a 'nominalist' interpretation of the *Tractatus* would admit that signs for properties and relations symbolize some kind of content, though a kind different from that possessed by objects. I do not profess to be able to make any sense of such a view as an interpretation of

the *Tractatus*, but in any case the argument which I am about to give is not directed against this kind of nominalist, or quasi-nominalist, interpretation either of the *Tractatus* or of position (2). The argument which follows is intended to show only that (2) is not nominalistic in the extreme sense in which signs for properties and relations are regarded as symbolizing no content whatever. (That the *Tractatus* cannot be nominalistic even in any more moderate sense will be shown later.) Still, although I do not claim that this argument is sufficient to compel the adoption of a full-fledged realist ontology, I will nevertheless subsequently contend that Wittgenstein's own return to realism in position (3) was, in fact, occasioned by his realization of the force of this argument and the closely related argument concerning the possibility of generalizing functions.

[10]This interpretation seems to have originated with Copi, "Objects, Properties, and Relations in the 'Tractatus'," and has been endorsed in its essentials by Anscombe, *An Introduction to Wittgenstein's Tractatus*, W. Sellars, "Naming and Saying," J.J. Thomson, "Professor Stenius on the 'Tractatus'," Pitcher, *The Philosophy of Wittgenstein*, and Anselm Müller, *Ontologie in Wittgensteins 'Tractatus'*, among others.

[11]*Notebooks*, p. 105.

[12]*Ibid.*, p. 110.

[13]*Ibid.*, p. 108.

[14]That is, if '$(\exists x, y)xRy$' has no content, then its 'existence' is guaranteed by that of the sign in the same sense that the 'existence' of logical constants is so guaranteed. In other words, there is no real question of there being a representation of existent contents here at all.

[15]His actual statement is: "All the problems that go with the Axiom of Infinity have already to be solved in the proposition '$(\exists x)x=x$'" (9.10.14).

[16]Unlike Russell, Wittgenstein sees no problem in supposing that a function-sign stands for a property.

[17]Wittgenstein does not explicitly say that 'ϕ' is an element, but he implies it, when he says: "I have here regarded the relations of the elements of the proposition to their meanings as feelers, so to say, by means of which the proposition is in contact with the outer world; and the generalization of a proposition is in that case like the drawing in of feelers; until finally the completely general proposition is quite isolated" (15.10.14). Though he then goes on to question this account of generalization, even for this account to be entertained requires that 'ϕ' be regarded as an element from which a feeler is supposedly withdrawn.

[18]See also the discussion of 14.6.15.

[19]Anscombe's translation reads: "any sort of names or other denoting signs", which obscures the point of the qualification by leaving open the possibility that symbols for universals might just be one *sort* of name. Wittgenstein's own phrase

'*irgend einen Namen*', however, means 'any name' or 'any name at all', where there is no suggestion that names themselves might be of different sorts.

[20]See also the discussion from 19.6.15 through 21.6.15.

[21]*Notebooks*, p. 15, translator's footnote.

[22]*Ibid.*, p. 119.

[23]*Ibid.*, p. 101.

[24]*Ibid.*, p. 116.

[25]Until now, the distinction between Wittgenstein's three positions has been made predominantly at the level of language rather than the level of ontology, i.e., as concerning symbols rather than the entities symbolized. This emphasis on language has been to facilitate the exposition and not necessarily to reflect Wittgenstein's own priority of interests. That is, the linguistic distinction between dependent and independent symbols is the common denominator according to which all three positions can be characterized, whereas an ontological distinction between dependent and independent entities can be straightforwardly invoked only to contrast (1) and (3), since at least on Wittgenstein's own view of (2) nothing at all corresponds to dependent symbols on the ontological level. Although we avoid complications by keeping the comparison of the three positions at the level of language, the formulation of (3) in the *Tractatus* is in fact made primarily at the level of ontology. Universals and particulars are both dependent *objects*, which are therefore both represented by dependent *symbols*. Accordingly, the following discussion of the *Tractatus* will focus on the ontological level, even though (3) continues to admit of an adequate characterization solely at the level of language.

[26]Actually, the status of objects as contents is not even mentioned until 2.025, so exclusively is the initial focus on this idea of an object's form.

[27]David Keyt, "Wittgenstein's Notion of an Object," p. 290. Keyt has informed me that his total opposition to a realistic interpretation of the *Tractatus*, as found in this article as well as in "Wittgenstein's Picture Theory of Language," has mellowed somewhat in his subsequently written review, "A New Interpretation of the Tractatus Examined." My criticism of Keyt will be confined to the views advanced in his two earlier articles.

[28]Pitcher, *The Philosophy of Wittgenstein*, p. 114.

[29]Müller, *Ontologie in Wittgensteins 'Tractatus'*, pp. 82ff.

CHAPTER THREE

[1]When I write a function-sign as a single letter, say 'f', it should be understood that a strictly correct representation includes a set of empty parentheses and/or a variable to indicate the argument-place.

[2]Pitcher, *The Philosophy of Wittgenstein*, p. 117.

[3]G.E.M. Anscombe, "Mr. Copi on Objects, Properties, and Relations in the 'Tractatus'," p. 187. In her book on the *Tractatus*, Anscombe attempts to support the claim that 'aRb' might represent infinitely many objects by arguing that, although Wittgenstein speaks of propositions of the form '$\phi(x)$' or '$\phi(x, y)$' in 4.24, "...it must not be supposed from this that Wittgenstein intends '$\phi(x, y)$' to represent an atomic fact consisting of three objects. He has only just remarked (4.2211): 'Even if the world is infinitely complex, so that every fact consists of infinitely many atomic facts and every atomic fact is composed of infinitely many objects, even so there must be objects and atomic facts.' So when he writes '$\phi(x, y)$', nothing whatever is indicated about how many names may be covered by the sign of the function; there might, on the hypothesis that he has just mentioned, be an infinite number" (*An Introduction to Wittgenstein's Tractatus*, p. 99). I would argue, on the other hand, that the only conclusion we can draw from 4.2211 is that there may not *be* propositions of the form 'f(x)' or '$\phi(x, y)$'. It is merely taken for granted in 4.24 that there are subject-predicate propositions and relational propositions of two terms, but as Wittgenstein admits in 5.55: "Since...we are unable to give the number of names with different meanings, we are also unable to give the composition of elementary propositions." Also, "[i]t would be completely arbitrary to give any specific form" (5.554). That is, he does not claim to know that there are propositions of the form '$\phi(x, y)$; for all he knows, every proposition might be a relational proposition with infinitely many terms, the point of 4.2211 being only that even if this is the case, the process of analysis must finally lead us to objects and states of affairs. Significantly, the version of 4.2211 found in the *Proto-Tractatus* puts the matter hypothetically, when it says that even if the world *were* infinitely complex, etc., there would still have to be objects and states of affairs. This shows even more clearly than in the case of the *Tractatus* that *Proto-Tractatus* 5.4103 (which corresponds to 4.2211 of the *Tractatus*) is not intended to imply that the forms mentioned in *Proto-Tractatus* 4.2212 (which corresponds to the relevant part of *Tractatus* 4.24) might actually represent infinitely many objects. Also, we may observe that the close proximity in the *Tractatus* of 4.2211 to 4.24, which Anscombe uses to justify her interpretation of 4.24, does not occur in the *Proto-Tractatus*, where the two remarks occur in entirely different contexts. I conclude that Anscombe has no basis for supposing that Wittgenstein regards a proposition of the form '$\phi(x, y)$' as involving something more than two particulars and a relation.

[4]Some commentators would say that 'R' represents the *structure*, and not the form, but I would contend that this is, in any case, a mistake, since the structure of a fact is determined, not only by the way the objects are configured, but also by which objects are in configuration, so that 'aRb' and 'cRd' would be propositions of the same form but of different structures. To this extent I agree with McGuinness (though he still goes on to contend that, in 'aRb', 'R' represents the form)

when he says: "A fact and its picture may have the same form (must have, indeed) but cannot have the same structure. Each fact that we are aware of has its own structure: that *these* objects stand in *this* arrangement constitutes *this* structure" (B.F. McGuinness, "Pictures and Forms in Wittgenstein's 'Tractatus'," pp. 144-145.

[5]*Notebooks*, p.11ff.

[6]See Pitcher, *The Philosophy of Wittgenstein*, pp. 116-117, and also Anscombe, *An Introduction to Wittgenstein's Tractatus*, p. 109, where she expresses the contrast as being between functions and individuals.

[7]Russell, *Problems of Philosophy*, p. 92.

[8]*Ibid.*, p. 100.

[9]Elizabeth Ramsden Eames, in her introduction to Russell's *Theory of Knowledge*, states that "[t]he 'shilling shocker', *The Problems of Philosophy*, was 'hated' by Wittgenstein..." (p. xx).

[10]Of course, what the content of a particular could be, on this view, is problematic. I discuss this problem further in Chapter Six.

[11]See Russell, *Principles of Mathematics*, #440.

[12]We may note, in passing, that no matter what Wittgenstein means by an object's being temporal, the notion of a temporal object is pleonastic, unless there are objects which are not temporal. The nominalist interpretation allows us to suppose only that there are two kinds of *particulars*—temporal and non-temporal— while the realist interpretation provides us with a more plausible candidate for a non-temporal object, viz., a universal.

[13]Russell, *Principles of Mathematics*, #438.

[14]*Ibid.*, #443.

[15]One could argue that *Problems of Philosophy*, though changing the emphasis of this earlier position, is not really a change of view, since, in *Problems of Philosophy*, Russell also characterizes space and time as a collection of particular points and instants (pp. 93 and 146) and characterizes the existence of an object as its relation to one or more instants (p. 100). Still, in an article roughly contemporaneous with *Problems of Philosophy*, Russell speaks as if particulars themselves are mutable and is willing to count particulars as indestructible substances only if they continue to persist throughout time. (See Russell, "On the Relation of Universals and Particulars," p. 122.) From *Principles of Mathematics* to *Problems of Philosophy*, then, Russell's view on this matter have undergone considerable modification.

[16]Russell, *Principles of Mathematics*, #428.

[17]This claim is defended in the Appendix.

[18]These remarks are made on 13.5.15, and since it is around this time that a preoccupation with topics discussed in *Our Knowledge* is evidenced by various

remarks in the *Notebooks* (see Appendix), we can plausibly suppose that *Our Knowledge* inspires these remarks on space and time as well.

[19] See *Notebooks*, p. 93ff.

[20] Russell, *Our Knowledge of the External World*, p. 92.

[21] *Ibid.*

[22] *Ibid.*, p. 93.

[23] *Ibid.*, p. 92.

[24] *Ibid.*, p. 116.

[25] That his remark is meant to apply to space in the usual sense, and not just to a metaphorical 'logical' space, is shown by the specific illustration of 2.0131.

[26] The only commentator who discusses the *Tractatus'* conception of space and time in any detail is Müller, who contends that the *Tractatus* holds a relative, rather than an absolute, view of space and time. (See Müller, *Ontologie in Wittgensteins 'Tractatus'*, p. 107.) The only evidence he offers from the *Tractatus* itself, however, is 6.3611, which says that "...the description of a temporal course (*Verlauf*) is possible only if it is based on another process. Something quite analogous holds for space." Whatever Wittgenstein is trying to say here, I see nothing that implies that space and time are relative. That "[w]e cannot compare a process with 'the passage of time'—there is no such thing—but only with another process..." (6.3611), is an observation quite compatible with a view of time as absolute, for we can easily suppose that Wittgenstein admits the existence of instants without also wanting to admit the existence of the 'passage' of these instants. Müller also cites the letter to Russell of January, 1914, in which Wittgenstein puts forward the idea that the law of causality implies the relativity of space and time, because if there were one solitary particle in the world which suddenly began to move, we see that "...*no a priori* insight makes such events seem impossible to us, *except in the case* of space and time's being relative" (*Notebooks*, p. 129). But this letter cannot be taken seriously as evidence for the views of the *Tractatus*. The tentativeness of its conclusion is made clear by the fact that in the *Tractatus* the law of causality is no longer regarded as being capable of excluding anything *a priori*. "What can be described can also happen..." (6.362), and since the *Tractatus* would therefore regard as possible that which the letter to Russell describes, but regards as impossible, Wittgenstein's basis in the letter for advocating the relativity of space and time has no rationale in the context of the *Tractatus*.

[27] Max Black, *A Companion to Wittgenstein's 'Tractatus'*, p. 50.

[28] That Wittgenstein intends to make the second, parenthetical sentence of 2.0131 a comment on the first sentence is confirmed by the corresponding version of the *Proto-Tractatus*, which reads: "Suppose that things are material points with infinite space around them. It is clear that a material point in unthinkable without infinite space" (2.0141). "On this interpretation, a spatial point is an argument-

place" (2.01411). Here, the status of the remark about argument-places as an elucidation of the notion of an object's being situated in infinite space is obvious, first, from the fact that the second remark is subsumed under the first in virtue of their respective decimal numbers, and secondly, by the occurrence of the expression 'on this interpretation', which must refer *Proto-Tractatus* 2.01411 back to the interpretation advanced in 2.0141. On Black's view of what Wittgenstein means by 'argument-place', 2.01411 would be totally irrelevant as a comment on 2.0141.

[29]In the essay "Totality and System," included in Appendix A of Waismann's *Ludwig Wittgenstein und der Wiener Kreis*, we again find Wittgenstein describing spatial points as 'places', where it is even clearer than in the *Tractatus* that he is talking about spatial positions rather than features of the symbolism, since he says 'spatial-place' rather than 'argument-place'. Thus: "Can we describe a spatial point by specifying which objects are found at this spatial-place? No, for we do not know how we should arrive at this spatial point. It is essential to a spatial description that it *gives* us the *way* that we are to arrive at a spatial-place. Specifying a spatial point means specifying a method for arriving at the spatial point" (p. 215).

[30]See *Tractatus* 3.26. The one exception would be Wittgenstein's reference to the general form of the proposition—the one genuine logical constant—as a primitive sign (5.46), which could, however, be argued to be an uncharacteristic and even figurative use of the expression, given the unique status of the one logical constant as representing only a form and no content.

[31]In the 'old' logic, concept and property amount to the same thing. I can say either that the object John falls under the concept redness or that the object John has the property redness. (See Frege, "On Concept and Object," p. 51.) That Wittgenstein follows Frege here can be seen by 4.126, where he implies that concepts are represented by means of functions and that properties are expressed by means of functions, both in contrast to formal concepts and properties. Unless we want to read some subtle distinction into the expressions 'represents' and 'expresses', for which there seems to be no basis, the evidence of 4.126 is that Wittgenstein equates concepts with properties.

[32]The problem, as previously discussed in Chapter one, is that concepts cannot be identified with functions, because only the former, and not the latter, are propositional constituents. Wittgenstein seems not to have noticed this difficulty for the Russellian view, probably because no similar difficulty exists for his own view, in which individuals are quite unproblematically represented by unsaturated signs.

[33]It should be noted that, although in the sense in which Frege uses the term 'object', concepts are never objects because (according to Frege) concepts are, and objects are not, unsaturated, nevertheless Frege would grant that concepts are objects in the sense that concerns us here, viz., concepts are included among those entities which constitute the meaning (*Bedeutung*) of primitive signs.

[34]Anscombe, *An Introduction to Wittgenstein's Tractatus*, pp. 108-109.

[35]Waismann, *Ludwig Wittgenstein und der Wiener Kreis*, p. 220. Concerning the dating of this material, McGuinness remarks: "Although it is probable that the material found in Appendix A was typed and duplicated in late 1930...it is nevertheless possible that the conversations from which this material was derived took place before December 1929" (B.F. McGuinness, editor's foreword to *Ludwig Wittgenstein und der Wiener Kreis*, pp. 20-21). A perusal of Appendix A shows this possibility to be a high probability, since the outlook, and even the wording, of these notes is extremely close to the *Tractatus*, whereas by 1930 Wittgenstein's views had begun to change radically. Also, McGuinness himself tells us (p. 20) that Engelmann's recently discovered copy of these notes bears the title "Dictated orally by L.W. (recorded before 1930)."

[36]*Philosophische Grammatik*, p. 58.

[37]*Ibid.*, pp. 200-201.

[38]I should mention, in anticipation of my subsequent argument, that nothing said by Wittgenstein in either of these two passages implies that at the time of their writing he altogether denies objecthood to, say, colors. From his statement that "[a] complex consists of its parts, which are things of the same kind (*gleichartigen Dingen*)..." (*Philosophische Grammatik*, p. 200), I take his point to be only that colors and shapes, or bricks and spatial relations, are not objects of a *sufficiently similar kind* to be properly spoken of as constituting complexes. Possibly there is the further implication that not only are colors and shapes sufficiently unlike one another to disqualify them from being fellow-constituents in the same complex, but that *no* properties or relations, just because they are not particular things, should be allowed the status of constituents of complexes. In either case, the denial that, e.g., the color red is a constituent in a complex is not the denial that this property is an object of some kind. It is true that Wittgenstein does go on to say that "[t]he root of this confusion is the muddled use of the term 'object'" (p. 201), but the context indicates that the muddle does not consist in applying the term 'object' to properties and relations, but rather in thinking of the fact as 'consisting' of its members, i.e., in treating the fact itself as a kind of (complex) object.

CHAPTER FOUR

[1]See I.M. Copi, "Objects, Properties, and Relations in the 'Tractatus'," p. 182, W. Sellars, "Naming and Saying," p. 261, Anscombe, *An Introduction to Wittgenstein's Tractatus*, p. 99, Pitcher, *The Philosophy of Wittgenstein*, p. 114, and Müller, *Ontologie in Wittgensteins 'Tractatus'*, p. 89.

[2]Müller, *Ontologie in Wittgensteins 'Tractatus'*, pp. 90-91.

[3]Russell, *Our Knowledge of the External World*, p. 47.

[4]*Ibid.*, pp. 47-48.

⁵I have argued that in fact Russell did quite probably equate individuals with particulars by the time of *Our Knowledge of the External World*, but it is questionable whether Wittgenstein was even aware that Russell had changed his position; in any case, it is not this aspect of Russell's position that Wittgenstein is trying to express by the parenthetical reference to individuals in 5.553.

⁶This interpretation is advanced by Anscombe, *An Introduction to Wittgenstein's Tractatus*, p. 122, Pitcher, *The Philosophy of Wittgenstein*, p. 113, Müller, *Ontologie in Wittgenstein's 'Tractatus'*, p. 93, and Copi, "Objects, Properties, and Relations in the 'Tractatus'," p. 181.

⁷I am, of course, assuming that the distinction between 'concept' and 'object' which runs throughout 4.126 means that 'object' is here being used in the narrow sense, in contrast to 'concept'.

⁸This argument is advanced by Copi, "Objects, Properties, and Relations in the 'Tractatus'," p. 183, and by Pitcher, *The Philosophy of Wittgenstein*, p. 115.

⁹Copi, "Objects, Properties, and Relations in the 'Tractatus'," p. 183.

¹⁰Pitcher, *The Philosophy of Wittgenstein*, p. 116.

¹¹Müller, *Ontologie in Wittgenstein's 'Tractatus'*, pp. 86-87.

¹²*Ibid.*, p. 84.

¹³*Ibid.*, p. 71ff.

¹⁴I assume that by the introduction of 'expression' Wittgenstein means to provide a term which, like 'name', designates a unit of meaning, but which, unlike 'name', is neutral to the question of whether that which is represented is simple or complex.

¹⁵Müller, *Ontologie in Wittgensteins 'Tractatus'*, p. 85.

¹⁶*Ibid.*, pp. 85-86.

¹⁷Copi, "Objects, Properties, and Relations in the 'Tractatus'," p. 182.

¹⁸Granted, examples are given in 3.333 of functions which have other functions as arguments, but Wittgenstein's point—viz., that we do not need a theory of types to tell us that a function cannot be its own argument, since this impossibility is shown by the form of the function itself—need not be taken as a concession that functions *can* have other functions as arguments. He might simply be adopting Russell's viewpoint for the sake of argument and then saying that even if functions could serve as arguments, we would not in any event need a theory of types to tell us where they could so serve.

¹⁹It might be supposed that 5.55, which says that "...we are not able to give the number of names with different meanings..." is evidence that Wittgenstein does regard the number of particulars, or of objects generally, to be contingent. I suspect, however, that our inability to give the number of objects is thought by him to be a matter only of our having not yet succeeded in reaching the ultimate analysis of propositions, the results of which, though presently unknown to us, are neverthe-

less not contingent. In any case, Copi would not profit by arguing against my interpretation of 5.55, since, if the number of particulars *were* contingent, then the contingency of properties would not count against their status as objects either.

[20]Copi, "Objects, Properties, and Relations in the 'Tractatus'," p. 183.

[21]Edwin B. Allaire, "The 'Tractatus': Nominalistic or Realistic?" p. 338ff.

[22]David Keyt, "Wittgenstein's Notion of an Object," pp. 290-291.

[23]*Ibid.*, p. 290. See also Pitcher, *The Philosophy of Wittgenstein*, p. 114, and Müller, *Ontologie in Wittgensteins 'Tractatus'*, p. 84.

[24]Keyt, "Wittgenstein's Picture Theory of Language," p. 383.

[25]*Ibid.*, pp. 383-384.

[26]F.H. Bradley, *Appearance and Reality*, pp. 32-33, quoted in Russell, *Our Knowledge of the External World*, p. 14.

[27]An interesting comparison can be made here with a passage in the *Philosophical Remarks* which resembles 2.03 of the *Tractatus* in its general purport and, in doing so, gives a realistic treatment to colors: "It is clear that there is no relation of 'finding oneself' which exists between a color and a place in which the color 'finds itself'. There is no middle-member between color and space. Color and space saturate one another" (p. 257).

[28]There is one other prominent critic of a realistic interpretation of the *Tractatus*—James Griffin, in *Wittgenstein's Logical Atomism*—whose viewpoint I have not specifically examined, as his arguments overlap those already considered. It might be worth pointing out that one of Griffin's main theses, which he attempts to support by his nominalist interpretation of the *Tractatus*, viz., that Wittgenstein's notion of analysis in the *Tractatus* is very much different from Russell's—Griffin's contention being that analysis for Russell consists in shifting descriptions from the subject to the predicate position, whereas for Wittgenstein descriptions are broken up into sub-descriptions which remain in the subject position (p. 48), this process continuing until all general terms are analyzed away—is not only contradicted by my contention that general terms are *not* analyzed away, but also by Wittgenstein's remark in *Grammar*: "I have myself in earlier times spoken of a 'complete analysis', with the thought that philosophy had to dissect all propositions completely in order to clarify all connections and to eliminate every possibility of misunderstanding. As if there were a calculus in which this dissection were possible. I imagined something like the kind of definition which Russell had given for the definite article" (*Philosophische Grammatik.* p. 211). This shows that Wittgenstein conceived his own programme of analysis along Russellian lines rather than according to the alternative theory of descriptions which Griffin proposes. (Further evidence that the early Wittgenstein is basically in sympathy with Russell's early theory of descriptions is to be found in the *Notebooks*, p. 128, and in *Philosophische Bemerkungen*, pp. 200-201.)

CHAPTER FIVE

[1]*Blue Book*, p. 17.

[2]This claim is defended further on p. 119ff.

[3]*Blue Book*, p. 17.

[4]I should point out that the later Wittgenstein no longer regards concepts as a kind of ontological item. As *Investigations* #532 shows, he now thinks of a concept as a use of words. Accordingly, I will henceforth usually indicate the subject-matter of a concept by single-quotes to indicate that this subject-matter is itself linguistic rather than ontological.

[5]*Brown Book*, p. 130.

[6]Renford Bambrough, "Universals and Family Resemblances," p. 193.

[7]Wittgenstein's argument in *Investigations* #88 that there is no ideal standard of exactness does not affect the point I am making here. I am not maintaining that there is an absolute standard of exactness which renders the normal, wide use of 'same' incorrect, but only that this wide use would be loose and misleading in a context where the purpose is to express one's detection of the slightest observable differences in color.

[8]Admittedly, in normal use even 'yellow ochre', like 'blue', is applied to more than one shade of color, ranging from a pale yellow to an orangish or reddish yellow; still, it is clear from the context of #72 that 'yellow ochre' is here being used, not to cover a whole range of shades of a color, but rather to refer to a specific shade of color which is the common quality of a number of things. Otherwise, the intended contrast in #72 between 'yellow ochre' and 'blue' would be pointless.

[9]This reference to 'pure colors' shows that Wittgenstein thinks that even terms like 'blue', 'green', 'red', and 'yellow' can be used to name specific color-qualities; as we shall later see (especially in Chapter Six), there are many instances when, presumably to avoid making cumbersome and irrelevant qualifications, Wittgenstein uses 'red' as just such a name. 'Red', in fact, is his favorite example of the name of a color.

[10]In *Remarks on Colour*, Wittgenstein also speaks of 'exactness' in the context of making such comparisons (III, #166, #256, #264-265), a way of speaking at cross-purposes with a treatment of colors exclusively in terms of family-resemblances.

[11]W.E. Kennick, "Philosophy as Grammar and the Reality of Universals," p. 176.

[12]*Ibid.*, pp. 182-183.

[13]*Ibid.*, p. 182.

[14]*Ibid.*, p. 179.

[15]*Brown Book*, p. 82.

[16]*Ibid.*, p. 80.

[17] *Ibid.*

[18] *Ibid.*

[19] *Ibid.*, p. 176.

[20] *Ibid.*, p. 174.

[21] Wittgenstein means that Augustine's description is right only to the extent that the individual words of this language are all names of objects. Augustine's other assumption, viz., that learning a language requires the making of inferences (presumably in one's own private language) concerning the inner, mental states of language-users on the basis of their outward behavior, is repudiated by Wittgenstein without qualification.

[22] But see *Investigations* #18, which warns us against a simplistic view of the notion of a 'kind'.

[23] It could, of course, be argued that on this question of the status of sensations, Wittgenstein's examination of linguistic practices is not as careful as it should be, but my present point is only that he certainly intends that his judgement should be determined on this basis, and not on some pre-conception of the way language works, or ought to work.

[24] Alice Ambrose, "Wittgenstein on Universals," p. 336.

[25] *Ibid.*, p. 339. This is also Kennick's professed view of what Wittgenstein is doing, but in practice Kennick treats Wittgenstein's arguments as having the effect of *denying* the truth of realism.

[26] *Ibid.*, p. 352.

[27] Some metaphysicians, on the other hand, would say that philosophy is simply the most general level of *empirical* inquiry. See, e.g., Whitehead, *Process and Reality*, p. 5.

[28] Wittgenstein's notion of a 'grammatical fiction' almost assuredly derives from pp. 98-99 of Ogden and Richards' *The Meaning of Meaning*. For an account of the influence of this work on the later Wittgenstein, see the Appendix.

[29] "Notes on Privacy," p. 314.

[30] The extent to which commentators have failed to grasp the point of this relatively straightforward 'grammatical' criticism is evidenced by the frequency with which a passage like *Investigations* #304 has been misunderstood. When Wittgenstein says that a sensation "...is not a *something*, but not a *nothing* either!" he is not contending with Specht that a sensation is indeed a something, only not a private something (*The Foundations of Wittgenstein's Late Philosophy*, p. 93), nor with Pitcher that a sensation is a private something, only that it plays no part in language-games and is therefore 'as nothing' in such language-games (*The Philosophy of Wittgenstein*, p. 300), nor with Donagan that a sensation is a private something that does play a part in public language by being referred to, though it is still irrelevant to the use of names telling us what is referred to, since these names require

public criteria of application ("Wittgenstein on Sensation," pp. 345-346). Against Pitcher and Donagan, Wittgenstein cannot be conceding that a sensation is a private something, because he has argued that the very notion of a private object is unintelligible. It is equally gratuitous, in light of Wittgenstein's insistence that a sensation is not a something, to suppose as Specht does that pain is a public something. Obviously, the point of #304 is to correct that misconception of the grammar of sensation-words which interprets such words as names of objects, the only two alternatives being that the objects designated by such names do exist, just as there really are objects named by 'horse', or that they do not exist, just as no objects answer to the name 'unicorn'. Wittgenstein is saying that neither of these alternatives hold in connection with a word like 'pain' any more than they hold for a word like 'sake'. If someone contends that sakes exist, the proper answer is not to *deny* that sakes exist, but rather to show him that he has misunderstood the function of the word 'sake', whose use is not to designate an object at all. This is precisely the approach taken by Wittgenstein in his discussion of sensations. The status of private objects, and Wittgenstein's attack on privacy generally, is examined in more detail in Chapter Eight.

[31] Ambrose, "Wittgenstein on Universals," pp. 346-347. She might also have added that not everything that, in some sense, can be pointed to is really an object; e.g., we can ostensively explain what the number two is by pointing to a group of two pebbles.

[32] *Ibid.*, p. 338.

[33] *Ibid.*, p. 349.

CHAPTER SIX

[1] Against the claim of this distinction's exhaustiveness, however, see p. 177.

[2] For a further discussion of the distinction between Platonic and Aristotelian realism, as this distinction applies to Plato and Aristotle themselves, see my article "Forms in the Philebus," pp. 202-205.

[3] We have already seen that Wittgenstein is strictly committed to holding that colors are *not* simple properties, but that the *Tractatus*, for lack of better examples, sometimes treats them as such.

[4] I am indebted to David Keyt for this argument.

[5] The primacy of the name-object connection is implicitly acknowledged in *Tractatus* 3.13: "A proposition, therefore, does not actually contain its sense, but contains the possibility of expressing it.... A proposition contains the form, but not the content, of its sense." That is, the elements of the propositional sign have the same possibilities of arrangement as objects in reality, and so to this extent the sense of a proposition need draw only on the resources of language itself. But in order to tell what the arranged elements in a propositional sign mean, i.e., in order to give the sense of a proposition a content as well as a form, we must look beyond language to

the objects of reality. Names must be correlated with objects.

[6]In December of 1931, Wittgenstein commented on his earlier view as follows: "I wrote [in the *Tractatus*]: 'One cannot give a description of elementary propositions', and that was entirely correct. It was clear to me that here there are, at any rate, no hypotheses, and that one cannot approach this question like Carnap, assuming in advance that elementary propositions should consist of two-place relations, etc. But I still thought that at a later date the elementary propositions would be able to be described. Only in recent years have I freed myself from this error.... One cannot discover anything in philosophy. I still had not understood that clearly enough myself, however, and violated the very principle" (Waismann, *Ludwig Wittgenstein und der Wiener Kreis*, pp. 182-183). See also *Philosophische Grammatik*, pp. 210-212.

[7]"Some Remarks on Logical Form," p. 33.

[8]*Ibid.*

[9]*Ibid.*

[10]*Ibid.*, p. 34.

[11]Waismann, *Ludwig Wittgenstein und der Wiener Kreis*, p. 43.

[12]*Ibid.*

[13]For reasons we need not examine (see *Remarks on Colour*, I, #6, III, #26, #113, #128), Wittgenstein here and elsewhere includes green among the primary colors. Since nothing important hinges on this, I will, for the purposes of this discussion, adopt his classification.

[14]*Philosophische Bemerkungen*, p. 169.

[15]*Ibid.*

[16]*Ibid.*

[17]*Ibid.*, p. 168.

[18]*Ibid.*, p. 136.

[19]*Ibid.*, p. 163.

[20]Russell, in *The Analysis of Mind*, and Ogden and Richards, in *The Meaning of Meaning*, are the causal theorists Wittgenstein has particularly in mind. See *Philosophische Bemerkungen*, p. 63.

[21]*Philosophische Bemerkungen*, p. 65.

[22]*Ibid.*, p. 66.

[23]*Ibid.*, p. 67.

[24]*Ibid.*, p. 70.

[25]*Ibid.*, p. 110.

[26]A rough idea of what is meant by the grammatical relation between colors can be given in statements like: "Purple is more closely related to blue than to green", or "Orange is a mixture of red and yellow, but yellow is not a mixture of red and green", which are not meant as empirical statements about color pigments, or about

light waves, or about processes in our retinas, but are instead conceptual truths concerning the colors themselves in their purely phenomenological aspect. For further details, see *Philosophische Bemerkungen*, p. 273ff.

[27]*Philosophische Bemerkungen*, p. 79.

[28]All quotations are taken from the published version of *Philosophische Grammatik*, which was not written until 1933-34, but the earlier, unpublished version, written during the period 1930-32, articulates essentially the same position. See especially #13, #31, #54, #173, and #441.

[29]*Philosophische Grammatik*, p. 88.

[30]*Ibid.*, p. 97.

[31]*Ibid.*

[32]*Ibid.*, p. 88.

[33]Still, as close as he comes, he does not, in the *Philosophical Remarks*, take the final step. Thus, after conceding the difficulties involved in connecting language to reality, he nevertheless continues to hold that "[w]hat is characteristic of propositions of the kind 'This is...' is only, that in the symbol there somehow enters the reality outside of the so-called sign-system" (p. 120).

[34]*Philosophische Bemerkungen*, p. 73.

[35]Thus, p. 143 of *Philosophische Grammatik* says: "...the wish 'he should come' is the wish that really *he* should really *come*. And if one wanted a further explanation of this affirmation, we would say 'and by "he" I understand this here, and by "come" I mean the action...'. But those are explanations of grammar, which we create through language. Everything is carried out *within the language*."

[36]It is much more natural to think of a patch of color in a color-chart as an instrument of language than, say, the Eiffel Tower, though on Wittgenstein's account, both are part of the grammar in the context of being ostensively defined.

[37]*Philosophische Grammatik*, p. 142.

[38]*Ibid.*, p. 143.

[39]His discussion of the status of simple objects is complicated by his claim that there are no absolutely simple objects—simplicity being relative to the language-game—but for now we can ignore this qualification, since his chief argument against regarding colors, etc., as examples of indestructible substance is independent of the claim that no objects are absolutely simple. As we shall see in Chapter Seven, the qualification that no objects are absolutely simple is only part of a much more important qualification about ontological classification as such.

[40]*Philosophische Grammatik*, p. 95.

[41]*Philosophical Investigations*, p. 18.

[42]*Philosophische Grammatik*, p. 63.

[43]*Ibid.*, p. 137.

[44]*Ibid.*, p. 67.

CHAPTER SEVEN

[1]For a fuller discussion of the distinction between these various sorts of positions, see R.I. Aaron, *The Theory of Universals*, which criticizes nominalism and conceptualism from the standpoint of the same sort of moderate Aristotelian realism that I have argued—subject to the qualifications of this chapter—is the position of the later Wittgenstein. Ironically, in his interpretation of Wittgenstein, Aaron makes Bambrough's mistake of placing the whole burden on the family-resemblance strategy, thus turning Wittgenstein into a kind of resemblance-theory nominalist despite the affinity of Wittgenstein's position with Aaron's own.

[2]As it stands, the notion that the game is defined by its rules—which is Wittgenstein's initial characterization of his position in the early 1930's—will not do. Surely we want to allow (as Wittgenstein's more mature formulation of his position in the *Investigations* does allow, with his distinction in #564 between essential and inessential rules) that the identity of a game can persist through some rule-changes, though not through others.

[3]I will be using the expression 'formalism' to refer only to the position discussed by Frege, and not to the work of subsequent mathematicians such as Hilbert, who are also called 'formalists'.

[4]Gottlob Frege, *Grundgesetze der Arithmetik*, pp. 194-195.

[5]J. Thomae, *Elementare Theorie der analytischen Functionen einer complexen Veränderlichen*, quoted in Frege, *Grundgesetze*, pp. 183-184.

[6]Frege, *Grundgesetze*, p. 185,

[7]*Ibid.*

[8]*Ibid.*, p. 189.

[9]*Ibid.*, p. 188.

[10]*Ibid.*, p. 190.

[11]*Ibid.*, p. 191.

[12]*Philosophische Bemerkungen*, p. 53.

[13]*Ibid.*, p. 61.

[14]This is clearly directed at Frege, who writes as if the only sense in which we can treat of the possibility of movement of a chess piece in the context of a chess game is *qua* physical possibility of moving a particular piece of wood around on a chess board. See Frege, *Grundgesetze*, pp. 190-191.

[15]Waismann, *Ludwig Wittgenstein und der Wiener Kreis*, p. 105.

[16]*Ibid.*, p. 103.

[17]*Ibid.*, p. 105.

[18]*Philosophische Grammatik*, p. 53.

[19]*Ibid.*, p. 55.

[20]*Ibid.*, p. 56.

[21]*Ibid.*, p. 58.

[22]*Ibid.*, p. 59.

[23]*Ibid.*

[24]*Ibid.*, p. 60.

[25]*Ibid.*

[26]Also, in the *Blue Book* (p. 4) the meaning-is-use doctrine is introduced as a response to Frege's criticism of the formalists.

[27]*Philosophische Grammatik*, p. 63.

[28]*Ibid.*, p. 184.

[29]*Ibid.*, p. 185.

[30]Anthony Quinton, "Contemporary British Philosophy," p. 12.

[31]*Philosophische Grammatik*, p. 97.

[32]*On Certainty*, #559.

[33]George Pitcher, "About the Same," p. 122.

[34]*Ibid.*, p. 123.

[35]*Ibid.*, pp. 131-132.

[36]*Ibid.*, p. 133.

[37]I say 'finally', for clearly 'the way reality is' can be cited as a justification for a move within a language-game, though only as an intermediate step. Thus, for example, I could justify my claim that the cat is behind the couch by saying that I saw it go behind the couch a minute ago and that I now hear a purring noise coming from that direction. But if I then were asked what justification I had for regarding these observations as a justification for my original claim, I could only appeal to the rules—tacitly accepted and for the most part unarticulated—by which we play the language-game of giving evidence and which justify me–if, indeed, we are willing to suppose that the justificational demand could properly be taken even this far—in supposing that my evidence is strong enough to justify my original claim. And, of course, these rules, which form the framework of the language-game, are not themselves ontologically grounded. To approach the same example from a different angle, if I had given my evidence and were then asked how I knew that what I heard was (or even seemed to be) a purring noise, I could only appeal to the rules for the use of the words 'purring noise' to justify my description as being correct, and these rules themselves have no ontological ground. Therefore, the process of justification, in whichever direction we take it, ultimately terminates, not in the way reality is, but in grammatical rules. (See, however, *On Certainty*, #306-307, in which Wittgenstein argues that some empirical propositions are as certain as any grammatical rules which could be cited in support of them, and which therefore themselves constitute part of the justificational framework of language-games. Whether or not this admission of content-expressing propositions to the justifica-

tional framework requires a fundamental modification of the notion of a language-game is a question that I cannot consider here, although I should add that Wittgenstein himself recognizes the problem and tries to solve it, if not altogether convincingly, by treating such basic empirical propositions as descriptive norms and thus assimilating them to grammatical rules. See *On Certainty*, #95, #98, #308, and #321.)

[38]*Blue Book*, p. 55.

[39]It might be objected that, if to speak of colors in an ordinary way (e.g., saying that different shirts are the same shade of blue, etc.) is to commit one to a realist ontology with respect to colors, then this makes virtually everyone a realist. What should commit us to an ontology, however, is not what we ordinarily say about colors (or anything else), but the *philosophical analysis* we give of what we say. While this objection may have merit, we must remember that from a Wittgensteinian point of view (which is my concern here), the very notion of a philosophical analysis of our ordinary language-games is suspect, since analysis really amounts to the replacement of one (non-philosophical) language-game by another (philosophical) one, where the latter activity is the product of an artificial, intellectual fixation rather than a genuine manifestation of a form of life. This strikes me as an unduly narrow conception of philosophy, and we have in fact taken note of a number of Wittgenstein's unordinary, 'philosophical' remarks which articulate the specific ontological position I have been attributing to him. However, even if we allow Wittgenstein ontological neutrality *qua* philosopher, as his narrow conception of philosophy requires, I have argued that he cannot altogether escape ontological commitment, such as it is: if our non-philosophical language-games imply realism, then he, along with the rest of us, is a realist. Nominalism will still be a possible position, but it will be a legitimate position only if it flows from a form of life and not from a philosophical argument.

CHAPTER EIGHT

[1]See *Philosophical Investigations*, #324-325. That primitive beliefs, with an ostensibly empirical content, can form part of the justificational framework of language-games, apparently goes against my claim just previously made that the justificational process terminates in the grammatical rules of the language-game. However, as I indicated in n. 37 of Chapter Seven, the question of whether to include empirical propositions as part of the justificational framework of language-games was a source of difficulty for Wittgenstein himself and never adequately resolved.

[2]E.K. Specht, *The Foundations of Wittgenstein's Late Philosophy*, p. 170.
[3]*Ibid.*, p. 181.
[4]*Ibid.*, p. 182.

[5]*Ibid.*, p. 183.

[6]*Remarks on the Foundations of Mathematics*, p. 184.

[7]Specht, *The Foundations of Wittgenstein's Late Philosophy*, p. 183.

[8]*Ibid.*, pp. 183-184.

[9]See, for example, *On Certainty*, #34, #77-78, #110, #130, #146, #148, #150, #166, #175, #192, #204, #206, #212, #307, #359, #429, #474, #499, #559, #563, #612, #625.

[10]I use the word 'introspect' with caution, since admittedly one usually does not determine what one is imagining by inspecting one's mental image, as one might inspect a picture to determine its contents. Still, if I were asked to imagine a farmer and a cow standing side by side and, after I had done this, I were then asked whether the farmer stood to the right or to the left of the cow, there is surely an admissible sense in which I could be said to inspect my mental image to find out. Granted, my reported findings would be incorrigible, but why should incorrigibility count against saying that I had surveyed my mental image and had found out something about it? And, anyway, would a report concerning a comparable *public* picture be any more corrigible in most circumstances?

[11]A common objection to the claim that Wittgenstein does not acknowledge the existence of mental images is that he frequently talks as though we do have such images. He admits, for example, that a picture of a slab could come before a child's mind (*Investigations*, #6) or that one can describe what one imagines (#367). But we must not be misled into supposing that Wittgenstein is thereby conceding the existence of mental images. When he says: "One ought to say, not what images are or what happens when one imagines anything, but how the word 'imagination' is used.... [T]his question [as to the nature of the imagination] is not to be decided—neither for the person who does the imagining, nor for anyone else—by pointing; nor yet by a description of any process. The first question also asks for a word to be explained; but it makes us expect a wrong kind of answer..." (#370), I take this to mean that the mistake in asking what images are or what happens when we imagine anything lies in imputing to 'image' or 'imagination' the wrong grammatical function. Wittgenstein no more *denies* that people have mental images than he denies that they have pains; but, in either case, we create a 'grammatical fiction', according to him, if we suppose that there are things such as images or pains which are designated by the words 'image' and 'pain'.

[12]P.F. Strawson, "Review of Wittgenstein's Philosophical Investigations," p. 42.

[13]*Ibid.*, p. 46.

[14]*Ibid.*, p. 62.

[15]*Ibid.*, p. 49.

[16]*Ibid.*

[17]*Ibid.*, p. 46 and p. 63.

[18]It should be understood that this analysis is confined to Strawson's position as it presents itself in the *Investigations* review, and does not claim to be an accurate representation of his views as stated elsewhere.

[19]Norman Malcolm, "Wittgenstein's Philosophical Investigations," p. 97.

[20]*Ibid.*, p. 98.

[21]*Ibid.*

[22]*Ibid.*

[23]Strawson, "Review of Wittgenstein's Philosophical Investigations," p. 45.

[24]*Ibid.*, p. 46.

[25]Malcolm, "Wittgenstein's Philosophical Investigations," p. 101.

[26]*Ibid.*, p. 92.

[27]*Blue Book*, p. 24.

[28]Peter Geach, preface to Frege, *Logical Investigations*, p. vii.

[29]*Ibid.*, p. viii.

[30]Frege, *Logical Investigations*, pp. 14-15.

[31]*Ibid.*, p. 24.

[32]Thus, in discussing the meaning of number words, Frege says that "…number words are to be understood as standing for self-subsistent objects. And that is enough to give us a class of propositions which must have a sense, namely those which express our recognition of a number as the same again. If we are to use the symbol *a* to signify an object, we must have a criterion for deciding in all cases whether *b* is the same as *a*, even if it is not always in our power to apply this criterion…. When we have thus acquired a means of arriving at a determinate number and of recognizing it again as the same, we can assign it a number word as its proper name." *Foundations of Arithmetic*, p. 73.

[33]In *Wittgenstein and Phenomenology*, Nicholas Gier argues that in many respects the views of the later Wittgenstein are quite close to those of phenomenology. Like many other commentators, however, Gier seriously underestimates the extent of Wittgenstein's attack on private objects, saying that "…he does not deny their existence, he simply insists that we cannot talk about them the way introspectionists do" (p. 137). While this misinterpretation hinders Gier from seeing that phenomenology is not something which Wittgenstein, in view of his attack on privacy, ought to be eager to engage in, Gier nevertheless has correctly discerned Wittgenstein's tendencies to want to move in just such a direction.

REFERENCES

Aaron, R.I. *The Theory of Universals*. 2nd ed. London: Clarendon Press, 1967.

Allaire, Edwin B. "The 'Tractatus': Nominalistic or Realistic?" *Essays on Wittgenstein's Tractatus*. Edited by I.M. Copi and R.W. Beard. New York: Macmillan, 1966.

Ambrose, Alice and Lazerowitz, Morris, eds. *Ludwig Wittgenstein, Philosophy and Language*. London: Allen & Unwin, 1972.

Anscombe, G.E.M. *An Introduction to Wittgenstein's Tractatus*. Harper Torchbooks. New York: Harper & Row, 1965.

Anscombe, G.E.M. "Mr. Copi on Objects, Properties, and Relations in the 'Tractatus'." *Essays on Wittgenstein's Tractatus*. Edited by I.M. Copi and R.W. Beard. New York: Macmillan, 1966.

Bambrough, Renford. "Universals and Family Resemblances." *Wittgenstein: The Philosophical Investigations*. Edited by George Pitcher. New York: Doubleday, 1966.

Black, Max. *A Companion to Wittgenstein's 'Tractatus'*. Ithaca, N.Y.: Cornell University Press, 1964.

Canfield, John V. "Tractatus Objects." *The Philosophy of Wittgenstein, Vol. 2: Logic and Ontology*. Edited by John V. Canfield. New York: Garland, 1986.

Copi, I.M. "Objects, Properties, and Relations in the 'Tractatus'." *Essays on Wittgenstein's Tractatus*. Edited by I.M. Copi and R.W. Beard. New York: Macmillan, 1966.

Copi, I.M., and Beard, R.W. *Essays on Wittgenstein's Tractatus*. New York: Macmillan, 1966.

Donagan, Alan. "Wittgenstein on Sensation." *Wittgenstein: The Philosophical Investigations*. Edited by George Pitcher. New York: Doubleday, 1966.

Fahrnkopf, Robert. "Forms in the Philebus." *Journal of the History of Philosophy*. Vol. XV, number 2 (1977).

216

Frege, Gottlob. *The Foundations of Arithmetic*. Translated by J.L. Austin. Oxford: Blackwell, 1953.

Frege, Gottlob. *Grundgesetze der Arithmetik* (Vol. II, #86-137). Translated by Max Black. *Philosophical Writings of Gottlob Frege*. Edited by Peter Geach and Max Black. Oxford: Blackwell, 1966.

Frege, Gottlob. *Logical Investigations*. Edited by Peter Geach. Translated by Peter Geach and R.H. Stoothoff. New Haven: Yale University Press, 1977.

Geach, Peter, and Black, Max, eds. *Philosophial Writings of Gottlob Frege*. 2nd ed. Oxford: Blackwell, 1966.

Gier, Nicholas. *Wittgenstein and Phenomenology*. Albany: State University of New York Press, 1981.

Hacker, P.M.S. *Insight and Illusion*. Revised Edition. Oxford: Clarendon Press, 1986.

Kennick, W.E. "Philosophy as Grammar and the Reality of Universals." *Ludwig Wittgenstein, Philosophy and Language*. Edited by Alice Ambrose and Morris Lazerowitz. London: Allen & Unwin, 1972.

Keyt, David. "A New Interpretation of the Tractatus Examined." *Philosophical Review* 74 (1965).

Keyt, David. "Wittgenstein's Notion of an Object." *Essays on Wittgenstein's Tractatus*. Edited by I.M. Copi and R.W. Beard. New York: Macmillan, 1966.

Keyt, David. "Wittgenstein's Picture Theory of Language." *Essays on Wittgenstein's Tractatus*. Edited by I.M. Copi and R.W. Beard. New York: Macmillan, 1966.

Malcolm, Norman. "Wittgenstein's Philosophical Investigations." *Wittgenstein: The Philosophical Investigations*. Edited by George Pitcher. New York: Doubleday, 1966.

Marsh, Robert C., ed. *Logic and Knowledge: Essays, 1901-1950*. London: Allen & Unwin, 1956.

McGuinness, B.F. "Pictures and Forms in Wittgenstein's 'Tractatus'." *Essays on Wittgenstein's Tractatus*. Edited by I.M. Copi and R.W. Beard. New York: Macmillan, 1966.

Moore, G.E. "Wittgenstein's Lectures in 1930-33." *Philosophical Papers*. London: Allen & Unwin, 1959.

Müller, Anselm. *Ontologie in Wittgensteins 'Tractatus'*. Bonn: Bouvier, 1967.

Ogden, C.K., and Richards, I.A. *The Meaning of Meaning*. 8th ed. New York: Harcourt, Brace and Company, 1946.

Pitcher, George. "About the Same." *Ludwig Wittgenstein, Philosophy and Language*. London: Allen & Unwin, 1972.

Pitcher, George. *The Philosophy of Wittgenstein*. Englewood Cliffs, N. J.: Prentice-Hall, 1964.

Pitcher, George, ed. *Wittgenstein: The Philosophical Investigations*. Anchor Books. New York: Doubleday, 1966.

Quinton, Anthony. "Contemporary British Philosophy." *Wittgenstein: The Philosophical Investigations*. Edited by George Pitcher. New York: Doubleday, 1966.

Ramsey, Frank. "Critical Notice of the 'Tractatus'." *Essays on Wittgenstein's Tractatus*. Edited by I.M. Copi and R.W. Beard. New York: Macmillan, 1966.

Ramsey, Frank. "Universals." *The Foundation of Mathematics and Other Logical Essays*. Edited by R.B. Braithwaite. London: Routledge & Kegan Paul, 1954.

Russell, Bertrand. *The Analysis of Mind*. London: Allen & Unwin, 1921.

Russell, Bertrand. *Introduction to Mathematical Philosophy*. New York: Macmillan, 1919.

Russell, Bertrand. "Mathematical Logic as Based on a Theory of Types." *Logic and Knowledge*. Edited by Robert C. Marsh. London: Allen & Unwin, 1956.

Russell, Bertrand. *Mysticism and Logic*. Anchor Books. Garden City, N.Y.: Doubleday, 1957.

Russell, Bertrand. "On Scientific Method in Philosophy." *Mysticism and Logic*. Garden City, N.Y.: Doubleday, 1957.

Russell, Bertrand. "On the Relation of Universals and Particulars." *Logic and Knowledge*. Edited by Robert C. Marsh. London: Allen & Unwin, 1956.

Russell, Bertrand. *Our Knowledge of the External World*. A Mentor Book. New York: The New American Library, 1960.

Russell, Bertrand. "Philosophy of Logical Atomism." *Logic and Knowledge*. Edited by Robert C. Marsh. London: Allen & Unwin, 1956.

Russell, Bertrand. *The Principles of Mathematics*. 2nd ed. New York: W.W. Norton & Company, 1964.

Russell, Bertrand. *The Problems of Philosophy*. A Galaxy Book. Oxford: Oxford University Press, 1959.

Russell, Bertrand. *Theory of Knowledge—The 1913 Manuscript. Collected Papers, Volume 7*. Edited by Elizabeth Ramsden Eames. London: Allen & Unwin, 1984.

Specht, Ernst Konrad. *The Foundations of Wittgenstein's Late Philosophy*. Translated by D.E. Walford. Manchester: Manchester University Press, 1969.

Stenius, Erik. *Wittgenstein's 'Tractatus'*. Oxford: Blackwell, 1960.

Strawson, Peter. "Review of Wittgenstein's Philosophical Investigations." *Wittgenstein: The Philosophical Investigations*. Edited by George Pitcher. New York: Doubleday, 1966.

Thomson, Judith Jarvis. "Professor Stenius on the 'Tractatus'." *Essays on Wittgenstein's Tractatus*. Edited by I.M. Copi and R.W. Beard. New York: Macmillan, 1966.

Waismann, Friedrich. *Ludwig Wittgenstein und der Wiener Kreis*. Edited by B.F. McGuinness. Oxford: Blackwell, 1967.

Whitehead, Alfred North, and Russell, Bertrand. *Principia Mathematica to *56*. Cambridge: Cambridge University Press, 1962.

Whitehead, Alfred North. *Process and Reality*. Harper Torchbooks. New York: Harper & Bros., 1960.

Wittgenstein, Ludwig. *The Blue and Brown Books*. Harper Torchbooks. New York: Harper & Row, 1965.

Wittgenstein, Ludwig. *Lectures, Cambridge, 1930-32*. Edited by Desmond Lee. Oxford: Blackwell, 1980.

Wittgenstein, Ludwig. *Notebooks, 1914-1916*. Harper Torchbooks. Edited by G.H. von Wright and G.E.M. Anscombe. Translated by G.E.M. Anscombe. New York: Harper & Row, 1969.

Wittgenstein, Ludwig. "Notes Dictated to G.E. Moore in Norway, April 1914." *Notebooks, 1914-1916*. Edited by G.H. von Wright and

G.E.M. Anscombe. Translated by G.E.M. Anscombe. New York: Harper & Row, 1969.

Wittgenstein, Ludwig. "Notes on Logic, September 1913." *Notebooks, 1914-1916.* Edited by G.H. von Wright and G.E.M. Anscombe. Translated by G.E.M. Anscombe. New York: Harper & Row, 1969.

Wittgenstein, Ludwig. "Notes on Privacy." *Philosophical Review* 77 (1968).

Wittgenstein, Ludwig. *On Certainty.* Edited by G.H. von Wright and G.E.M. Anscombe. Translated by Denis Paul and G.E.M. Anscombe. Oxford: Blackwell, 1969.

Wittgenstein, Ludwig. *Philosophical Investigations.* 2nd ed. Edited by G.E.M. Anscombe and Rush Rhees. Translated by G.E.M. Anscombe. Oxford: Blackwell, 1967.

Wittgenstein, Ludwig. *Philosophische Bemerkungen.* Edited by Rush Rhees. Oxford: Blackwell, 1964.

Wittgenstein, Ludwig. *Philosophische Grammatik.* Edited by Rush Rhees. Oxford: Blackwell, 1969.

Wittgenstein, Ludwig. *Proto-Tractatus.* Edited by B.F. McGuinness, T. Nyberg, and G.H. von Wright. Translated by D.F. Pears and B.F. McGuinness. London: Routledge & Kegan Paul, 1971.

Wittgenstein, Ludwig. *Remarks on Colour.* Edited by G.E.M. Anscombe. Translated by Linda L. McAlister and Margarete Schattle. Oxford: Blackwell, 1977.

Wittgenstein, Ludwig. *Remarks on the Foundations of Mathematics.* Edited by G.H. von Wright, Rush Rhees, and G.E.M. Anscombe. Translated by G.E.M. Anscombe. Oxford: Blackwell, 1956.

Wittgenstein, Ludwig. "Some Remarks on Logical Form." *Essays on Wittgenstein's Tractatus.* Edited by I.M. Copi and R.W. Beard. New York: Macmillan, 1966.

Wittgenstein, Ludwig. *Tractatus Logico-Philosophicus.* Translated by D.F. Pears and B.F. McGuinness. London: Routledge & Kegan Paul, 1961.

Wittgenstein, Ludwig. *Zettel.* Edited by G.E.M. Anscombe and G.H. von Wright. Translated by G.E.M. Anscombe. Berkeley: University of California Press, 1967.

Peter J. Hadreas

IN PLACE OF THE FLAWED DIAMOND
An Investigation of Merleau-Ponty's Philosophy

American University Studies: Series V (Philosophy). Vol. 13
ISBN 0-8204-0211-7   185 pages   hardback US $ 30.30*

*Recommended price - alterations reserved

In Place of the Flawed Diamond offers a survey and comparative study of Merleau-Ponty's philosophy. In Peter Hadreas' view, Merleau-Ponty is influenced primarily by Husserl, Sartre and Heidegger. But the sources of Merleau-Ponty's thought cannot be circumscribed by an «intellectual narrative» which depicts his thought as an inheritance from celebrated intellectual forebears. Hadreas shows how Merleau-Ponty's thought differs from Husserl's, Sartre's and Heidegger's. The issues Hadreas discusses include Merleau-Ponty's revision of Gestalt psychology, his theory of the body-subject, and his posthumously published doctrines of the «flesh» and the chiasm. These last two issues, in particular, are contrasted with issues in Heidegger's later philosophy.

This book gives a comprehensive reading of Merleau-Ponty's philosophical work from The Structure of Behavior to The Visible and Invisible. It brings out clearly the continuities in Merleau-Ponty's thought and thereby casts much needed light on the, at first sight, strange new language and problems of Merleau-Ponty's last work. (Hubert L. Dreyfus, University of California, Berkeley).

PETER LANG PUBLISHING, INC.
62 West 45th Street
USA – New York, NY 10036